Internet Survival Cheat Sheet

tear here

UNIX Commands

Backspace	**Backspace**, **Ctrl-h**, **#**
Cancel an operation	**Ctrl-C**, **q**
Change directory	**cd** /*directoryname*
Change directory back one level	**cd ..** (leave a space after the d)
Change directory back to home directory	**cd**
Clear the command line	**Ctrl-U** or **@**
Copy a file	**cp** *oldname newname*
Copy a file to another directory	**cp** *oldname directoryname*
Copy several files to another directory	**cp** *firstpartofname* directoryname*
Current directory: show path	**pwd**
Delete a file	**rm** *filename*
List directory contents: full info and hidden files	**ls -al**
List directory contents: full information	**ls -l**
List directory contents: names only	**ls**
List directory contents: names only, several columns	**ls -x**
Logout	**Ctrl-d**, logout, exit
Move a file	**mv** *filename directoryname*
Password (change)	**passwd**
Read a text file	**cat** *filename*
Read a text file: page by page	**more** *filename*
Read the instruction manual	**man** *commandname* ??
Rename a file	**mv** *originalname newname*
Repeat command	**!!** or **r**
Search for text in a file	**grep** *"this text" filename*

Telnet to Archie

Search type, selecting	**set search** *type* (*type* may be regex, exact, sub, or **subcase**)
Search type, finding	**show search**
Searching	**prog** *filename*
Paging, turn on	**set pager**
Paging, turn off	**unset pager**
E-mail a list	**mail** *emailaddress*
E-mail, set e-mail address	**set mailto** *emailaddress*
Descriptive search	**whatis** *keyword*
View a list of FTP sites	**list**
View a list of Archie servers	**servers**
Maxhits, modify the number	**maxhits** *number*

Telnet Sessions

Connect to a telnet site	**open** *hostaddress* or **telnet** *hostaddress*
Connect to an IBM mainframe	**tn3270** *hostaddress*
Close telnet connection from telnet site	**quit**, **exit**, **Ctrl-d**, or **done**. Or try **Ctrl-]** followed by **close**
Close telnet connection from telnet> prompt	**close**
Close a telnet session	**quit**, **q**, or **Ctrl-d**
Select an escape character	**set escape** *character*
Turn echo on and off	**set echo**
Suspend the session	**z**
Restart session	**fg** (in most cases)
View help	**?**

Using FTP to Transfer Files

Account information	**account**
ASCII: prepare to transfer an ASCII file	**ascii**
Binary: prepare to transfer a binary file	**binary**
Change directory	**cd**
Change directory on *your* system	**lcd** (use like the UNIX cd command)
Change directory to previous	**cdup** or **cd ..**
Close the connection	**close** or **disconnect**
Close the connection and exit FTP	**bye** or **quit** or **Ctrl-d**
Confirm transfer type	**type**
Connect to an FTP site	**open** *hostaddress* or **ftp** *hostaddress*
Current directory: show path	**pwd**
Directory listing: full	**dir**
Directory listing: names only	**ls**
Directory listing: names only, several columns	**ls -x**
Directory listing: include subdirectories and put in a text file	**ls -lR** *filename*
Exit FTP	**quit** or **bye** or press **Ctrl-d**
Hash marks indicate transfer progress	**hash**
Help: a list of FTP commands	**help** or **?**
Help: describe a command	**help** *commandname* or **?** *commandname*
Read a text file	**get** *filename* -
Read a text file using "more"	**get** *filename* - "|more"
Transfer a file from the FTP site	**get** *sourcefile destinationname*
Transfer a file to your computer with Xmodem	**xmodem st** *filename* (text file)
	xmodem sa *filename* (Apple text file)
	xmodem sb *filename* (binary file)
Transfer a file *from* your computer with Xmodem	**xmodem rb** *filename*
Transfer a file to your computer with Zmodem	**sz** *filename filename etc* (text file)
Transfer multiple files *from* the FTP site	**mget** *filename filename etc* or **mget** *partialname**
Transfer multiple files *to* the FTP site	**mput** *filename filename*
Uncompress UNIX compress files	**uncompress** *filename*

que

Using WAIS (the swais version)

Start WAIS	telnet to a WAIS site or run from service provider's menu
Deselect all selections	**=**
E-mail a document	**m**
Enter keywords on which to search	**w** and then press **Enter** (Press **Ctrl-C** to cancel)
Move the cursor down one entry	**j** or **down arrow** or **Ctrl-n**
Move the cursor down one screen	**J** or **Ctrl-v** or **Ctrl-d**
Move the cursor up one entry	**k** or **up arrow** or **Ctrl-p**
Move the cursor up one screen	**K** or **Ctrl-u**
Move to a particular line	type the **number** and press **Enter**
Quit	**q**
Read about the highlighted database	**v** or **,** (comma)
Read a jumbled up document	Press **|** type **more**, and press **Enter**
Return to the listing	**s**
Search for a listing	Press **/** then type the **word** you are looking for and press **Enter**
Search selected entries with keywords	**Enter**
Select an entry (or deselect a selected entry)	**Spacebar** or **.** (period)
Select an entry and move to keywords field	**Ctrl-j**
View the Help screen	**h** or **?**

The

COMPLETE

IDIOT'S

GUIDE TO

the Internet

2nd Edition

by Peter Kent

A Division of Macmillan Computer Publishing
201 W. 103rd Street, Indianapolis, IN 46290

To Nick & Chris, who may, one day, learn to keep the volume down.

©1994 Que®

International Standard Book Number: 1-56761-535-X
Library of Congress Catalog Card Number: 94-78340

96 95   8 7 6 5 4 3 2

Interpretation of the printing code: the rightmost number of the first series of numbers is the year of the book's printing; the rightmost number of the second series of numbers is the number of the book's printing. For example, a printing code of 94-1 shows that the first printing of the book occurred in 1994.

Screen reproductions in this book were created by means of the program Collage Complete from Inner Media, Inc., Hollis, NH.

Printed in the United States of America

Publisher
Marie Butler-Knight

Product Development Manager
Faithe Wempen

Acquisitions Manager
Barry Pruett

Managing Editor
Elizabeth Keaffaber

Production Editor
Michelle Shaw

Copy Editor
Audra Gable

Illustrator
Judd Winick

Cover Designer
Scott Cook

Designer
Barbara Kordesh

Indexer
Bront Davis

Production Team
*Brad Chinn, Kim Cofer, Lisa Daugherty, David Dean,
Jennifer Eberhardt, David Garratt, Erika Millen, Beth Rago,
Bobbi Satterfield, Karen Walsh, Robert Wolf*

*Special thanks to Scott Parker for ensuring
the technical accuracy of this book.*

Contents at a Glance

Contents

Introduction

What have you gotten yourself into? Or what are you about to get yourself into? The Internet is a fantastic service. It currently provides an e-mail link to almost 30 million people, and that number is rising. It enables you to connect to government computers and find information about the most recent research or legislation. It enables you to connect to university computers and search thousands of different databases. It enables you to "meet" people who can help you with just about anything—from planning a trip to Papua New Guinea, to designing a scanning tunneling microscope. The Internet is the electronic highway at work. Forget the popular magazines' projections for the future—the Internet is here today.

But... (and it's a big But) using the Internet is like eating soup with chopsticks. If you wanted to create a system that would make its users think they were complete idiots, you couldn't do much better than the Internet. It's a mess of different ways to connect, strange acronyms (like PPP, SLIP, CSLIP, UUCP, and POP), and many different ways to find and get data. To the average user, it's a tangle of confusion—which is why the average user uses only a small percentage of what is available, and why many companies that provide the Internet service also provide training courses. The Internet is not something you'll "just pick up."

Welcome to The Complete Idiot's Guide to the Internet

The Complete Idiot's Guide to the Internet assumes that you're no idiot on your own territory. You know how to do your job well; you know how to do everything you need to do to get by—even to thrive—in modern life. But there's one thing you don't know: how to use the Internet.

I'm going to assume that you want to get onto the Internet and get some work done. Perhaps you just want to send e-mail, or do a little research on that book you've been planning for years. Perhaps you'd like to find a few "pen pals" on the other side of the world, or find people who share your passion for orchids. I'm going to assume that you don't really want to know how to use the Internet for its own sake; you want to get the job done, not become an Internet expert. For instance, you probably don't care about how the Internet Protocol works, as long as it gets your messages where they are supposed to go.

Sure, given the time and interest, you could learn all there is to know about the Internet. But do you have enough time? Are you really interested? I'm going to assume that the answer to at least one of those questions is No. You don't want to know every UNIX command and how the Internet might use it, but you do need to know practical stuff, such as:

➤ How to address an e-mail message

➤ How to find e-mail addresses

➤ How to transfer files from a computer on the Internet back to your computer

➤ How to copy and delete the files created during your Internet sessions

➤ How to connect to "newsgroups" and join in discussions on just about any subject you can imagine

➤ How to do research in government and university computers

While I'm making assumptions, I assume you know at least a little about computers: you know what a keyboard is, what a monitor is, that sort of thing. And I assume you have access to a computer or a computer terminal (a "dumb" system hooked up to a big computer), and know how to use it. If you want really basic beginner's information about using a PC, check out *The Complete Idiot's Guide to PCs* by Joe Kraynak (Alpha Books). If you are using another type of computer—a Mac, a UNIX machine, or whatever—the techniques described in this book will be similar for you.

How Do You Use This Book?

You don't have to read this book from cover to cover. If you want to find out about e-mail, go to the e-mail chapter; if you want to know how to use Gopher to search the Internet, go to the Gopher chapter. Each chapter is a self-contained unit that contains the information you need to use one aspect of the Internet.

I've employed a few conventions in this book to make it easier to use. For example, when you need to type something, it will appear in bold like this:

type this

If I don't know exactly what you'll have to type (because you have to supply some of the information), I'll put the unknown information in italics. For instance:

type this *filename*

In this example, I don't know the file name, so you'll have to supply it. Also, I've used the term "Enter" throughout the book (although your keyboard may have a "Return" key instead).

A word about UNIX. Most users will be working on a UNIX system. Even if your computer is an IBM-compatible PC or a Macintosh, usually the computer to which you are connected (and through which you work) will be a UNIX machine. Most users will be working with dial-in terminal accounts, which turn their computers into terminals of the computer to which they are attached. So I talk a lot about the various UNIX commands you can use. Although some users won't be on a UNIX machine, much of what you find in this book will be relevant. In a few areas, a particular command won't work on your system. Ask your service provider what command to use instead.

Sometimes I'll need to show you longer examples of what you'll see on the Internet. They will appear in a special typeface that's intended to mimic what appears on your screen (within this, text you type will still be bold):

```
CNS> telnet nxoc01.cern.ch
Trying 128.141.201.214 ...
Connected to www0.cern.ch.
Escape character is '^]'.
```

Some of the lines of a listing will be in actual English; some of them will seem to be in a mutant dialect of English. Don't panic when you see this. It's just a sort of discussion between you and the UNIX system.

If you want to understand more about the subject you are learning, you'll find some background information in boxes. Because this information is in boxes, you can quickly skip over it if you want to avoid the gory details. Here are the special icons and boxes used in this book that help you learn just what you need.

Skip this background fodder (technical twaddle) unless you're truly interested.

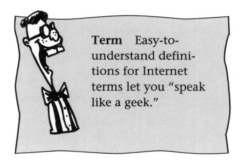

Term Easy-to-understand definitions for Internet terms let you "speak like a geek."

Acknowledgments

I would like to thank a number of people for helping me with this book.

First, I'd like to thank Art Smoot, an Internet consultant in Boulder, CO, for providing advice and technical editing on the first edition. I'd also like to thank Alpha Books' editorial staff for their help, in particular Faithe Wempen.

Trademarks

All terms mentioned in this book that are known to be trademarks or service marks are listed here. In addition, terms suspected of being trademarks or service marks have been appropriately capitalized. Alpha Books cannot attest to the accuracy of this information. Use of a term in this book should not be regarded as affecting the validity of any trademark or service mark.

America Online is a registered service mark of America Online, Inc.

Chameleon is a registered trademark of NetManage.

CompuServe is a registered trademark of CompuServe Incorporated, an H & R Block company.

Delphi is a registered trademark of General Videotex.

Free-Net is a registered service mark of NPTN.

GEnie is a registered trademark of General Electric Company.

MS-DOS, MS, and Microsoft are registered trademarks of Microsoft Corporation.

PC/TCP is a registered trademark of FTP Software, Inc.

Penthouse Online is a registered trademark of Penthouse International, Ltd.

PRODIGY is a registered trademark of Prodigy Services Company.

Windows is a trademark of Microsoft Corporation.

Part I
Untangling the Wires and Getting It Running

Maybe you already have an Internet account, or maybe you've heard so much about the Internet that you're ready to see what it's all about. Well, prepare to be overwhelmed. Most manuals and books you'll encounter will probably not be much help, because they're designed for programmers and experienced PC hackers—not for normal people like you. Fortunately, you've got this book to guide you through the maze.

In Part I I explain the basics of the Internet. I will help you select the sort of account you need and get the best price. I tell you what you need to connect to the Internet, how to get an account, and how to get up and running.

SKIP HAD SOME TROUBLE WITH THE NEW MODEM.

## Chapter 1

The Least You Need to Know

First of all, don't panic! There's nothing difficult in this book. The Internet itself is not difficult per se. It just assumes you know a lot of things that you may not already know (such as UNIX commands). Stick with me, and I promise you'll get out alive.

Don't try to learn everything at once; that will just give you a headache. For now, breeze through this list of important things you need to know. You'll learn more about each of them later.

1. The Internet is not the most user-friendly system you'll find. It takes some time to learn the right commands to use. Unfortunately, in some cases, you might find your service provider isn't particularly helpful either—unless you want to shell out a couple hundred bucks for a training course. One way or another, you need help to learn the Internet. (Which is why you bought this book, right?)

2. There aren't any fixed prices for services in Internet-land. Providers can charge whatever they want, and supply you with whatever services they decide upon. As you might imagine, this leads to some fairly wide variations (in both quality and price) among providers. Prices to get connected range from absolutely free (rarely) to very expensive, and the prices are not necessarily related to the level of service you receive. Spend some time looking around (see Chapters 3 and 4) before (and after) you choose a service provider.

3. There are four basic types of Internet accounts: permanent, dial-in direct, dial-in terminal, and mail. Most beginning individual users (as opposed to large companies) don't need anything more than a dial-in terminal account. It's relatively cheap and easy to use and, in most cases, you can access all of the Internet's services. However, if you find yourself becoming an Internet junkie, you may want to change to a dial-in direct account, which experienced users often find more convenient. See Chapter 3 for more information about account types.

4. Although different Internet service providers have different systems, most users will probably be working on a UNIX system. This is great news if you're a UNIX hacker. For the rest of us, however, it's a bit daunting, especially at first. Spend a little time in Chapter 9 figuring out how to use UNIX.

5. E-mail is the most-used service on the Internet. It's easy and convenient—once you know how to use it. You can send messages to practically anyone who's connected to the Internet. Give it a try! See Chapters 10–12 for more information.

6. To find e-mail addresses, try using the postmaster; finger, MIT's newsgroup directory; the Knowbot Information Service; Netfind; whois; and fred. There's no single directory of Internet users, but these odd-sounding systems will help you find that missing person. Chapters 13 and 14 explain how.

7. The newsgroups let you discuss any subject in the world with people from all over the world. They're similar to what some online services call *BBSs* or *message boards*. One person posts a message, another person posts a reply, and so on. You can read everyone's messages, and even post your own. Check it out in Chapters 15 and 16.

8. The LISTSERV groups are like newsgroups, but use e-mail to share messages. Chapter 16 has all the details.

9. Use telnet to "get onto" other computer systems to view files and search databases. If you like the idea of reading files and using databases or games on computers on the other side of the world, telnet's for you. How do you know which telnet site contains what? Use HYTELNET to search through a list of telnet sites for a subject that interests you. Chapter 17 explains the wonders of telnet.

10. Use FTP to grab files from computers anywhere in the world. Chapter 18 tells how to snag goodies from all over the world. Yes, that includes games.

11. One little detail I forgot to tell you in that last item is that most of the time, there *isn't* a friendly looking list of files available for the taking. That's why you need special utilities like Archie to find files. With Archie, you can search for file names or file categories. You'll meet Archie in Chapter 20.

12. Gopher (great name, huh?) can help you bypass much of the confusion of the Internet and go straight to information and files you can use. Dig around in Chapter 21 for more details.

13. WAIS is a relatively simple system for searching the world's computer databases. (I say relatively simple because nothing on the Internet is truly simple.) Try it out in Chapter 22.

14. The World Wide Web makes searching for information easy. It's a remarkably simple way to track things down. Get enmeshed in the Web in Chapter 23.

15. As with the real world, there are risks on the Internet. Chapter 24 teaches you how to make your e-mail *totally* secure, and warns you about the risks of Internet commerce and Internet socializing.

16. The Internet is rapidly becoming more user friendly through such systems as Mosaic and The Pipeline. See Chapters 25 and 26 for information about these systems as well as instructions for installing the SuperHighway Access sampler bundled on the disk at the back of this book.

17. To explain everything about the Internet would take several thousand pages, most of which you would never need to read. Remember that if you run into an unusual situation that you can't handle, you should talk to your service provider.

## Chapter 2

What Is This Thing Called the Internet?

In This Chapter

➤ What is a BBS?

➤ Why the Internet *isn't* a BBS

➤ How the Internet began

➤ Why the Internet can be so complicated

➤ The remarkable resources of the Internet

When I first started working with the Internet, I felt lost. The "documentation" I got from the company that provided my Internet account was a joke. It was badly organized and misleading, and omitted lots of important stuff. Technical support wasn't much better: phone calls went unanswered, and the help wasn't always helpful. I'll bet there's a good chance you feel the same about your Internet account (if you have one).

I shouldn't lay all the blame on a single company, though. One of the problems with the Internet is that of responsibility—who is responsible for which part? As you'll see in a moment, the way the Internet was born and has grown has been haphazard, to say the least. It's not like a typical *bulletin board system* (BBS), where you know who is responsible for the system in its entirety—the owner. With the Internet, it's never clear who (if anyone) owns what, and who (if anyone) has responsibility for getting you going. In other words, you may be left to your own devices.

It doesn't have to be confusing, though. This book will help you cut through the crud and easily find the information you need to get to the fantastic resources available on the Internet. This chapter starts you out with an overview of what the Internet *is*, and of how it has come together to become the world's largest network of computer users.

Let's Start with the Basics

Let's start right at the beginning: what is a *bulletin board system* (BBS), and what is a *computer network*? A BBS is a computer running special software that enables other computers to connect to it. (Actually, a BBS could be several computers connected together, but the principle is the same.) A computer user installs a *modem* in his computer, connects the modem to the phone line, uses *communications software* to dial the BBS, and voilá, he's "connected."

 The word modem is a combination of the words "modulate" and "demodulate." That's what the modem does with the digital signals from your computer when it converts them to the analog signals used by most telephone networks.

What can you do once you're connected to a BBS? Well, you can read messages left by other BBS users, reply to those messages (or leave your own), and copy files to and from the BBS. There also may be other services available: perhaps you can play an online game with another BBS user (chess, for instance, or some kind of arcade game); you might be able to "chat" with another user, typing what you want to say and reading the other user's almost-instant response; or you may be able to search a database or view photographs and weather maps stored on the other computer.

There are thousands of BBSs spread around the world. All you need to start a BBS is a computer, a phone line, BBS software (which you can find easily and for a low cost), a modem, and the money to pay the electric bill.

You've probably heard the names of a number of the larger BBSs, such as CompuServe, PRODIGY, GEnie, America Online, and even Penthouse Online. These services often don't use the term BBS; they might call themselves *online services* or *information systems*, but the principle is the same. They are computers or groups of computers to which computer users can connect to communicate with others, find computer files, play games, do research, and so on.

But That's Not the Internet!

The Internet is not a BBS. The Internet is a network of networks. A computer *network* is a group of computers that have been connected so they can communicate with each other. They can send messages to each other and can share information in the form of computer files. The Internet connects more than 18,000 of these networks, and more are being added all the time. On those networks are millions of computers, computer terminals, and users—about two million computers and as many as 30 million users, according to some estimates. And it's growing by around 1,000 computers *a day*. It's no wonder that the president of ISOC (the Internet Society) recently suggested that the Internet could conceivably reach 1 *billion* people in the not-too-distant future.

There's nothing astounding about computer networks. I have a small one in my home, connecting my work computer and my kids' "play" computer (which used to be my work computer until technology raced past). Many small companies have networks that connect anywhere from two or three computers to thousands of them.

But the Internet isn't just a network. It's a network of networks. Lots of different networks have been joined to produce the world's largest group of connected computers. Some of the networks are run by government bodies, some by universities, some by businesses, some by local community library systems, and some are even run by schools. Most are in the United States, but many are overseas, in countries ranging from Australia to Zimbabwe.

9

As remarkable as all this may seem, if that's all the Internet was, I wouldn't be writing this book. Sure, the Internet might make it possible for you to communicate with all these people on all these computer networks through electronic "mail," but that wouldn't be enough for a book.

What makes the Internet so special is the fact that many of the computers on the network are, in effect, BBSs. (Strictly speaking, most computers on the Internet are not set up as BBSs, but they do enable you to log in and do stuff, such as grab files or use databases.) That means that when you connect to the Internet, you have the opportunity to connect to thousands of different systems. Those computers contain government archives, university databases, local-community computing resources, library catalogs, messages about any subject you can imagine, and millions of computer files (over two million at last count) containing photographs, documents, sound clips, video, and whatever else you can put into digital form.

When you **log on** or **log in** to a computer system, you tell the system who you are, and it decides if it wants to let you use its services. A log-on (or login) procedure usually entails providing some kind of account name and a secret password.

The Internet is more like a data highway than it is like a BBS. Dial up a system on the Internet, or log on through an institution's terminal, and you're on the road. Then you have to navigate your way through the network to the city that has the data you need. When you dial up a service such as CompuServe, you are connected to a big room with a lot of computers. When you access the Internet, you might find yourself in a government computer in Washington D.C., a university's computer in Seattle, Washington, or a community computer system in Elyria, Ohio. Or, perhaps, the Centre Internationale de Rencontres Mathematiques in Marseilles, France.

It's Like the Phone System...

Perhaps the best analogy that one could use to describe the Internet is that it is like a phone system. A phone system has lots of different "switches," owned by lots of different companies, all connected to each other. When someone in Denver tries to call someone in New York, he doesn't need to know how the call gets through (which states and cities the call passes through, for example). A network of telephone companies handles it all for him. These private companies have decided amongst themselves the mechanics—the electronics—of the process, and the average caller doesn't care one whit how it's done, as long as his call gets through. The Internet works in much the same way: just as there's no single telephone company, there's no single Internet company.

So What's the Catch?

The Internet's resources dwarf those of other online systems, but there is a catch. The Internet is relatively hard to use. Systems such as CompuServe, PRODIGY, and America Online make money each time someone uses their services, so it's a good idea for them to make their services easy to use. If it's too hard, people will log off and won't come back.

Actually, some of these services haven't done such a great job at making their *user interfaces* easy to use. (A user interface is what the user sees when he or she sits at the computer and tries to use a program or system.) However, they are still way ahead of the Internet. If you use CompuServe, for example, there are a number of different programs, called *navigators*, that you can use to customize the user interface and make it simpler for you. Some of these programs are made by CompuServe's own programmers, and some are made by independent companies.

Although the Internet has the equivalent of navigators, they generally are not as sophisticated, and because of the complexity of the Internet, producing a good "all-around" Internet navigator is very difficult. (Still, Internet software is getting better, as you'll see in Chapter 25.)

"Sorry, It's Not Our Problem"

Unfortunately you may run into a case of "it's not our problem." While most *service providers* (organizations that can connect you to the Internet) claim to provide great technical support, many of them are small non-profit organizations that have trouble keeping up with the demand. And because the Internet is such an amorphous creature, these organizations can always claim that your problem lies in another area.

11

The Internet has grown so fast in the past year or two that some service providers are providing lousy service. For instance, if you are having trouble getting your Internet connection working, they may point you in the direction of your software manufacturer. Complaints that it's hard to get a connection and that calls and messages for technical support go unanswered are becoming more common.

Why, then, is the Internet so difficult to use? Well, it's because of the way the Internet was born, the way it has grown, and the way it is managed.

The Internet was originally intended to be a non-commercial system, so many service providers are non-profit organizations. They are often understaffed and underfunded, and don't have the incentive of the "profit motive." In recent years, the Internet has opened up to commercial service providers, and the result seems to be easier-to-use software and better service.

Who Owns the Internet?

BBSs are owned by someone. A company or individual buys a computer, puts it in a room somewhere, then sells the general public time on the computer. (Or, in many cases, the company lets interested parties onto the BBS for free. Many computer companies have BBSs for their customers so the customers can contact technical support, find the latest program files for their systems, and so on.)

There are literally thousands of such BBSs, from the giants we named earlier down to the small systems owned and run by one person. Take a look at a local computer newspaper, and you'll see dozens of BBSs listed, designed for use by everyone from *Star Trek* fans to computer-game nuts to swingers. In each case, though, *someone* owns the BBS, whether it's H & R Block (who owns CompuServe) or Fred down the street (who owns The Wizard's Secret Games BBS).

Nobody Owns the Internet

The Internet's not like a BBS in that respect. Nobody "owns" the Internet. As a comparison, consider who owns the nation's—or the world's—telephone network. Nobody does. Sure, each component is owned by somebody, but the network as a whole is not owned by anyone; it's a system that hangs together through mutual interest. The world's telephone companies get together and decide the best way the "network" should function. They decide which country gets what country code, how to bill for international calls, who pays for transoceanic cables, and the technical details of how one country's lines connect to another. The Internet is very similar.

The origin of the Internet can be traced back to ARPANET, a Department of Defense computer system developed in the early '70s that was intended to test methods of making computer networks survive military attack. Through these tests, researchers found that by dispersing the network over a wide area and using a web of connections between the computers, a system could continue functioning even when portions of it were destroyed, by redirecting communications through the surviving portions of the network. (This system works so well that it caused the Department of Defense plenty of frustration when Iraq used it during the Gulf War to keep its "command and control" computer system in operation.)

The NSF (National Science Foundation) gave the Internet a real boost when the Foundation realized that it could save money by creating several super-computer centers connected to a network, giving researchers all over the country (in major universities, for example) access to them and the information they stored. In the past decade, all sorts of organizations have gotten in on the act, each one connecting its own network with its own particular configuration of hardware and software. In this way, the Internet has grown tremendously.

So if nobody owns the Internet, who decides how it all hooks together? ISOC, the Internet Society, is a group of interested people (you can join if you want) who elect a "council of elders." This council, known as the Internet Architecture Board (IAB), gets together and decides how the network will function. They are advised by the Internet Engineering Task Force (IETF), another volunteer organization that studies technical problems.

...And That's the Problem.

The problem with the Internet, therefore, lies in the way it has come to be. It's a problem of planning, and it's an inevitable result of the way the network grew. As an example of this theory, compare the cities of Dallas and London. London is a confusing mesh of intertwining roads, while Dallas is laid out on a sensible grid system. London wasn't planned, it just grew. Dallas was planned almost right from the start.

The Internet wasn't developed as a single, planned system. It just grew. There is no Internet, Inc.—no single company that decides what the network should look like (which makes it a little confusing when you decide you'd like to use the Internet). Instead, the Internet is governed by consensus, by diverse organizations getting together to figure out the best way for it all to work.

Going out alone into Internet-land is like venturing on foot across London without a guide or map. It'll be interesting, but you may not find what you're looking for. So take this book along as your guide.

What's in It for YOU?

Why would you want to use the Internet, anyway? There are about 20 or 30 million reasons. That's how many people already have a way to use the Internet, so that's how many people you could send messages to, if you had the time.

Okay, there really aren't that many active users. Most people rarely or never use anything but their own organization's computers, and have little idea of what lies out there in Internet-land. When you consider that most Internet users are in the United States, it seems improbable that there are 20–30 million people with even potential access to the Internet (that would be one American in ten).

But there are plenty of other reasons for using the Internet. Are you going on vacation to Costa Rica and want to check out some good scuba locations? Then take a look at a scuba *newsgroup*, and find out if anyone's been down there recently. Leave a public message and see if you get any responses (you probably will).

Would you like to talk with collectors of antiques and vintage articles? How about talking with people who share your interest in high-fidelity audio equipment, interactive multimedia, the importance of romance in love, *Star Trek*, or tastelessness?

How about checking out Project Gutenberg, an ambitious attempt to convert works of literature to an electronic form? Go online and select from hundreds of works of copyright-free literature. You could check out the Journalism Periodicals Index at the University of Western Ontario, or Project Hermes, which stores decisions of the U.S. Supreme Court.

You could research a book or magazine article you are working on using CARL, Denver's online library index-search for books or magazine articles, without ever leaving home. Or use the Reader's Guide to Periodical Literature to search for your subject in virtually every popular U.S. magazine.

It's difficult to give a good idea of what is on the Internet because there's just so *much*. There are even drink machines connected to the Internet. They don't normally do you much good, but the students in various colleges' Computer Science Departments can use the Internet to determine if the machine has any Cokes left, and if they've been in the machine long enough to cool down. It saves them walking to the basement only to find the machine empty.

The Internet is huge. You will find many sources of information listed in this book, but I can only mention a fraction of what's out there.

➤ Chapters 15 and 16 discuss *newsgroups*, in which you can leave messages for and read messages from people with similar interests. These chapters name a few of the newsgroups and tell you how to find a list of them.

➤ Chapters 18 and 19 discuss how to download files from other computers, Chapter 17 explains how to connect to another computer so you can use its files and databases, and Chapter 28 lists computers to which you can connect using these techniques (and how to find more of those computers).

➤ Chapters 20–23 tell you how to find other sources of information using tools such as Archie, gopher, WAIS, and the World Wide Web.

The Least You Need to Know

In this chapter you learned a little background information that will help you understand how the Internet fits together. You don't have to remember the details, but at least remember these basics:

➤ The Internet is a network of networks.

➤ Because some of those networks contain what are, in effect, BBSs, the Internet is a pathway to thousands of different sources of information.

➤ Nobody owns the Internet. It's a cooperative venture linking a multitude of companies, government bodies, universities and schools, and community computer networks.

➤ Think of any subject. You can find information about it *somewhere* on the Internet.

➤ Okay, so the Internet can be complicated. That's why you need a good guide. Read on.

PSST. YOU WANNA GET WIRED FOR NOTHIN'?

## Chapter 3

So You Wanna Get Wired? For Free?

In This Chapter

➤ Types of Internet connections

➤ Advantages and disadvantages

➤ Finding a free Internet connection

➤ Finding a Free-Net

➤ An almost-free connection in D.C.

In this chapter, we're going to look at how to get connected to the Internet. Even if you already have an Internet account, you might want to skim through this chapter because it explains the *types* of accounts and the pros and cons of each. And for those who don't have an Internet account yet, we'll look at *how* to get one (it's not as straightforward as you might imagine). For most readers, "money's no object" doesn't hold true, so you want to find the cheapest way to connect to the Internet (or a free way, if possible).

Unlike systems such as CompuServe and PRODIGY, there's no set charge for connecting to the Internet. Most BBSs and online information services have a standard set of fees. You might be able to pick one fee schedule from several, but all customers have the same choices. Not so with the Internet. Because there is no Internet, Inc. (no single organization running the Internet), what you are buying is *access* to the network. You need a connection on a computer through which you can connect your own computer or terminal.

Companies and non-profit organizations called *service providers* or *Internet Access Providers* buy computers, connect them to the Internet, and sell connections to anyone who has the money to spare. These service providers set their own rates, and, as you'll see in a moment, those rates vary considerably.

Types of Connections

There are four standard ways to connect to the Internet, plus a few variations:

➤ Permanent connections

➤ Dial-in direct connections

➤ Dial-in terminal connections

➤ Mail connections

You won't necessarily hear these terms elsewhere, though. In fact, different service providers use slightly different terms, and the terminology can become blurred. It gets confusing, but the following definitions should help to clarify things.

Permanent Connections

A *permanent connection* means your computer is connected directly to a TCP/IP network that is part of the Internet, or that your organization has a large computer connected to the network, and you have a terminal connected to that computer. (You may even have a computer that is acting as a terminal; that is, all the work is done by the other computer, and your computer is simply passing text to and from your screen.) This type of connection is also known as a *dedicated connection* or a *permanent direct* connection.

Permanent or dedicated connections are often used by large organizations such as universities, groups of schools, and corporations. The service provider places a *router* at the organization's office and

leases a telephone line that connects the
router to the service provider's computer
(known as a *host* computer). The details
vary: the service provider might provide the
router, or they might tell the organization
which router to buy. But once this is established, the organization can connect its
computers and terminals to the router.
Because the organization has a *leased line*, it
is always connected to the Internet and
doesn't have to make a telephone call to
reach the service provider's computer.
Instead, the user simply *logs on* to the
Internet from his terminal. Once on the
Internet, he can transfer files between his
organization's computer and other computers on the Internet.

TCP/IP stands for
Transmission
Control Protocol/
Internet Protocol. A
protocol defines how
computers should
talk to each other.
It's like a language: if a group
of different people all agree to
speak French (or English, or
Spanish), they can all understand each other. Communication protocols provide a set
of rules that define how
different modems, computers,
and programs can communi-
cate.

This sort of service is very expensive,
costing thousands of dollars to set up, and
thousands of dollars to run. Getting a
dedicated line is, of course, way beyond the scope of this book (which
is a computer-writer's euphemism for "let's not get into that").

Dial-In Direct Connections

A *dial-in direct connection* is often referred to as a *SLIP* (Serial Line
Internet Protocol—pronounced like the undergarment), *CSLIP* (Compressed SLIP—pronounced see-slip), or *PPP* (Point-to-Point Protocol)
connection. (You may also hear the term XRemote, although you
probably won't be offered this variation.) This is also a TCP/IP connection, like the permanent connection, but it is designed for use over
telephone lines instead of a dedicated network.

This type of service is the next best thing to a permanent connection. While a permanent connection is out of the price range of individuals and most small companies, it can be quite cheap to get a SLIP
account. Prices have dropped considerably in the past year. You can get
a dial-in direct account for a $30 to $40 setup fee (sometimes no setup
fee at all) and connect rates that are the same as for dial-in terminal
accounts.

Because this is a "dial-in" service, you'll need a modem in your computer, and you'll have to dial a telephone number that the service provider gives you. Once you have connected to the service provider's computer and logged on, you can't tell any difference between a SLIP account and a dedicated account (other than speed). You can transfer files to and from your computer exactly as if it were a host computer. In fact, it will be identified on the network as a host.

There is one important way in which you'll see the difference between dial-in direct and permanent connections: file transfers between your computer and others, as well as "telnet" sessions, will be much slower than those between your service provider's computer and others on the Internet.

Also, depending on the software you are using, you may be able to run multiple sessions at the same time. That is, in the same way that the service provider's computer can let dozens of people work on the Internet at the same time, you will be able to do several different things on the Internet at the same time using multiple program windows. For example, you could transfer files from computer A in one window, search a database on computer B in another window, and work in your own file directories in another window.

Don't confuse this service with what some service providers call a *dial-up* connection. A dial-up service (what I call dial-in terminal service) also requires you to dial a telephone number, but it provides slightly more limited service than SLIP (as we'll see in a moment).

Dial-in direct accounts work very differently from dial-in terminal accounts, and in this book I'm assuming that you have a terminal account. For more information about dial-in direct accounts, see Chapter 25. If you need detailed information about setting up a dial-in direct account, pick up *The Complete Idiot's Next Step with the Internet*, also published by Alpha Books.

Dial-In Terminal Connections

With this type of connection you'll have to dial into the service provider's computer. It's confusing that this connection is often called a *dial-up* service, because you have to dial a call in order to connect to a

SLIP account as well. (To differentiate, some service providers call this an *interactive* service, which seems only slightly less ambiguous.) I've called it a *dial-in terminal connection* because you dial the call to your service provider and, once connected, your computer acts as a terminal.

Unlike with a permanent or dial-in direct connection, your computer won't appear as a host on the network when you use a dial-in terminal connection; it'll simply be a terminal of the service provider's computer. All the programs you run are actually run on the service provider's computer. That means that you can transfer files across the Internet to and from your service provider's computer, but not to and from yours. You have to use a separate procedure, normally a transfer procedure such as zmodem or xmodem, to move files between your computer and that of the service provider. (You'll learn more about data transfers in Chapter 18 and after.)

You can still use all the services that are available on a permanent connection or dial-in direct connection. However, as you'll see in Chapter 25, the tools available to permanent dial-in connections are far better.

In one way, the permanent connection and dial-in terminal connection are very similar: in both cases your computer is nothing but a terminal of the host computer. (In contrast, with a dial-in direct connection, your computer temporarily becomes a host computer.) But there's an important difference between permanent and dial-in terminal. In the case of the dial-in terminal connection, you don't really want your data stored on the host computer, and you have to mess around to get it back. In the case of a permanent connection, either you are used to having your data stored on your organization's large computer (you are using a terminal and can probably print directly from the host computer, for instance), or you have the networking tools that let you transfer data readily between the host computer and the computer sitting on your desk.

Mail Connections

There are several different mail connections to the Internet. In fact, you may already have one. If, for instance, you have a CompuServe or America Online account, you automatically have an Internet mail connection. You can send mail to the Internet and have friends and colleagues on the Internet send mail to you. On CompuServe you simply precede the Internet mail address with **INTERNET:**. (For more information about sending mail to and from CompuServe, see Chapter 10.)

To send a message from the Internet to CompuServe, your associates would replace the comma in your CompuServe ID with a period and add **@compuserve.com** at the end (for example, **71234.5678@compuserve.com**).

You can even send mail across the Internet to other, non-Internet BBS accounts. And it's possible to use Internet's LISTSERV and mailing list systems to take part in Internet discussions on just about any subject through your CompuServe account. (See Chapter 16 for more about LISTSERV.) I don't advise this, however, because CompuServe will charge you 15 cents per message; it'll break the bank. These types of mail connections are also known as *network gateways*, systems by which networks connect to the Internet in a rather limited way.

By the way, CompuServe and the other online services are getting into the Internet business. America Online has several Internet services, and CompuServe recently added newsgroups and plans to add most or all Internet tools and systems in 1995. See Chapter 25 for more information.

UUCP stands for UNIX-to-UNIX Copy Program. It's a system by which mail can be placed in files and transferred to other computers.

Another form of mail connection is one in which you connect to the Internet in the same way as a dial-in terminal connection, but all you're allowed to do is get to the mail system. And finally, you could get a UUCP connection. This is a simple mail connection that uses software intended for this purpose (instead of a general purpose communications program). All you can do is send and receive mail and USENET newsgroup messages (which we'll look at in Chapter 15).

The Bottom Line: Pros and Cons

I'm assuming you have (or are going to acquire) one of the first three types of connections: a permanent, dial-in direct, or dial-in terminal connection. I'm going to ignore the mail connections because they are so limited in capabilities.

You're probably not quite ready to decide which of these three types of services you want. There are some other factors, such as cost, to consider. But let's at least compare the services to get an idea of the pros and cons of each.

Permanent Connection

A permanent connection is expensive, but may look like a good deal for a large company. Once connected, you can have as many users as your company's computer and the leased line can manage; there's no charge for individual users. If you have lots of users, it may turn out to be cheaper than giving each person his or her own account, especially if most of them use the Internet infrequently or for just a few minutes a day (to check for messages, for instance). But dedicated service is way out of the price range for most of us. If you are an individual looking for a way to get onto the Internet, forget about dedicated service.

Dial-In Direct Connection

A dial-in direct connection is the next best thing to a permanent connection. It can be quite affordable, and provides you with all of the benefits of dedicated service once you are logged on. You'll need a modem, of course, but since 14400 bits per second modems sell for as little as $100 or less these days, it's not too steep a cost. You'll need a fast modem—9600 bps at the very least. Anything less will be too slow.

Unlike a dial-in terminal connection, which can be established with any simple terminal program, a dial-in direct connection requires special software. You'll sometimes hear it referred to as "SLIP software" because SLIP is one of the most common types of dial-in direct connections. The available software has improved greatly in recent months, and is getting much easier to install and much cheaper. Some service providers, though by no means all, even provide the software when you sign up.

Bits per second is a measurement of how much data a modem can transmit. Computer data is stored in the form of bits, each bit being either a one or zero. String enough of these ones and zeros together, and you can describe anything, from a single character to a large document (or picture, sound, etc.). The actual rate at which your modem transmits will vary depending on the telephone line condition, what's happening on the computer at the other end, and so on.

Some service providers will be very helpful and will lead you through the process step by step. Others will set up your account on their computer and then tell you that you're on your own; it's up to you to figure it all out.

Although dial-in direct accounts do cost more to set up, they often cost no more than a dial-in terminal connection to run—that is, the same charge per hour. However, if you do a lot of research and often copy files from other computers, you're likely to spend less time on the Internet using the dial-in direct account than you would if you were using the dial-in terminal account. With the direct account, you will be able to copy files directly from other computers to your computer's hard disk. (In contrast, if you have a dial-in terminal account, you'll have to copy the files to your service provider's computer, and then do a file transfer to copy them from that computer back to yours.) And if you want to use all the fancy graphical user interfaces, with pictures, sounds, and even video, you'll need a dial-in direct account. See Chapter 25 for more information about these accounts.

Dial-In Terminal Connection

A dial-in terminal connection is a good, low-cost service for the casual user. The setup fee will often be a little less than for a dial-in direct connection ($20 as compared to $30 or $40, for instance), but the charge per hour may be the same, and, of course, you'll still need a modem. You can usually get away with a slower modem, though, (perhaps just 2400 bps), because the host computer is doing most of the work, sending screens of text to your monitor which doesn't take much effort. (However, if you plan to copy lots of files from other computer systems, a slow modem means slow transfers between your computer and the host computer. Large files can easily take an hour or more.)

With dial-in terminal, you'll be able to do almost anything on the Internet that you can do with a dial-in direct connection, except that some procedures will take a few more steps. To get a file from a computer in, say, Australia, you'll have to copy it to your service provider's computer, and then do a file transfer to get it to yours. (With a dial-in direct connection, the file would come straight from Australia to you.) And dial-in terminal doesn't come with the neat programs available to dial-in direct accounts.

You may find that the difference in capabilities between dial-in terminal and dial-in direct is so slight that you don't want to pay the extra setup money. And you might also lean toward dial-in terminal service if you find you can get it for free. Whereas you probably won't find any community computer networks providing free dial-in direct access to the Internet, as we'll see, there are a number that provide free dial-in terminal access.

Let Someone Else Pay

The best way to connect to the Internet is to use OPM—Other People's Money. Most Internet users are connected through an organization that has a dedicated connection to the Internet. Many large companies have their own computers connected directly to the Internet and allow their employees access to it.

IBM, for instance, is connected to the Internet, and claims to have 250,000 employees who could, if they wished, find their way onto the network. These employees don't have to pay anything to use Internet; they just have to get permission from the company. Many government departments have Internet access, and many universities also have connections and let students access the network for free. Most medium-sized and larger colleges have an Internet connection.

Talk with the person in your organization who's in charge of the Internet connection. You may find that you have to use the Internet from a terminal in the organization's building (in the office or from a university department building), or you may be able to dial in from home to your organization's computer and then get onto the Internet. This depends on the type of software and hardware that the organization has available.

If you don't know who's in charge of your Internet access (or if your organization is even hooked up), ask around. Ask the head of the computer department, computer center, information services department, or whatever. Ask the people who spend much of their time maintaining, installing, and fixing computers. It may be that only a few people in your organization use the Internet, and you won't get on without a bit of searching and diplomacy. Of course, most small companies won't have an Internet connection, but if you work for a medium-sized or large business, it may.

Find a Free-Net

If you can't get an account through your company or college, the next step is to look for a *Free-Net*. These are community computing systems, which may be based at a local library or college. You may be able to use the Internet from a terminal at the library, or perhaps you can even dial in-to the system from your home computer. And, as the name implies, they don't cost anything. (Well, some may have a small registration fee—$5 perhaps—but if they're not actually free, they are pretty close to it.)

Free-Nets offer a variety of local services, as well as access to the Internet. You may be able to find information about jobs in the area, local events, and recreation. You may be able to search the local library's database, find course schedules for local colleges, or ask someone questions about social security and Medicare.

 Even if you're not a student, you may be able to get onto a college's Internet system. Call your local college, see if they have a connection, and find out the requirements for network use. You may be able to use it if you are a part-time student (though you probably won't be able to dial in from home). So sign up for Basket Weaving 101.

Free-Nets usually have a "menu" of options based on a simulated "town." There's the Community Center, Teen Center, and Senior Center. There's an Administration Building, where you can go to register your account on the Free-Net; a Social Services and Organizations Center, where you can find support groups and local chapters of such national organizations as the Red Cross; and a Home and Garden Center, where you can find out about pest control and "Family Preparedness Planning." There might even be a Special Interests Center, where you can chat about UFOs, movies, religion, travel, or anything else. And Free-Nets also have a system that lets you send messages to other users.

You'll see the terms Free-Net, freenet, FreeNet, and maybe other variations. All these terms are service marks of NPTN (National Public Telecommuting Network), who prefer to use the term Free-Net.

Even without their Internet links, Free-Nets are a great community resource, especially for home-bound people such as the elderly and handicapped. (It's a shame that the very people who could benefit most from a computer system such as this are the least likely to have computers. Maybe that will change in the next few years.)

At the time of this writing there were a few dozen Free-Nets, mostly in the U.S., but also in New Zealand, Canada, and Finland. This number is expected to grow quickly. To find a Free-Net, e-mail info@nptn.org, or call the NPTN (National Public Telecommuting Network) at 216-498-4050. If you can't find a Free-Net, maybe you should start one in your town. NPTN can tell you how.

An Almost-Free Account in Washington

You can also get a free dial-in terminal account from the International Internet Association. This organization has received some criticism because, although they say the accounts are free, they make money if you dial in on their 800 number. Still, the account *is* free if you are in the same area code (202). The 800 number costs 20 cents/minute ($12/ hour). This service is also reportedly very busy and may be difficult to connect to (but then, it won't cost much to try it, will it!).

If you want to find out more about this offer, call (202) 387-5445, fax a request to (202) 387-5446, or write to The International Internet Association, Suite 852, 2020 Pennsylvania Ave., N.W., Washington, D.C., 20006.

More Freebies

There are more free sites around. Take a look in *Boardwatch* Magazine, *ComputerShopper*, *Online Access*, and other such magazines (which you can find in many bookstores, these days). Also, check your city's local computer publications and ask other Internet users you run into. You'll find bulletin board systems advertising Internet access, but you'll also find listings of free BBSs with Internet access. For example, in Denver there's NYX, a system at a local university. On NYX, you can get a free account, some Internet access, and even free international e-mail—not bad.

If you can't figure out where to find a free or almost-free Internet connection, you're going to have to pay—but pay as little possible. The next chapter explains how. For now, keep these things in mind:

The Least You Need to Know

➤ There are four main types of Internet connections.

➤ A permanent connection is the best type of connection, but it's expensive. You may have one if you are an employee of a large corporation or a member of an organization (such as a university).

➤ A dial-in direct (SLIP or PPP) connection is the next best thing.
It can be complicated to set up and is more expensive up front, but it may be easier and cheaper to use in the long run. (See Chapter 25.)

➤ A dial-in terminal connection is the most common type of
connection for individuals buying their own accounts. It's cheap and easy to set up, and you can use just about any data communications program.

➤ If you have an account with a computer "information service," such as CompuServe or America Online, you already have an Internet mail connection. You could also get a UUCP mail
connection from an Internet service provider.

➤ Ask your employer or local college if you can use their Internet connection.

➤ Find a Free-Net or another type of free BBS for free Internet access.

➤ If you are near Washington D.C., see if you can get a free account from the International Internet Association.

If You Have to Pay: Picking a Provider

If you've looked around and found no way to get a free account, the next stage is to find the service provider with the best rates and the services you need. In this chapter, we'll take a stroll around the block of paid providers, so you can see what's for sale.

How Do I Know What's out There?

When we first published *The Complete Idiot's Guide to the Internet*, we included a list of service providers, but since that time, the number has grown tremendously, making it impossible for us to list any significant portion of them. So, how do you find one?

Look in your city's local computer publication for ads. If you already have access to Internet e-mail, or you know someone who does, send a message to **info-deli-server@netcom.com** (see Chapter 10 for information on working with Internet e-mail). In the body of the message type **Send PDIAL**. The recipient automatically returns a message that includes a large list of service providers in the United States, some of which have international access.

What if you are in China, or India, or someplace else where Internet access is hard to find? (I recently received CompuServe e-mail from someone in China asking this very question.) Talk to everyone you know who works with computers. Maybe someone will have an idea.

Also, you may want to get a copy of the publication *Internet Access Providers* (Mecklermedia, $30). It's an international directory of service providers, regional networks, and bulletin boards, all with Internet access. (You can order it through your local bookstore by calling 800-632-5537, calling 203-226-6967, calling 071-976-0405 in the UK, or by sending e-mail to **info@mecklermedia.com**.)

And be sure to check out the coupons in the back of this book. There you'll find service providers who are offering discounts to *Idiot's Guide* readers.

Home-Town Operations

Look for all service providers with service in your area, not just the ones that are headquartered near you. Even if a provider is in, say, Maine, they may be able to provide local telephone number support all over the country by buying phone service in lots of different cities. You may find that the service closest to you is *not* the cheapest deal; a service based in another city may have a local phone number in your city, with lower rates.

One-Eight-Hundreds

Some services provide a 1-800 number you can call, regardless of where in the United States you happen to be. (Others have 800 numbers that work only within their home states.) You won't pay for the phone call connecting you to their computer, but you *will* pay a higher per-minute rate while you are connected than you normally would. For instance, if a service provider normally charges $1/hour for evening use, you may pay $6/hour if you are using their 1-800 number.

Still, there are two benefits to using a service provider with a 1-800 number: if you travel a lot, you can continue to use the Internet when you're out of town, and if you're far from a local-number connection, you can get onto the network without paying for long distance calls. The extra $5 or so per hour may still be less than the long distance charges.

Data Networks

Depending on where you're located, you may be able to use a data network to connect. It's like this: a number of companies have leased telephone lines and numbers all over the country. A service provider can sign up with one of these companies, so the data network is linked to the service provider's computer.

For example, a service provider named The World has telephone numbers only in the Boston area. But users in, say, Phoenix or Dallas who want to use The World's services can sign up with CompuServe Packet Network or PC-Pursuit (Sprint Data Services). These two companies have local numbers all over the country, so a user can dial the CompuServe or Sprint number, log onto the network's computer, and then log onto The World's computer.

You don't need to have a CompuServe Information Service account in order to use CompuServe's Packet Network.

Of course there's a charge, perhaps $5 or $6 per hour. (Some services are as low as $1/hour during evenings and weekends.) If you find a service provider with low rates but no local number, ask them if they have a data network through which you can connect; then figure out the total cost.

The standard of service you'll get can vary widely. Some service providers are very helpful and have responsive technical support, good documentation, and even setup programs that will lead you through installing a dial-in direct connection. Others will set up an account for you on their end, but leave the rest for you to figure out. Also, some services are currently overused, in which case you'll run into busy signals when trying to connect, and may find that the system seems to "hang" when you try to type a command. If you know other Internet users, ask for a recommendation. Otherwise, you'll just have to pick a service and see what it's like.

Use an Online Service

You may already have access to the Internet if you are a member of an online service. I'm not talking about the capability to send mail to and from the Internet, which most online services offer. I'm talking about being able to log onto your service provider and use Internet tools such as Gopher, FTP, telnet, and so on. Delphi, for example, already provides full Internet access. America Online has Gopher, WAIS, and thousands of newsgroups. (Look in the back of this book for Delphi and America Online coupons). CompuServe has newsgroups, and plans to add all sorts of things in 1995. Even PRODIGY is talking about adding Internet access.

Comparison Shopping

Once you've found a few promising service providers with local numbers, data networks, or 800 numbers, call or write them to get their rates. Before you buy, compare. Making the best deal can save you hundreds of dollars in setup fees, and hundreds of dollars a year in *connect fees* (the money you are charged for actually using the service).

Shopping for Permanent Connections

Shopping for a permanent connection is way beyond the scope of this book. If you are an individual, you don't want a permanent connection (at least, you don't want to pay for one). Permanent connections require routers, leased lines, and all sorts of other expensive items. Startup costs are in the thousands of dollars, and yearly costs in the tens of thousands. Anyone shopping for a permanent connection should probably be reading a different, much more in-depth, book.

Shopping for Dial-In Direct

If you want dial-in direct service, you may have to pay a one-time connection fee of $30 or $40. You'll find a great variety in the way you pay and how much you pay, so compare as many providers as you can. These days dial-in direct hourly rates are about the same as those for dial-in terminal accounts.

And remember that the best deal depends on your circumstances. For some users, $175/month for unlimited dial-in direct use is a good deal. That averages about 1.9 hours a day at $3/hour; if you use it more than that, the price per hour will drop. If most of your use will be during the evening, $175 would buy you 2.9 hours each evening at the $2/hour rate, but will you really use that much? For many users, a 15-hour/month minimum is a better deal.

Shopping for Dial-In Terminal

You can find dial-in terminal accounts for as low as $10 to $25/month for unlimited use, which seems very reasonable. Often, they go for a little more, such as $3/hour with a $15/month minimum and a $100/month maximum (once you've paid for $100 worth of online time, the rest is free). And you may have lower hourly rates at certain times of day; for example, $2 in the evenings and $1 at night.

Remember to check into which services are available. Some service providers that sell dial-in terminal accounts may not provide you with full Internet access.

Shopping for Mail Connections

Simple mail connections are selling well these days as people become more interested in e-mail connections they can use while on the move. There are a number of ways to get an e-mail connection: through CompuServe, GEnie, or America Online, and through true Internet service providers. So if you want to send and receive Internet mail through an online service of which you are already a member, it's simply a matter of using an Internet mail address. Keep in mind that you may be charged a small fee for each message. CompuServe charges a fee, America Online doesn't. Some service providers charge as little as $10/month for unlimited messages.

Explaining What You Want

When you first contact a service provider, make sure you are both talking about the same thing. If you don't understand the account types they are talking about (and there are plenty of variations, with many service providers creating their own product names), make sure they clarify what they are offering.

If you want a dial-in terminal account, say:

"I want an account that I can dial into with a simple telecommunications program, and which allows me full access to the Internet—mail, FTP, USENET, telnet, and so on."

Okay, so you don't know what these terms mean. That's okay. You will eventually, and (more importantly) the service provider does now.

If you want a dial-in direct account, say:

"I want a SLIP, CSLIP, or PPP account."

If all you are interested in is sending electronic mail, and you don't want to use all the other fancy Internet capabilities, say:

"I want a simple mail account."

You may hear a service provider use one of these names for the types of service we've been discussing:

Permanent may be called direct, permanent direct, or dedicated service. **Dial-in terminal** may be called interactive or dial-up service. **Dial-in direct** may be called SLIP, CSLIP, PPP, or TCP/IP service. **Mail** may be called UUCP, e-mail, or messaging service.

Of course if you are reviewing information sent in the mail, you'll have to dig through it carefully to figure out the different options.

Once you are both talking about the same thing, you can use the following list of questions to compare the rates of different service providers. This list is intended for use in comparing dial-in direct services, dial-in terminal services, and mail connections. I do not discuss permanent connections, as those are far more complicated and beyond the scope of this book.

➤ *How much is the connect or startup cost for dial-in terminal and dial-in direct services?* To get started, you may have to pay a setup charge, which is a one-time fee and runs between $20 and $45.

➤ *Do you provide free software for dial-in direct accounts?* It's possible to get dial-in direct accounts quite cheaply, but you may have to provide your own software. Other service providers may charge more but give you the software. Some service providers provide shareware that you can install—though it's not always easy to do so (unless you read *The Complete Idiot's Next Step with the Internet*, that is). Others, such as NETCOM and The Pipeline, have their own software. Or you can buy commercial dial-in direct software for around $100 and up. (See Chapter 25.)

> The differences between accounts are starting to blur. For instance, NETCOM sells NetCruiser (a program that runs with a PPP account) that is so easy to install, you don't realize you are setting up a dial-in direct account. And The Pipeline has a hybrid system. It's a Windows system that is neither dial-in direct nor dial-in terminal, yet it has many of the advantages of dial-in direct. (It's actually a *Pink SLIP* system—see Chapter 25.)

➤ *Is there a fixed fee?* The amount you pay per hour can vary tremendously. Some service providers don't charge by the hour; they charge a single monthly fee and provide unlimited time on the Internet ($15 a month for unlimited use, for instance). Also, some service providers charge different fees for different modem speeds. Make sure you get the price for the speed of the modem you are using.

➤ *If there's a fixed fee, is it for limited access?* If the service provider is charging a fixed fee, make sure you know what hours you will be allowed onto the system. Some providers may have a low fixed fee account, but will only let you on in the evenings.

➤ *How much do you charge per hour during weekdays?* Many providers charge an hourly rate, such as $3 an hour for online time between, say, 8:00 a.m. and 8:00 p.m. during the week. You may have to make a few notes along with the numbers. For example, some providers charge a minimum which gets you a few free hours ($10/month with four free hours) and then charge a set fee for subsequent hours (say, $4/hour for the fifth and subsequent hours). In addition, some providers may have two or more payment plans for the same service, so you may need more than one column for each provider when you're comparing services. And remember to check rates for your modem speed.

➤ *How much per hour in the evening?* What hours do you consider "evening"? Rates are usually lower from 8:00 p.m. to midnight.

➤ *How much per hour at night?* What hours do you consider "night"? Rates are often lower still between midnight and 8:00 a.m., perhaps around $1/hour.

➤ *How much per hour during weekends?* Check to see if there's a lower rate during weekends. Some service providers use the same schedule for all seven days, the only variation being the time of service and not the day.

➤ *Is there a minimum number of hours I must use each month?* The service provider will probably charge a minimum monthly fee. This may be combined with an hourly rate. For instance, you may have to pay $15/month minimum (which might get you 5 hours at the highest $3/hour rate or 15 hours at the lowest $1/hour rate) and then pay an additional amount when you've used up the $15 worth. Or perhaps the minimum buys you a set number of hours at a low rate, and the rate goes up once you've used those hours.

➤ *Can I pay for a maximum number of hours, after which all hours are free?* If a service provider charges by the hour, they may have a maximum. For example, once you've paid $150 in hourly fees, everything is free for the rest of the month.

➤ *Do you have a local number?* Ideally, you want a service provider with a telephone number in your area code, so you don't have to pay long distance charges.

➤ *Is there a surcharge on that local number?* Some service providers charge you extra to use their local number—perhaps as much as $9 an hour! Ideally you want a *free* local number.

➤ *Do you have 1-800 access? What is the surcharge? Is it national, or state only?* Some service providers have 1-800 numbers you can use. You'll pay a surcharge (maybe $5–$12/hour), but if you live in the boonies with no Internet number in your area code, you might find it cheaper to use the 1-800 number than to pay long distance charges. The 1-800 number is also convenient for people who want to be able to use the Internet while away from home.

➤ *Do you have data network access? What is the surcharge?* Some service providers have data networks they work with. The surcharge will vary from $1/hour to about $6/hour, depending on the time of day that you use the Internet.

➤ *What modem speeds do you support?* The slower the connection, the more time everything will take, and the more expensive your online work will be—in terms of both money and time. If all your service provider can manage is 2400 bps (bits per second), it's probably too slow. They should have at least 9600 bps, and preferably 14400 bps (many will soon be operating at 28800 bps). Of course, the data-transmission speed you want to use is limited by the speed of your computer's modem. If you have a 300 bps modem, it doesn't matter if the service provider has 14400 bps modems; *your* connection will be at 300 bps.

If a service provider says it has a **POP** (Point of Presence) in your area, it means they have a local telephone number in your area. You won't have to pay for long distance calls to connect to the Internet.

Many people use the term *baud* instead of bps. The two terms are pretty much interchangeable, although they're not exactly the same—and purists will tell you that bps is the more correct of the two when referring to your modem's throughput. Baud is named for J. M. E. Baudot, who invented the Baudot telegraph code, and refers to the modulation and demodulation rate of the modem (the rate at which the modem converts between the computer's digital signal and the phone line's analog signal).

➤ *How much is disk space per megabyte per month?* Your service provider will probably charge you if you store too much stuff (messages and files) on his computer's hard disk. This doesn't have to be a problem, though. A provider may let you use up to 1 MB (megabyte) for free, then charge from 50 cents to $2–$3 a month for each additional MB. You can store a lot of messages in 1 MB, and you can make sure you always move files from their computer to yours so you don't go above the limit. (If you have a dial-in direct connection, files will land directly on your computer's hard disk anyway—not on your service provider's.)

➤ *How much is domain service?* When you get a dial-in direct account you can establish your own *domain name* or use the service provider's (we'll discuss the pros and cons later, in Chapter 6). Establishing your own domain name may be free, or it may cost $10 or $20.

➤ *Do you provide a discount for* Complete Idiot's Guide *readers?* Some service providers have agreed to give readers of *The Complete Idiot's Guide to the Internet* a special discount. (See the coupons at the back of this book.)

➤ *Are there any other charges?* There are as many ways to charge you as there are service providers. Check the fine print.

The Least You Need to Know

➤ Don't look at just the service providers close to you; some non-local ones may have local numbers.

➤ If you are a long way from a service provider's coverage area, look for one with a 1-800 number or data network access.

➤ Remember to check the service provider's modem speed. Some still use slow modems.

➤ Compare costs carefully—rates vary widely.

➤ Check the coupons in the back of this book to see if a service provider is offering a discount to readers.

## Chapter 5

Let's Get Physical: What You Need to Get Started

In This Chapter

➤ The type of computer you need

➤ How to pick a modem

➤ The type of software you need

➤ Account names and passwords

If you've decided that the Internet's for you, you need to decide if you've got what it takes—if you have the computer hardware and software you'll need. Internet's hardware demands are not extreme, but there are a few things to consider. You are going to need the following:

➤ An Internet account (of course)

➤ A computer or terminal

➤ A modem or connection

➤ Simple communications software

➤ Mail software (maybe)

➤ A login name

➤ A password

Get Your Account!

The first thing you're going to need is an *Internet account*. Until you've figured out how to get one, there's not much point in trying to figure out the rest. So if you haven't yet decided on the type of account (and where you're going to get it), go back to Chapters 2 and 3 and do so.

I'm going to use the term **Internet account** (or simply, **account**) throughout this book to mean "access to the Internet." You may also hear the terms Internet access, Internet service, or Internet connection. These all mean the same thing: the capability to "get onto" the Internet and use its services.

A Screen to Read, a Keyboard to Type On

You need some electronic means of communicating with the Internet. If you are getting your account from an organization with a permanent connection, the system manager will provide you with something or tell you what you need. You might get an actual computer, or you might only get a *dumb terminal*, a keyboard and a monitor that is hooked up to the organization's computer.

If you are directly connected to the service provider's computer (usually if you are part of the organization or company), you don't need to establish the connection yourself. However, if you are dialing into your account (whether it's dial-in direct or dial-in terminal), you'll need an actual computer with a modem and some communications software. That's because the computer must call the service provider's computer and "log on."

 The term *dumb terminal* means that your piece of equipment has no actual computing power; all it has is the capability to send and receive text. When you sit and type, the terminal sends the text to the computer. The computer does whatever it's supposed to do with the text; then sends some more text back to your terminal to tell you what it's just done. One of the most common types of dumb terminals is the VT100. Originally a Digital Electronics Corporation terminal, it has become a standard, and many manufacturers' terminals now emulate the way the VT100 works. That is, they imitate it by working the same way.

What type of computer should you use? You've got a wide choice. You can use any IBM PC-compatible, Macintosh, Apple, UNIX workstation, or any other computer that can have a modem installed (or to which you can connect a modem) and that can run communications software. For a dial-in terminal connection, you don't need much of a computer. You don't need the latest Pentium PC with a 24-bit color monitor. As a matter of fact, you can use the earliest 8086 PC with a monochrome monitor if you want (which you can pick up for $100 or less if you look hard).

If you are going to use a dial-in direct connection, you may need a little more computer. There are dial-in direct programs for DOS, but most of the really neat programs for IBM-compatible PCs are designed for Microsoft Windows. To run Windows, you'll need a 286 at the very least, and a 386 or later is better. There are also dial-in direct programs for the Mac, but you'll find a wider selection in the IBM PC world.

Getting Connected

If you are using a dumb terminal, all you need is a connection to the organization's computer. You don't need to worry about that, though. The system manager will figure out how to connect a wire between the two.

If you are using a dial-in direct or dial-in terminal account (both of which require your computer to "dial in" to the service provider's system), you will need a modem. Modems come in two types: internal and external. An *internal modem* is a computer board that plugs into a slot inside the computer, with the phone line plugged into a socket on the edge of the modem. An *external modem* is a box that contains a board much like the internal modem board, but which connects to the outside of your computer with a cable running to the computer's serial port (one of the plugs on the back). The phone line then plugs into the modem box.

Internal and external modems are the same thing, they are just located in different places. They vary slightly in price: external modems are a bit more expensive because they need a box and an extra socket (for power). In addition, they use up your serial port, which can be a hassle (many computers have the mouse plugged into the serial port, and may not have a spare one).

The faster your modem, the better. If you are going to use a dial-in direct connection, you *must* have a fast modem. You'll find anything less than 9600 bps is too slow, and even 9600 bps may be frustrating. You're better off with 14400 bps. (At the time of this writing, service providers were talking about upgrading their systems to 28800 bps, so by the time you read this, that may be an option as well.)

Help! Which Modem Should I Buy?

I can't tell you which modem to buy, because your choices are directly related to the type of computer you are using. If you already have a modem, use it; it'll probably work fine. If you don't have one yet, you might want to talk to the service provider and ask for a recommendation. Sometimes modems run into compatibility problems. It's possible (though unlikely) that the modem you buy will have trouble connecting to the service provider's computer. The service provider should be able to give you a list of modems that they know to work well, and perhaps even a list of modems that have problems connecting.

 Doubling the speed of your modem doesn't cut your costs in half. The modem speed affects only the transmissions between your computer and the service provider's computer, such as when you're uploading or downloading files. Unfortunately, much of your online time will be spent waiting for other computers to do their work. Still, fast modems will save you money.

You'll probably find that your service provider is using fairly advanced modems with fancy specifications such as V.32*bis*, MNP-5, V.42, V.42*bis*, and so on. (These describe the way in which modems communicate and handle problems during a transmission.) As a result, your service provider might recommend a top-of-the-line modem that costs $300 to $500. Don't do it. You can buy a fast (14400 bps) high-quality modem for $100 to $150 if you look around, and prices are dropping all the time. Try buying from a reputable mail-order company, such as MicroWarehouse (800-367-7080), PC/Mac Zone (800-258-2088), or Direct Micro (800-288-2887). Ask your service provider the modem specifications you must match; then buy a modem that matches. You're better off buying a name brand modem, but not necessarily "top-of-the-line."

There are no guarantees, of course. If there's a bug in your modem's *firmware* (the software that makes the modem run), you might have problems even if your modem matches. Although it's unlikely, this does happen (as thousands of purchasers of fax/modems from a certain major computer manufacturer—which will remain nameless—can attest). But if you buy from a reputable mail-order company, you can always return the modem and try another one.

One day (soon, perhaps) you won't need a modem. Your phone line will connect to a special card in your computer that transmits digital signals straight to the other computer—no need to modulate them into analog signals and demodulate from digital signals. The real advantage is that such digital transmissions are *very* fast.

Picking the Software You Need

If you have been given a permanent connection Internet account by your company or college, you probably don't need communications software. Your computer or terminal is already connected directly to a computer that is (in turn) connected directly to the Internet. Your system administrator (the guy or gal in charge of the organization's Internet accounts) chooses which system to use.

However, if you are going to use a dial-in account, you'll need a *communications program*. This program tells your modem what to do when it's communicating with the service provider's computer, and displays the session (the text that you send and receive while working on the Internet) on your computer screen.

If you are using a dial-in terminal account, you probably don't need to buy communications software. Most modems these days come with a program such as Qmodem or Crosstalk, and if your computer uses Microsoft Windows, you have Windows Terminal. If you use an *integrated package* (a program that integrates several mini-programs, such as a word processor, spreadsheet, and database), you may be in luck: many of these also include a simple communications program. And a simple program is all you need to get onto the Internet using a dial-in terminal account.

If you do have to buy a communications program, they start at around $50, although you can find shareware communications programs for much less. To find out about available shareware communications programs, call Public Brand Software (800-426-3475) or Software Labs (800-569-7900) for PC-based shareware. Make sure you get a program that can do *xmodem* data transfers (most can these days) or, better still, *zmodem* transfers.

The more sophisticated communications programs have a lot of advantages (of course). For instance, they enable you to write "scripts" for logging onto the Internet so the program will automatically enter your login name, password, and so on. Some programs can even "learn" the logon procedure from you: the program watches the first time you log on, and then duplicates the procedure the next time.

When I provide examples of using a communication program, I'll use Windows Terminal because so many people have it and because it's a fairly basic, straightforward program (though not without its problems). Whichever program you get, though, spend some time playing with it and figuring out how it all works. You need to know how to enter the setup information (modem speed, telephone number, terminal type, and so on). You also need to know how to use the program to connect to a BBS, how to capture text files, and how to do *binary transfers* (xmodem or zmodem transfers, for instance).

If you are using a dial-in direct connection, you won't use a simple communications program. Instead, you will work with programs designed to work on TCP/IP connections. For more information, see Chapters 6 and 25.

If you managed to find a Free-Net connection, I've pretty much covered what you need to get started: a computer, a modem, and a communications program. Dial the Free-Net and follow the instructions. You'll be told about how to register and how to select a login

Shareware is distributed for free or at a very low cost. A shareware communications program from a distributor may cost around $5 or $10. If you like the program, you must register it and pay for it. Fees vary, but they start around $10 for the simplest communications program and go to as much as $90 for the most sophisticated.

Windows Terminal is actually easier to use than many telecommunications packages, but it's not the world's finest piece of programming. And it doesn't have all the "bells and whistles" available with a more advanced program. Eventually you may want to find something better.

name and password. And at some point (perhaps not the first day), you should be able to get onto the Internet itself, which we'll get into in later chapters.

I've Got a Name

To get connected, you will need a *login name*. (You will also see the terms *username* and *account name*.) This is the name of your account, the name you will type each time you access the Internet. It tells the service provider who you are so that he or she knows whether to let you on the network (and knows who to bill for the time). Your login name will also be part of the "address" that other users type when they want to send messages to you.

A login name can be up to eight characters, and it is *case-sensitive*. In other words, Pkent is not the same as pkent or pKENT or PKENT. You will always have to type in your login name in exactly the same way (actually, you'll probably get your communications software to do it for you). A login name is usually made up of the account owner's name, such as *pete*, *pkent*, *peterk*, or *peterwk*, but you can make yours anything you want.

If you are using a dial-in direct connection, you will also need to know your host number and domain name. See Chapter 6 for details on these.

The Password Is...

You also need a *password*, a secret "code" to type when the system asks you to do so. Since the computer assumes that if it receives the correct password, the correct person is trying to log on, you shouldn't let anyone else learn your password.

Why do you care if someone else is able to log on as you? Well, first of all, you don't want to pay for the time someone else spends working or playing on the Internet. Nor do you want someone reading your messages, sending messages under your name, deleting your files, or communicating

This isn't just theory. There really are people who want to break into your account. The press has reported that many service providers' systems have been "broken into" recently, forcing at least one organization to close down for a while.

in the newsgroups as you. There are people out there who would like to get your password, and who know a few (computer) tricks to help them do so. They work on the basic assumption that your password is easy to figure out because it's a name or a word.

In most cases, passwords can be up to eight characters (check with the service provider). And, like the login name, your password is case-sensitive. If you are using 1n=9YT% as a password, you can't type 1N=9YT% or 1n=9yt%. (It should go without saying that this is only an example.)

Passwords: Pick a Good One

So how do you pick a good password? It shouldn't be a recognizable name or word—not the name of one of your kids or your dog, not a description of your job ("bookie" or "boss," for example), not the name of your house or a character from *The Simpsons*. It also shouldn't be a meaningful number, especially not your Social Security number or your date of birth.

Here are a few tips for picking a good password:

➤ The best password is a random jumble of characters (1n=9YT%, for example).

➤ Because random jumbles are difficult to remember, create what *appears* to be a random jumble, even if it isn't. For example, mix special characters with several short words, such as I&you%in. You could pick three short words at random from the dictionary.

➤ Don't give your password to anyone else; if you have to, change it as soon as he or she is finished using it.

➤ Don't type your password while someone is watching; if you must, change it as soon as he leaves.

➤ Change your password regularly, such as every month. (Some systems may force you to do so by stopping you from logging in until you create a new password.)

➤ Don't write your password online (in messages, for instance) or anywhere else.

➤ The longer your password, the better. Five characters is too short. Ask your service provider the maximum password length (probably eight characters).

When you are first given an account, you may be able to tell the service provider what password you want to use, or they may simply assign you one. Log onto the system as soon as possible and change the password; while your paperwork has been lying around the service provider's offices, several people have probably seen it.

> If you forget your password, don't worry. Call the service provider. Someone there will be able to assign you a new one. Use it to log on; then change the password immediately.

Do You Need Mail Software?

If you are getting a mail connection to the Internet through a service provider, they may give you (or sell you) some *mail software*. These programs enable you to read and write your mail messages when you're not connected to the Internet (and therefore not paying online charges). The program will then go online, drop off your messages, and pick up the ones waiting for you. You can tell the program to do this immediately, or schedule it so it does so at regular intervals. If you want to learn more about mail programs and mail readers, see the **comp.bbs.waffle** and **comp.os.msdos.mail-news** newsgroups (you'll learn about newsgroups in Chapter 15). Be warned, however: setting up shareware programs for Internet communications can be complicated. If you are a novice and value your time, you may want to buy what your service provider offers, since it is probably set up correctly to run with their system.

The Least You Need to Know

If your organization provides you with an account, don't worry about this; they'll tell you what you need. If you are setting up any other type of account, remember these basic guidelines:

➤ If you are getting your own account, you'll need a computer and a fast modem (as fast as possible).

➤ Ask your service provider to recommend a modem, and buy one that matches the specifications they give you (though not necessarily the exact modem they recommend).

➤ Ask the service provider if they know of any modems that *won't* work with their system.

➤ For dial-in terminal accounts, just about any simple data communications program should work.

➤ Pick a sensible password: make it long and seemingly random. Don't select real words, names, or numbers that have a meaning to you.

O.K. PEOPLE, LISTEN UP!!

THE DIAL-IN DIRECT FOLKS ASSOCIATION

Special Stuff for Dial-In Direct Folks

If you've decided that dial-in direct is the way to go, you've got some extra things to think about. Are you beginning to think that a dial-in terminal might be a lot less hassle? In most cases it is, and the casual user may be better off with a dial-in terminal account. The software is easier to install, the connection is cheaper, and the headaches are fewer—in most cases. But if you're planning to spend a lot of time on the Internet, it may be worth it for you to slog out the details of a dial-in direct account. This chapter should help.

You Need TCP/IP Software!

If you are going to use a dial-in direct account, you need *TCP/IP software* (Transmission Control Protocol/Internet Protocol—now you can forget what it means; most people do). So where do you find this TCP/IP software? When we published the first edition of this book, this software was hard to find, even harder to install, and expensive ($300 to $400). But in the past year, the market has really taken off. To get an idea of the TCP/IP software available, take a look at Chapter 25. See Chapter 26 for information about the dial-in direct software on the disk included with this book.

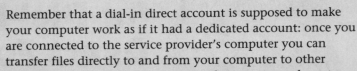

Remember that a dial-in direct account is supposed to make your computer work as if it had a dedicated account: once you are connected to the service provider's computer you can transfer files directly to and from your computer to other computers on the Internet. (With a dial-in terminal account, you have to copy files from the other computers to the service provider's computer, and then copy them over to your computer.)

There are a number of commercially distributed TCP/IP programs, such as Chameleon, a Microsoft Windows program sold by NetManage (408-973-7171, richard@netmanage.com); PC/TCP, a DOS and Windows program from FTP, Inc. (508-685-4000); and Air Navigator and Internet in a Box, both sold by SPRY (see the coupon in the back of this book). And, of course, there's also SuperHighway Access, which you can try out by using the "sampler" on the disk included with this book (see Chapter 26). There are also programs available for other computers. Ask your service provider what he or she recommends.

TCP/IP Shareware

There is a multitude of shareware programs, including Windows programs, for dial-in direct connections. But as I mentioned before, setting up shareware TCP/IP communications packages on the Internet is no simple matter; it's probably beyond the average novice, unless he wants to invest dozens (hundreds?) of hours figuring it all out and seeking information. And even many experienced users will find installing the Windows TCP/IP systems quite a challenge. The documentation provided with most shareware is generally difficult to work with. However, PC owners may want to check out *The Complete Idiot's Next Step with the Internet*. In that "sequel" to the book you are now reading, I provide detailed instructions for installing and using TCP/IP shareware for IBM PC-compatibles. And in *The Complete Idiot's Guide to World Wide Web*, I explain how to set up a TCP/IP connection and a web browser (such as Mosaic) for both Windows and the Macintosh.

If you've decided that you need a dial-in direct account, you'll probably want to start with the software SuperHighway Access Sampler on this book's disk (see Chapter 26). Once that's installed, you can check out more of the SuperHighway Access suite of programs by downloading from the Frontier Technologies FTP site (see Chapter 27). And with the SuperHighway Access TCP/IP stack installed, you can even run Windows TCP/IP shareware, such as Mosaic, Cello, WinWAIS, and many other programs. (You'll find lots of information about this stuff in *The Complete Idiot's Next Step with the Internet*.)

There's shareware not only for IBM-compatible PCs, of course, but also for Macs, Amigas, Sun workstations, other UNIX computers, and so on.

Host Numbers: A Bit of Techie

If you are getting a dial-in direct account, you will need a host number. In effect, your computer will be registered as an Internet *node*, with communications passing from your "host" through the service provider's host and vice versa. For instance, your host number will look something like this: **192.94.50.236**. You will get your host number in one of two ways. Either your service provider gives you a number (and you enter that number into your TCP/IP software), or the system uses some method of dynamically assigning you a number each time you log on. With the first method, the number is always yours. With the second method, the number you get when you log on may be different each time. It really doesn't matter too much which method is used, but it does affect the way in which you set up your TCP/IP software (see Chapter 27).

When you sit down to work with the Internet, your computer (or your computer terminal) is connected to a computer that is connected to the network. For instance, with a dial-in terminal account, you use your PC to connect to another computer, which in turn is connected to the Internet. The computers that are connected directly to the Internet are known as *hosts*, and each one is assigned a unique number. That

The host computers are connected to **routers**, which are computers that connect various parts of the network and route messages between different areas. The lines between the routers may be telephone lines, or they may be local area networks (cable links among multiple computers) in a company or on a university campus.

number is the *address* that the Internet uses to send the messages to their correct destination. It's made up of numbers identifying the network on which the host may be found (remember, the Internet is a conglomeration of networks) and numbers identifying the *routers* used to get the message to the particular host. For instance, the address used by Colorado SuperNet is **128.138.213.21.**

Domain Names: Not Quite So Techie

An Internet user is identified by his username and *domain name*, such as **fredflint@bedrock.com**. In this address, the username is **fredflint**, and the domain name is **bedrock.com**. The host number is used by the computer equipment itself, but in order to make it easier for mere mortals to use, the system also assigns a domain name to each host.

No matter what kind of Internet connection you have, it wouldn't hurt for you to understand domain names. Consider reading this material and writing it on your heart, even if you're sure you don't want anything fancier than a dial-in terminal account.

The Domain Name System (DNS) uses subsets of domains to identify computers and groups of accounts on a computer. For example, one domain is named **gov**. Not surprisingly, that's the domain used by the U.S. Government. In addition, that domain has other domains associated with it, one of which is named **whitehouse**. (Actually it's more correctly named **whitehouse.gov**, because a domain is always identified in relation to the domain of which it is a part.) And yes, **whitehouse** is the domain at the White House. Each level in this system is known as a domain, so one domain may have several domains "under" it, each of which may have several more associated domains. Think of these as "subdomains."

Here's another gov domain: **fdabbs.fda.gov**. This identifies the domain in which you'll find the Food and Drug Administration's bulletin board (**fdabbs**), which is part of the FDA domain (**fda**), which is part of the U.S. Government domain (**gov**). You can log onto this computer and find consumer information, news releases, information about drugs, and so on. And here's the domain I currently use: **csn.org**. That's the computer used by Colorado Supernet (**csn**, the service provider I work through), which is part of a group of "other organizations" (**org**).

As you can see, the lowest-level domain is the left part of the name, the highest-level is the right part. Here are a few more high-level domain names you may see:

➤ **edu** A national group of educational institutions (most universities and schools are part of this domain)

➤ **com** Commercial organizations (businesses)

➤ **mil** Military domains

➤ **ca** Canadian domains

➤ **cf** Central African Republic domains

➤ **co** Colorado

As you can see from the last two in this list, there are also country and state domains. Most countries have been assigned codes, though not all are on the network. You probably won't be seeing any **cf** domain messages anytime soon, but there's a domain name waiting for them as soon as they are ready.

Domain names can also be geographical names. For instance, **golden.co.us** is a domain in Golden, Colorado, in the United States of America.

Want Your Own Domain?

When you get an Internet account, you may have no choice about the domain name. If you are getting access through a company or university, you will be told what domain name to use. But if you are buying access from a service provider for yourself, your company, your school, or whatever, you can pick a domain name. Instead of using the host computer's domain name, you can create your own.

When you ask your service provider to give you a particular domain name, the provider has to register the name with the NIC (Network Information Center), which takes about ten days. This group makes sure that domain names are unique and are correctly associated with the number that identifies the actual computers used by that domain. Domains that are members of the same higher-level domain are not always directly and physically connected through the same hardware. Domains are simply used to help people figure out how the network is organized. What really counts (as far as the computers are concerned) are the host numbers, and the domain name tells you nothing about the actual host computers involved.

Let's say you have a company called Acme Potato Peelers, Inc. How about using **apotpeel** as the lowest-level domain? You could then create a name that shows where you are, for example, **apotpeel.golden. co.us**. Or you could make your company part of the **com** domain (commercial, a domain of businesses). Thus your domain name could be **apotpeel.com**.

The capability to create a domain name is important to an organization, of course. Once you have your **apotpeel.com** domain name, you can then add a few more domains, such as one for each department: **sales.apotpeel.com**, **mgt.apotpeel.com**, and so on. However, there's another advantage to a business or an individual having a domain name for an Internet account. Once you have a domain name, it's yours, regardless of the service provider you use. So if the one you are currently using decides to double its prices or reduce its service, you can jump ship and take your domain name with you. The new service provider will have to register a change with the Network Information Center, so the host-computer number associated with your domain name will now be the one used by the new service provider's computer.

You may have to pay $10–$20 if you want to create your own domain name, or it may be free. Libraries, universities, schools, and governmental organizations use special naming conventions, but individual companies can create domain names in any form they wish.

Although your service provider may encourage you to, you don't have to create a domain name. You can use the service provider's domain name, if you want. If you are buying access from Colorado Super-Net, you can use their domain name, **csn.org**. So if you picked a login name of **joebloe**, your Internet address would be **joebloe@csn.org**.

It's Not So Easy...

When I wrote the first edition of this book, I didn't spend too much time writing about dial-in direct accounts for two reasons. First, few people had them. Second, they are not always easy to set up, and there's a large choice of programs that you can work with.

Since then, however, a lot has changed. Dial-in direct accounts are *much* cheaper (sign up fees are down to around 20% of the price they were a year ago) and, therefore, more people are using them. And because there's much better TCP/IP software available, they're getting easier to set up, too.

Still, we are left with a real problem. Explaining how to choose the right software, install it, and use it could take an entire book. In fact it *does* take an entire book. In *The Complete Idiot's Next Step with the Internet,* for example, I devote one entire chapter to telling you all the questions you have to ask your service provider before you try to set up a dial-in direct account. Then there's information about installing dial-in direct software for DOS; getting Trumpet Winsock (a TCP/IP "stack" for Windows); running, installing, and using Mosaic; and... well, it's a big subject.

Most people are still working with dial-in terminal accounts. This book explains the basics of Internet use for *all* users, but describes the actual tools that dial-in terminal users are working with. If you want to check out what's available for dial-in direct accounts, see Chapter 25. Then see Chapter 26 for information on installing SuperHighway Access Sampler, the free TCP/IP software bundled with this book. Read Chapter 27 to find out how to use this software—and how to get more of the SuperHighway Access suite of programs. If you still want to know more about TCP/IP software for DOS and Windows (both shareware and commercial products), read *The Complete Idiot's Next Step with the Internet.*

The Least You Need to Know

➤ For dial-in direct accounts, you need TCP/IP software. Expect to pay around $100 or more.

➤ Host numbers are the addresses that the computers on the Internet use among themselves to identify one another; domain names are the text equivalents preferred by humans because they're easier to remember and decipher.

➤ You can select your own domain name, but you may have to pay for the privilege.

➤ See Chapter 25 for more information about dial-in direct software, and read *The Complete Idiot's Next Step with the Internet* for information on selecting, installing, and using dial-in direct programs.

➤ Better still, use the free software that comes with this book—see Chapter 26.

## Chapter 7

Your First Trip to the Internet

In This Chapter

➤ Connecting with different types of accounts

➤ Setting up your software

➤ The info you need to know before you start

➤ The actual logon

➤ Changing your password

➤ Getting the heck out of there

Well, it's about time, huh? You're finally ready to get onto the Internet. In this chapter, I'm going to describe how to *log onto* the Internet, and a little about what you'll find once you are logged on. You'll also learn how to change your password and how to log off.

The procedure for logging on is different depending on which kind of connection you're using—whether it's a dedicated link, a dial-in direct account, or a dial-in terminal account.

Easy Street: Logging On with a Permanent Connection

A permanent-connection account is simplest to log onto because you don't have to worry about setting up communications software. You simply sit at one of your organization's terminals or computers, and enter the commands that the system administrator gave you. I can't say what those commands might be, except that at some point you'll have to enter your login name and password. Your terminal may show your terminal name and a **login:** prompt. Type your login name and press **Enter**, and the system prompts you for your password. To get to the Internet itself, you'll have to enter another command or two. Check with your system administrator for more information.

Log on/Log in The process of identifying yourself before you use a computer system (whether a single computer, a small network, or a large network such as the Internet).

A Real Challenge: The Dial-In Direct Connection

Dial-in direct accounts (such as SLIP or PPP) are more complicated. A dial-in direct account enables you to use the Internet as if you were using a permanent connection account. Your computer appears to be an Internet host computer, making it possible for you to communicate directly with the Internet. You can copy files directly to and from your computer's hard drive and, depending on your software, you may be able to run several sessions at once.

To get to this stage, however, you have to install and run special software. To do so, follow the instructions that came with your software (see Chapters 26 and 27 for information on starting SuperHighway Access, for example). Once the software is up and running, use it to call your service provider's computer and log in.

If you have a dial-in direct connection, how you work will depend on the software package you are using. This book can help you learn the Internet basics—what each tool is, how it works, and so on. However, it cannot show you precise keystrokes and mouse-clicks, because each dial-in direct system is different.

Do-It-Yourself with Dial-In Terminal Accounts

Getting onto the Internet using a dial-in terminal account is like calling any BBS and logging in. I'm going to use Windows Terminal as an example, partly because millions of PC users already have it. If you aren't using Terminal, you'll need to read your documentation carefully to figure out how to work with it. If you are using a program other than Terminal, but you are not already familiar with communications software, you might want to read the following description of preparing Terminal. It'll give you an idea of what is involved in preparing for a transmission.

You need to begin by telling the program what sort of modem you have, what port it's connected to, the type of data communications protocol you are going to use, and so on. You should be able to get this information from your service provider; at a minimum, they should tell you what to use for the data bits, stop bits, parity, and flow control settings. If you are not sure about any other settings, be sure to ask.

Of course, before you can begin, you have to start the program. In the case of Microsoft Terminal, you will double-click on the **Terminal** icon in the **Accessories** program group.

Who Ya Gonna Call?

First things first: enter the phone number and settings you need. In Terminal, open the **Settings** menu and select **Phone Number** to see the dialog box shown here.

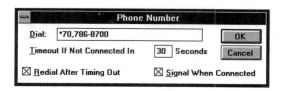

Enter the service provider's number and a few other details in the Phone Number dialog box.

In the **Dial** text box, type the telephone number that your service provider gave you. If it's a long distance number, remember to include 1 plus the area code. You can also precede the number with other numbers and codes. For instance, if you work in an office and need to get an outside line, you may want to put a 9 first (or whatever number you need to dial to get a dial tone).

 If the line you are using has call waiting, you need to turn off that feature before you call the Internet. (Call waiting tones can disturb your Internet session, and even cause you to lose data.) To turn it off, dial the code (probably *71 or maybe 1170) that turns it off. You may be able to find the code you need in the front of your local phone book.

When entering the number for your modem to dial, you can separate numbers with commas. For most modems, a comma means "pause for one second." For instance, if you type

   9,,123-4567

your modem will dial 9, wait for two seconds, and then dial the telephone number.

Notice that there are three other items in this dialog box. Use the **Timeout If Not Connected In** box to indicate the amount of time you want to wait after dialing the call. If your modem hasn't connected to the service provider's modem within that time, it stops trying. **Redial After Timing Out** tells the program to try to dial the call again if it was unable to connect within that time (if, for instance, the line was busy). The **Signal When Connected** control tells the program to sound the computer's beep when the connection is made.

Some programs have more options, of course. You might be able to define when and how often to redial, what sound should play when the computers connect, and so on.

What Type Is Your Terminal?

Once your computer is connected to the service provider's computer, it's going to act as a *terminal*, that is, as if it were a piece of equipment designed to interface with that computer. In Windows Terminal, open the **Settings** menu and select **Terminal Emulation** (see the following figure). Terminal has only three options: TTY, VT100, and VT-52. Unless your service provider has told you otherwise, select **VT100**. Other communications programs will have more options, but again, select VT100 (or **VT102**, if you don't have VT100), unless you're told otherwise. If you prefer a different terminal emulation type, ask your service provider about it; they may be able to work with many different types.

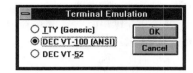

Use the Terminal Emulation dialog box to tell Terminal how to act once connected to the service provider's computer.

Next you need to configure your terminal preferences. Open the **Settings** menu and select **Terminal Preferences**. The Terminal Preferences dialog box appears (shown in the figure below). You can define various factors related to how your computer will act while it is "emulating" a terminal. Leave **Line Wrap** selected; this tells Terminal to wrap long lines onto two lines if necessary, instead of just throwing away the text at the end of the line.

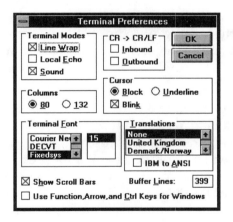

Use the Terminal Preferences dialog box to define terminal characteristics.

Leave **Local Echo** unselected unless you run into problems later. Most systems these days are what is known as "full duplex." When you type a character, the modem sends it to the other computer, which instantly "echoes" it back so it appears on your computer screen. If you are going to be connected to a computer that is "half duplex" (unlikely), you will want to use Local Echo so Terminal itself displays the text you type, without waiting for it to be sent back from the other computer.

The **Sound** option is not important; it lets the other system get to your computer's beeper, which few systems will try to do anyway. You can usually leave the **CR->CR/LF** options turned off, as well. These tell Terminal to add a *linefeed* (that is, move to the next line) each time it gets a *carriage return* instruction from the other computer (that is, an instruction to move back to the left column). Most computers do this automatically, so you won't have to worry about it.

You can also set up the number of text **Columns** you want (you'll probably want to use 80, though you might use 132 if you have a large screen) and what the text **Cursor** should look like. The **Terminal Font** area simply defines what the characters in the window will look like while you are working, and the **Translations** box is used if your computer is using a character set different from the one used by the service provider's computer. Again, you'll generally leave this alone.

The **Show Scroll Bars** and **Buffer Lines** controls enable you to set up how Terminal will handle text as it scrolls out of the top of the window—whether you want to be able to use scroll bars to go back and re-read the text, and how many lines of text should be kept. (Once you've exceeded the number of buffer lines, the oldest lines are lost as new ones arrive.)

Finally, there's the **Use Function, Arrow, and Ctrl Keys for Windows** check box. You need to make sure this check box is clear. If it's selected, you won't be able to use the arrow and Ctrl keys, which your service provider's computer will almost certainly expect you to be able to do. Some other Windows communications programs will automatically turn off these keys, so if you want to select text from the screen during a session, you have to use the menu commands—not the Ctrl-c command.

Telling Your Modem How to Behave

Select the **Communications** option from the **Settings** menu. In the Communications dialog box (shown in the following figure) you set up communications parameters, which govern the manner in which your computer and modem communicate with the service provider's system. Select the maximum speed of your modem at the top of the box in the **Baud Rate** area. If the box doesn't include your modem's speed, select the next highest; for example, if your modem's speed is 14400, but that's not available, select 19200.

62

Purists would say that modem speed is not really baud rate, it's bps (bits per second). But many communications programs use the term baud rate instead, and many people regard the two as the same.

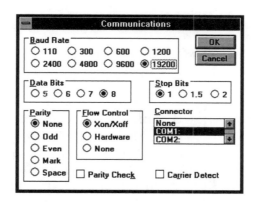

Here's where you tell your modem how to do its job.

You should also select the **Data Bits**, **Stop Bits**, **Parity** (most systems use 8 data bits, 1 stop bit, and no parity), and **Flow Control**. This is all information that your service provider should give you, and it's related to exactly how the modem should transmit the information. Use the **Connector** box to indicate the computer port that you are using to transmit the data (usually COM1 or COM2 on a DOS computer). The **Parity Check** option tells Terminal to display a question mark when it receives a character that it knows has an error (a character with a "parity error"). If you don't select the Parity Check option, the computer simply displays a garbage character, even if it knows that it's wrong. You probably won't need **Carrier Detect**; you use it only if your modem is unable to connect to the service provider's computer (assuming you are sure that everything else is set correctly).

Helping Your PC and Modem Talk

In order for your computer to communicate with another computer, it first has to know how to communicate with its own modem. Open the **Settings** menu and select **Modem Commands**. The Modem Commands dialog box appears, as shown in the following figure.

Modem Commands			

Commands

	Prefix:	Suffix:
Dial:	ATDT	
Hangup:	+++	ATH
Binary TX:		
Binary RX:		
Originate:	ATQ0V1E1S0=0	

OK
Cancel

Modem Defaults
- ● Hayes
- ○ MultiTech
- ○ TrailBlazer
- ○ None

Use the Modem Commands dialog box to tell Terminal how to communicate with the modem.

If your telephone line is a "pulse" line, you should change the **Dial** entry to **ATDP**. Few lines these days are pulse, though—most let you use either pulse or tone phones.

You can select one of the **Modem Defaults** from the box on the right. Because most modems these days are "Hayes compatible" (that is, they work in the same way as a Hayes modem), select the Hayes option button if you are not sure. If you don't have a Hayes-compatible modem, nor any of the other modems listed under Modem Defaults, select **None**, and then see your modem's manual (or call the technical support line) to find out what to enter in the **Originate** text box. You can generally leave the rest of the dialog box alone.

Psst! Wanna Know a Shortcut?

Now let's set up a few function keys to make it easier to work online. You will be able to use the function keys by pressing the key itself, or by clicking on a "key" that will be displayed at the bottom of the Terminal window. Open the **Settings** menu and select **Function Keys**. The Function Keys dialog box appears, as shown in the following figure.

Each function key has a line on which you can enter a label and the text that you want to transmit. The bottom of the Terminal window will have two lines of keys: the top line will have F1, F3, F5, F7, and the bottom line will have F2, F4, F6, and F8. The figure on the following page shows the function keys. The list that follows describes what they do.

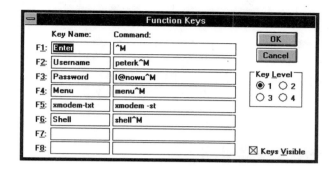

Use the function keys to help speed up your online session.

F1 Enter   Pressing F1 or clicking on the F1 button at the bottom of the screen is the same as pressing the Enter or Return key. (The code ^M means Enter.)

F2 Username   This will type my username and press Enter.

F3 Password   This will type my password and press Enter.

F4 Menu   This will type menu and press Enter. On the system I'm about to log onto, this will take me to a menu of options.

F5 xmodem-txt   This will type the command that is used to transmit a text file from the service provider's computer back to mine.

F6 Shell   Instead of typing *menu* and pressing Enter, I can make Terminal type *shell* and press Enter. This will take me to a UNIX command line.

Other Stuff You Can Change

That's all we need to look at right now. There are other options, however, such as the capability to automatically print the text as it appears on your screen, to "capture" the text in a text file, and to transfer binary files. Spend some time figuring out what your communications program can do for you, and you'll save time in the long run.

Save It!

Don't forget to save your settings. Open the **File** menu and select **Save**. Terminal asks you to provide a file name. Type **INTERNET** or something similar and click **OK**. The next time you want to use the Internet, you can open the existing settings file; you won't have to go through this mess of options each time.

Before Going Online

Before you actually go online, you need to know what you are going to do once you get there. Your service provider should give you a list of options. For example, the service provider I'm currently using gives me these choices once I've entered my password:

menu   If I type **menu** and press **Enter**, I'll see a menu of choices.

shell   If I type **shell** and press **Enter**, I'll see a UNIX command line.

Actually, there are lots of other choices (such as commands that enable members of certain groups to access certain programs), but you really don't need to know all of them, because they are either for system maintenance or for people other than you. Your service provider or system administrator should tell you what options you have.

Let's Go!

Now you are ready to go online. Open the **Phone** menu, select **Dial**, and Terminal dials the number you gave it. (I'm going to assume you've installed your modem!) The following figure shows the beginning of our session.

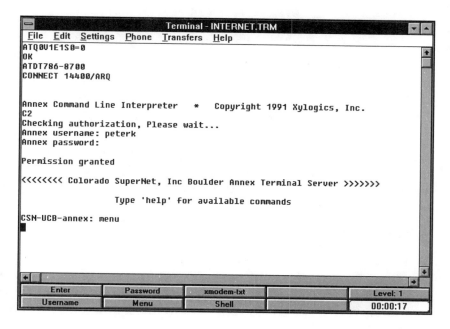

```
                    Terminal - INTERNET.TRM
 File  Edit  Settings  Phone  Transfers  Help
ATQ0V1E1S0=0
OK
ATDT786-8700
CONNECT 14400/ARQ


Annex Command Line Interpreter   *   Copyright 1991 Xylogics, Inc.
C2
Checking authorization, Please wait...
Annex username: peterk
Annex password:

Permission granted

<<<<<<< Colorado SuperNet, Inc Boulder Annex Terminal Server >>>>>>>

              Type 'help' for available commands

CSN-UCB-annex: menu
```

| Enter | Password | xmodem-txt | | Level: 1 |
| Username | Menu | Shell | | 00:00:17 |

Getting online is straightforward once you understand what's going on.

Let's go through this session piece by piece:

```
ATQ0V1E1S0=0
```

This line tells the modem to get ready because the modem's about to dial.

```
OK
```

This is from the modem, telling me it got the message.

```
ATDT786-8700
```

This line tells the modem to dial the number.

```
CONNECT 14400/ARQ
```

This tells me that the modem has connected with the service provider's modem.

```
Annex Command Line Interpreter   *   Copyright 1991 Xylogics, Inc.
```

This is a header sent by the service provider's computer. I press **Enter**. Some systems require that you do so to "get their attention."

```
Checking authorization, Please wait...
```

Another line sent by the service provider's computer. Just wait.

```
Annex username: peterk
```

The service provider's computer sends a line asking for my username. I type **peterk** and press **Enter**. (Actually, I click on one of the function buttons I set up at the bottom of the Terminal window, but it's the same thing.)

```
Annex password:
```

The service provider's computer now asks for my password. I type it and press **Enter** (or click on the password function button). Just in case someone's looking over my shoulder, the service provider's computer doesn't "echo" the password back to my computer, so it doesn't appear on my screen.

 UNIX has an irritating habit of not telling you if you entered your login name incorrectly. If you mistype the name, UNIX will ask for your password and then tell you that you made a mistake, without letting you know if the mistake was with the password or the login name. That's supposed to confuse bad guys trying to break into your account. It may confuse you, too.

```
Permission granted
```

The system checks my username and password and tells me it's okay.

```
<<<<<<< Colorado SuperNet, Inc Boulder Annex Terminal Server >>>>>>>
```

Another "header" line. It just identifies where I am.

```
Type 'help' for available commands
```

This just reminds me that I can type **help** (and press **Enter**) at the next line.

```
CSN-UCB-annex:    menu
```

When this line appears, I can type one of the options. I type **menu** and press **Enter**, so I can go to the system's Main Menu.

Problems?

There are a few problems you may run into. Some of those potential problems and their solutions are listed here.

You see garbage on the screen. If you see something like __p/__#£ä__, you've probably set something incorrectly. Check your baud rate, stop bit, parity, and flow control settings.

You see something like this: ~~xx~xxx~xx. Your baud rate may be set incorrectly.

You see something like this at the beginning of lines: ^7M or ^K or ;H2J;H2J24. You may be using the wrong terminal type.

Instead of seeing your service provider's menu system, you see a jumbled mess. You're probably using the wrong terminal emulation.

You can't see the characters you type. Turn Local Echo on.

You see every character you type twice. Turn Local Echo off.

There's a blank line after each line of incoming text. Turn off Inbound CR/LF.

There's a blank line after each line of outgoing text. Turn off Outbound CR/LF.

Incoming text is displayed on one line. Turn on Inbound CR/LF.

Not all problems are at your end; your service provider can also screw up and enter your account information incorrectly. When you've checked everything at your end, if you are still having problems, call your service provider and describe the symptoms. In particular, make sure you are using the correct login name, password, and terminal type.

What Now?

I'm going to explain how to work on your service provider's computer in Chapter 8. But before we move on, let's learn two more things: how to change a password and how to log off.

A word about UNIX. Most users will be working on a UNIX system. Even if your computer is an IBM PC-compatible or a Macintosh, the computer to which you are connected and through which you work is probably a UNIX machine. Since that is the case, I've talked a lot about the various UNIX commands you can use. For those users who aren't on a UNIX machine, much of what you'll find in this book will still be relevant. In a few areas, though, a particular command won't work on your system; ask your service provider what command to use instead.

Changing Your Password

You'll remember that I told you to change your password when you log on the first time. If you do so, only you and the system administrator have access to your account, not anyone else who may have seen your password on your account's paperwork.

The system may check the new password before it accepts it (to make sure it's valid and not used elsewhere) and then rewrite the entire password file that contains all users' passwords. So changing your password may take several minutes, depending on what else the computer is doing at the same time. Be patient.

To change your password from the UNIX shell, use the **passwd** command. You'll know you're in the shell if you see something like this on the last line by itself: **teal%**. You probably won't see teal (that's the name of the computer, you'll see something different). And in some cases the % will be replaced by **$** or some other symbol. Still, what you are seeing is the *prompt*, the line that's waiting for you to type something. So, type **passwd** and press **Enter**. (You'll learn more about the UNIX shell in the next chapter.)

If you are using a menu (some service providers have a list of options from which you can choose), there'll be a menu option for changing the password somewhere. (On the system I'm using, for example, I select **14. SuperNet Services/** and then **3. Change Your Password**.)

Either way, you'll be asked to enter your current password, then you'll have to enter the new one twice. Because the password won't be echoed back to you, you won't see it on your screen when you type it. Typing it twice makes sure you actually typed what you thought you typed.

Logging Out

When you are finished, it's time to log out of your service provider's computer. You don't want to just hang up your modem—that's rude. (And anyway, your service provider's computer will continue billing you until it realizes that you've gone.) There is a proper way to end a session.

If you are working with a menu system, you'll have to type a particular character. On my system, I type **q**, and the system asks if I want to exit. I type **y**, and my connection is closed. Or, I can type **Q**, and the connection is closed without the menu system asking me for confirmation first.

If you are at the UNIX shell, there are a few ways of logging out, depending on the type of shell. You may be able to press **Ctrl-d**; or type **logout** and press **Enter**; or type **exit** and press **Enter**. Or maybe any of the above. Try them all, and use the one you find easiest, or add a shortcut to your communications program. For instance, if you are using Terminal, you can enter the logout command for a function button, so that all you have to do is click on the button to log out.

Windows Terminal requires that you also hang up after logging out by selecting **Hangup** from the **Phone** menu. Many (perhaps most) communications programs will hang up your modem for you once they realize the other end has hung up.

The Least You Need to Know

➤ Each system's logon procedure will be slightly different, so get the details from your service provider.

➤ Spend some time learning your communications program. It has lots of useful features.

➤ As soon as you log on, change your password.

➤ To change your password, use the **passwd** command at the UNIX shell prompt, or find the Change Password option on the menu if you have one.

➤ Log out using **Ctrl-d**, or by typing **exit** or **logout** and pressing **Enter**. If your service provider's system has a menu, you'll probably type **q** or **Q**.

OH MY!

MENUS
MENUS
SHELLS
SHELLS

## Chapter 8

Menus and Shells, Oh My!

In This Chapter

➤ What is a UNIX Shell?

➤ Using a service provider's menu system

➤ % and other UNIX prompts you might see

Once you've logged onto your service provider's computer, what are you going to find? If you're lucky, there'll be a menu system. If you're not (and there's a very good chance you won't be) you'll probably have to use a command line—the UNIX *shell*. In this chapter, we'll take a quick look at shells and menus. In Chapter 9 you'll learn some UNIX commands you can practice at the shell. (Although most users are connected to the Internet through UNIX machines, you may find yourself working with a non-UNIX system. If so, check with your service provider for information about working at the command prompt. If you have a dial-in direct account, spend some time looking through your program's documentation.)

If you're used to working with DOS, the term "shell" may be misleading. In DOS, a shell is something that takes you away from the command line and lets you work on the system using menus or a graphical user interface. In UNIX, the shell is where you type commands, the equivalent of the DOS command line.

Using a Menu (If You're Lucky)

If you're lucky, your system has some kind of menu. This insulates you from the UNIX command line for the most part, but not completely. At some point, you'll have to go to the command line to do something. (So you'll want to read the information about the UNIX shell later in this chapter even if you do have a menu to work with.)

You and UNIX speak different languages. You can't understand UNIX, and UNIX can't understand you. Luckily, you have a shell to act as translator for you. You type commands into the shell, and it translates them into UNIX language. When UNIX wants to tell you something, it tells it to the shell, and the shell translates it into something you've got at least a small chance of understanding.

Even if you're lucky enough to have a menu, the menu systems used by most service providers are usually not very good. Get a group of Internet users together, and you'll hear descriptions such as "pretty primitive" and "horrible." One comment I heard recently, "It's not painless, but it's not awful," might actually be considered a compliment, relatively speaking.

Of course I can't tell you what your system will do. You'll likely have a series of menus that help you select important commands and that lead you to different areas of the Internet, and there may even be a system by which you can use most services by pressing a single keystroke. Whatever you have, it probably won't be comprehensive; it will probably miss bits and pieces, leaving you to fall back on the shell. Spend some time figuring out what the system can do for you, though. Take a look at your service provider's documentation, as awful as it may be, and spend an hour or two just exploring.

As an example of the options you might have, let's take a look at the menu in the system I'm using on Colorado SuperNet. As we saw in Chapter 7, during the logon procedure I'm presented a prompt from which I can choose between a shell and a menu. If I type **menu** and press **Enter**, this is what I'll see:

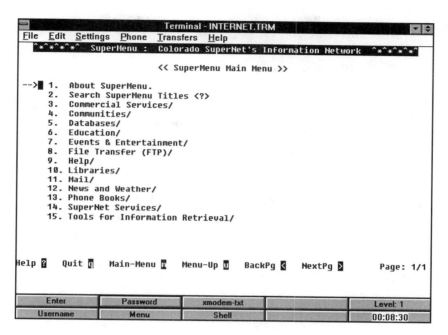

```
┌─────────────────────────────────────────────────────────────────────┐
│ ═                    Terminal - INTERNET.TRM              ▼ │ ≑ │
│ File  Edit  Settings  Phone  Transfers  Help                          │
│ ^*^*^*^     SuperMenu :   Colorado SuperNet's Information Network  ^*^*^*^ │
│                                                                       │
│                       << SuperMenu Main Menu >>                       │
│                                                                       │
│   -->█ 1.  About SuperMenu.                                           │
│        2.  Search SuperMenu Titles <?>                                │
│        3.  Commercial Services/                                       │
│        4.  Communities/                                               │
│        5.  Databases/                                                 │
│        6.  Education/                                                 │
│        7.  Events & Entertainment/                                    │
│        8.  File Transfer (FTP)/                                       │
│        9.  Help/                                                      │
│       10.  Libraries/                                                 │
│       11.  Mail/                                                      │
│       12.  News and Weather/                                          │
│       13.  Phone Books/                                               │
│       14.  SuperNet Services/                                         │
│       15.  Tools for Information Retrieval/                           │
│                                                                       │
│                                                                       │
│ Help ▯   Quit ▯   Main-Menu ▯   Menu-Up ▯   BackPg ▯   NextPg ▯   Page: 1/1 │
│                                                                       │
│ ┌──────────┬──────────┬─────────────┬──────────────┬───────────┐    │
│ │   Enter  │ Password │  xmodem-txt │              │  Level: 1  │    │
│ │ Username │   Menu   │    Shell    │              │  00:08:30  │    │
│ └──────────┴──────────┴─────────────┴──────────────┴───────────┘    │
└─────────────────────────────────────────────────────────────────────┘
```

A typical Internet menu from a service provider.

Note the arrow on the left side of the screen; it indicates which menu option is currently selected. I can choose an option in two ways: I can move that arrow up and down the list using the arrow keys on my keyboard, and press **Enter** when it's pointing to the option I want; or I can press the number of the option and press **Enter**.

Actually, there are a few more ways to get around. Pressing **k** moves the arrow up, pressing **j** moves it down, and pressing the right arrow selects an option. And once I've selected an option that leads to another menu of choices, I can press **u** (or the left arrow) to take me back to the previous menu.

Then there's **m**. If I find myself in a menu lower down the "tree" of menus, I can press **m** to return to the Main Menu. Pressing **?** displays help information. Pressing **q** displays a message asking if I want to exit the menu; if I press **y** (as in yes), I'll be logged off the system. Pressing **Q** logs me off the system without even confirming the action.

Well, now that you know how to navigate the menu and choose options, you may be wondering what all these menu options do for you.

About SuperMenu   Displays information about how the menu system was created. Turns out it's based on Gopher, a public-domain program usually used for digging through the Internet to find information. We'll learn more about Gopher in Chapter 21.

Search SuperMenu Titles   Lets me search for information about my service provider's services by typing a keyword key.

Commercial Services   Takes me to some businesses (I can enter the databases of several booksellers: O'Reilly, UTC, Quantum, and SoftPro to search for a book or even place an order). And I can contact a company that sells UNIX add-in and add-on peripherals.

Communities   Takes me to a list of Free-Nets to which I can connect using telnet (I spoke a little about Free-Nets in Chapter 3, and you'll learn about telnet in Chapter 17.)

Databases   Lets me "telnet" to other computers, so I can search their databases.

Education   Also lets me telnet to other computers, but specifically computers at universities or colleges.

Events & Entertainment   Accesses a short list of local events.

File Transfer (FTP)   Takes me to an automated FTP (File Transfer Protocol) system. FTP is used for finding and transferring files from other computer systems. We'll look at FTP in Chapter 18.

Help   Displays a list of subjects I might need help with, such as changing my Backspace key or checking how much online time I've used.

Libraries   Lets me search various library and research databases. The menu takes me to many of these resources by telnetting.

Mail   Lets me send and receive e-mail.

News and Weather   Lets me view news and weather, and oddly enough, reach the newsgroups. (Newsgroups on the Internet are the equivalent of CompuServe forums or BBS message areas; they are not what we normally think of as the "news." See Chapter 15.)

Phone Books   Lets me track down people using various directories such as whois (see Chapter 14) and directories on other computer systems (using FTP).

SuperNet Services   Lets me find billing information, change my password, use the UNIX shell, and so on.

Tools for Information Retrieval   Lets me use various tools for tracking down information, such as Gopher (Chapter 21), WAIS (Chapter 22), and World Wide Web (Chapter 23).

A menu is a great help. You can do plenty without ever seeing the UNIX shell or knowing UNIX commands, but you won't be able to do everything. You may find that you can't use the menu system to ftp or telnet to some systems; you may not be able to transfer files to and from your computer (if you have a dial-in terminal connection); and so on.

If you are lucky enough to have such a system, take the time to learn it. Read the documentation and find out what's available. You'll save a lot of time if you know what it can do for you.

Playing with Shells

Now, let's look at the UNIX shell. Even if you have a menu, you'll eventually want to go to the shell to do something, because the menu probably won't have everything you need. You might need to go to the shell to transfer files back to your computer or to view files stored in your home directory on the hard disk (more about the home directory in a moment).

How do you get to the shell? It may be there immediately when you log in; if not, you can choose it from the menu that appears instead. You'll remember that when we logged in (Chapter 7), we were given a choice of the type of access we wanted. On my service provider's system, I can type **shell** or **menu** and press **Enter**. Shell takes me to the UNIX operating system. If I am at the menu and decide I want to go to the shell, I can choose a menu command that takes me there. Based on the options available from my service provider, I select **14. SuperNet Services** and then **14. Unix Shell (Suspend Supermenu Temporarily)**. What do I see when I get to the UNIX shell? Something like this:

```
teal%
```

Teal is the name of my service provider's host computer, and % is the UNIX prompt, the character that says, "Okay, let's go… type something."

If you are used to working on a DOS computer, you are used to seeing > as the prompt; the % is the same thing. You may see a **$** prompt instead, depending on the type of UNIX shell you are using. (If you are used to working on a Macintosh, you are used to no prompt at all, but you've probably heard other users gripe about them.)

Is That All?

Hardly. To use the shell, you need a basic understanding of UNIX commands, which is unfortunate since very few DOS users study UNIX in their spare time. Luckily for you, Chapter 9 presents some UNIX basics to help get you up to speed.

The Least You Need to Know

➤ Depending on your service provider's setup, you will either be presented with a menu or with a shell interface when you log into the Internet.

➤ If your service provider has a menu system of some kind, spend some time reading the documentation and figuring it out. Menus can save you a lot of time!

➤ If your Internet connection consists only of a shell, you'll probably see a UNIX prompt, such as % or **$**.

➤ Don't despair if you don't understand UNIX commands; just turn to Chapter 9.

A UNIX Survival Guide

In This Chapter

➤ Don't be afraid—it's only UNIX!

➤ Directories: what's in them and how to move around

➤ Files: copying, deleting, moving, and so on

➤ Reading and finding files

Most Internet users eventually find themselves at a UNIX prompt, wondering what they should type next. (As I mentioned in Chapter 8, some systems are not UNIX-based, in which case you are going to have to find more information from your service provider on your dial-in direct program's documentation.)

Although UNIX can seem intimidating to a new user, it's actually quite straightforward—once you know what to type. Read this chapter, and while you are working online, refer to the commands on the handy, tear-out reference card in the front of this book. You'll soon get into the swing of it.

A Quick Directory Primer

Most of you probably know a little about directories already, but for those of you who don't, here goes. The service provider's computer (and your computer, probably) stores data on a hard disk. It doesn't matter what a hard disk is or why it's hard. It's simply a box with a circular disk in it that stores information in the form of computer files. These files can contain words, sounds, pictures, programs, or anything else that can be converted to a format the computer can read.

My computer has about 4,000 files on its hard disk. A service provider's computer has tens, maybe hundreds, of thousands of files. That gets complicated, especially when those files are owned by hundreds, maybe thousands, of different people. So to organize all of this, we use directories. A *directory* is like a compartment into which you can place computer files or other directories. A directory within a directory is called, not surprisingly, a *subdirectory*. Subdirectories can also hold computer files and other subdirectories.

This information storage system is like a filing cabinet that contains hundreds of file folders, which may contain documents and other document folders. And many of those document folders might contain not only documents, but also smaller folders—which may also contain documents and smaller folders. We call this the *directory tree* because it's a branching system. It makes finding and using the files on a hard disk much easier.

Each Internet account has a *home directory* on the service provider's computer. For instance, the path of my home directory is **/home/clients4/peterk**. A directory path describes how to travel along the directory tree to a particular directory. In this case, for example, the path tells us that the hard disk contains a directory named **home**. This directory contains a directory called **clients4**. The **clients4** directory contains a directory called **peterk**, which is my home directory. The **clients4** directory contains other directories, hundreds of them, one for each of the client accounts. But I don't care about those directories (and even if I did, the computer wouldn't let me get to them because they don't belong to me).

Checking Out Your Home Directory Files

Each time you log onto a UNIX system (the service provider's computer), you are placed "in" your home directory. That is, the computer assumes you are working in the home directory and that (for instance) new files you create will be placed there. If you transfer files from another computer using FTP (which you'll learn about in Chapter 18), they'll be placed in the directory you were in when you started FTP (though you can select a different directory if you wish).

What, then, can we do with this directory? First, let's take a look at it. Type **ls** and press **Enter**. You'll see a list that looks something like this:

```
my.signature network.guide newlist.txt s-list.txt sig.txt
temp/winq200a.zip winsuper.txt xmodem.log
teal%
```

This list shows the files and directories in your home directory. Notice the *temp/*. The front slash (/) indicates that this is a directory. The other words, which are separated by spaces, are files. (On some systems, the / won't appear unless you type **ls -lf**. The f switch also causes the list to include "hidden" files. In UNIX, files beginning with a period are normally hidden.)

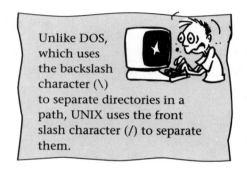

Unlike DOS, which uses the backslash character (\) to separate directories in a path, UNIX uses the front slash character (/) to separate them.

Let's get some more information. Type **ls -l** and press **Enter**. You'll see something like this:

```
-rw----   1 peterk       25 Oct  8 12:28 my.signature
-rw----   1 peterk    22942 Sep 30 08:05 network.guide
-rw----   1 peterk     5972 Oct  6 13:48 newlist.txt
-rw----   1 peterk    10985 Oct  5 08:13 s-list.txt
-rw----   1 peterk      255 Oct  7 09:15 sig.txt
drwx----  2 peterk      512 Oct  8 12:48 temp/
-rw----   1 peterk   282126 Oct  1 09:18 winq200a.zip
-rw----   1 peterk    15599 Oct  1 09:28 winsuper.txt
-rw----   1 peterk    17911 Oct  8 12:29 xmodem.log
teal%
```

You can see the file or directory name on the right of each line, but there's more. Let's take a look at two lines in particular:

```
drwx----  2 peterk      512 Oct  8 12:48 temp/
-rw----   1 peterk   282126 Oct  1 09:18 winq200a.zip
```

81

d or -   The first character indicates whether the entry is a file or directory. A hyphen (-) means it's a file; a **d** means it's a directory.

r   The second character indicates whether the owner of the object can read it. If he can't, there's a hyphen instead of the **r**.

w   The third character indicates whether the owner of the object can modify it (write). If he can't, there's a hyphen instead of the **w**.

x   The fourth character indicates whether the owner of the object can execute it—whether he can get into the directory, or execute the file (run it) if it's a program file. If he can't, there's a hyphen instead of the **x**.

The next characters are related to what *other* people can do with the file. The fifth, sixth, and seventh characters define what members of the user's group can do, and the last three characters define what users who are not group members can do. (Each user on a UNIX computer is a member of a group, but we don't really need to get into that.)

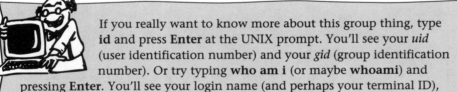

If you really want to know more about this group thing, type **id** and press **Enter** at the UNIX prompt. You'll see your *uid* (user identification number) and your *gid* (group identification number). Or try typing **who am i** (or maybe **whoami**) and pressing **Enter**. You'll see your login name (and perhaps your terminal ID), along with the date and time.

The first number on the line shows the *link count*, which we don't want to get into. Ignore it.

Next comes the *owner name*. That's generally you (although it's me in this example). After the owner name, you might see the *group name*, but not in this example. Next you'll see the file size, the number of bytes (characters) in the file, the date and time the file or directory was created (or last modified), and the file name or directory name.

Directory Management, UNIX Style

No, this is not going to turn into a book on UNIX. But you need to know a few simple UNIX commands to be able to conquer the shell. (I've also included a quick reference table of UNIX commands on the tear-out card at the front of the book.) The following sections introduce you to some UNIX commands you can use to work with directories.

Computer files contain two parts: a listing in a table some-where, and the actual data, which is stored on the disk and referenced by the listing. UNIX lets you use different names for the same block of data on the disk (using the **ln** command). The link is the information that connects the particular table entry to the particular block of data. So if a file has two names, it has two links. The link number next to a directory name is the number of subdirectories in the directory, plus two. Why "plus two"? Because UNIX adds the current directory and the parent directory.

Viewing the Contents

Use these commands to see what you've got.

ls	Shows a simple list of files and directories.
ls -l	Shows the list with the file sizes and other information.
ls -al	Lists everything, including hidden files.
**ls	more**	Stops the list after every page. (Press **Enter** to show the next line, or press **Spacebar** to show the next page.)
ls -l |more	Gives the full-information listing, broken down page by page; you may be able to use the DOS **dir** command (the equivalent of **ls -l**) to show a full listing.

Your Backspace key doesn't seem to work? Try pressing **Ctrl-h** or **#** instead.

Moving Around

When you first log on, you are in the home directory. This is also the current or working directory (that is, the directory you are in at the moment). To play around in a different directory, you can change the working directory using any of the following commands:

cd ..	Moves you back to the previous directory level. Important: note that there's a space between the **cd** and the .. (unlike in DOS).
cd *directory name*	Takes you directly to a different directory. For instance, type **cd /home/clients4/***othername* and press **Enter**.
pwd	Tells you what your current location is, in case you're not sure.

Creating and Removing Directories

Now and again, you'll need to create new directories, and sometimes you'll want to delete them. When you do, use these commands:

mkdir *directory name*	Creates a new subdirectory in the working directory.
mkdir */existingname/ newname*	Creates a subdirectory in a particular directory.
rmdir *name*	Deletes an empty directory.

What About Those File Names?

Actually, UNIX is not so very different from the DOS so many of us know and love. But what about those file names? These are not your traditional "8.3" DOS names (eight characters in the name itself, followed by a period, followed by three characters in the extension). How about this for a name, for instance:

```
Where-can-I-find-the-source-to-C-news?
```

Yes, this really is a file name. Here are a few rules for naming files in UNIX:

84

➤ Names are *case-sensitive*, which is tech-speak meaning that the computer regards uppercase and lowercase letters differently (unlike DOS). Therefore, FILENAME.TXT is not the same as filename.txt. This is very important; remembering it could save you hours of confusion.

➤ While old versions of UNIX limited you to 14 characters in a name, new versions have no limit.

➤ Don't use these characters: / | \ ! @ # $ ^ & * ( ). In addition, some UNIX versions don't like you to use ? or – (minus sign).

➤ You may be allowed to put spaces in file names, but don't, because it may upset some programs.

➤ You can use periods to separate words, such as Where.can.I.find.the.source.to.C.news?. UNIX doesn't have file extensions (as DOS does). It simply regards the period as a character like any other.

UNIX: The Sensitive Operating System

UNIX is case-sensitive in general, not just in its handling of file names. In other words, you have to type all commands correctly: you can't type RM if you want to delete a file (the correct command is **rm**). This can be confusing at times. Sometimes when UNIX fails to carry out a command, it'll quickly be obvious why; you typed text.txt instead of Text.txt, for instance. But sometimes you'll have to put your thinking cap on to figure it out, especially when you're using long names. For instance, if you type

```
rm Textwin7thOct93.zip
```

and UNIX tells you that the file doesn't exist, maybe you mistyped a character. Or maybe you used a zero instead of the uppercase letter O in Oct. (On many machines, in fact, you may not be able to tell the difference between a zero and an O. If your communications program allows it, select a font in which the characters are distinct.)

Messing with Files

If you are using a dial-in terminal connection, you'll be copying files from other computers into your directories on the service provider's computer. What are you going to do with all these files? At some point

85

you may want to do a file transfer to get them onto your computer. (We'll explain that in Chapter 19.) But eventually you'll want to delete some, rename some, and even move some. The following sections explain how to work with files.

Deleting Files

Use the **rm** command to delete a file:

```
rm delete.this.file
```

Moving Files

Use the **mv** command to move a file:

```
mv filename directoryname
```

Renaming Files

You can use the **mv** command to rename a file:

```
mv oldfilename newfilename
```

Copying Files

To copy a file, use the **cp** command:

```
cp originalfilename newfilename
```

To copy the file to another directory, type

```
cp originalfilename directoryname
```

To copy the file to another directory with a new name, use

```
cp originalfilename directoryname/newname
```

Viewing a Text File

There are a couple of ways to view the contents of a text file. If it's a short file, type

```
cat filename
```

and the file will be displayed on-screen. If it's long, type

```
more filename
```

and it will be displayed page by page. (Press **Spacebar** to see the next page, or press **Enter** to move line by line.) Press **q** to stop viewing the file.

Finding Lost Files

UNIX has some neat little tools for finding files. If you know the name of the file you want, but aren't sure where it is, type

```
find . -name filename -print
```

If the file is in the working directory (the one you are in when you use the command), UNIX will simply repeat the name to you, like this:

```
./filename
```

If the file is in another directory, UNIX will show you which one, like this:

```
./directoryname/filename
```

The find command will only search through the working directory and its subdirectories (and their subdirectories). It won't go the other way and search the directory of which the working directory is a subdirectory. And remember, make sure you type the name correctly, with each letter in the correct case. Don't type lost.file if you are looking for Lost.File.

Using grep

If you don't know the name of the file you need, but you do know some of the text inside it, you can use the **grep** command to find the file. To use **grep**, type **grep** *"these words"* *. For instance, you might type

```
grep "IBM main frames" *
```

and press **Enter**. The asterisk tells grep to search all the files in the current directory. You can enter a file name if you want to specify which file or files; you can omit the quotation marks if you are only looking for one word. For instance, if you type

```
grep IBM work.txt
```

UNIX searches for *IBM* in the file called work.txt. If you type

```
grep IBM w*
```

UNIX searches for *IBM* in all the files that begin with the letter w. When grep finds what it's looking for, it names the file in which it found the text, and displays the line or lines containing the text, like this:

```
winsuper.txt:in IBM main frames, workstations and personal
computers
```

Using this command, you'd better get the case of the specified text correct; if you typed **ibm**, your system wouldn't find IBM. But if you are not sure of the case, use the **-i** switch. For example, you could type

```
grep -i "these words" *
```

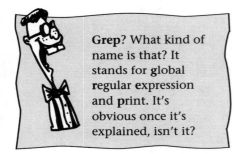

Grep? What kind of name is that? It stands for global regular expression and print. It's obvious once it's explained, isn't it?

The command now finds matches regardless of the case of the letters. The only problem with this is that you are also telling grep to search for partial matches. If you are searching for *she*, the system will also stop on *sheet*, *shear*, and *sheaf*.

If you don't want to see the line containing the matching text (you just want the file name), you can use the **-l** switch:

```
grep -l -i "these words" *
```

There's plenty more you can do with the **grep** command, and there are even **egrep** and **fgrep** commands. But that is (you guessed it) beyond the scope of this book.

More Useful UNIX Stuff

Here are a few more useful UNIX commands:

Repeating the last command   If you want to repeat the command you just carried out, type !! and press **Enter**. This works only in the C shell, though. If you are using the Korn shell, try **r** instead. Tough luck if you are using the Bourne shell.

Canceling what's happening   If you want to stop what is happening, try pressing **Ctrl** and **c** at the same time (**Ctrl-c**). If that doesn't help, try **Ctrl-x** or **q**.

Finding Help   You can see instructions explaining a command using the **man** (as in "manual") command. Type **man** *commandname* | **more**. For example, if you type **man grep** | **more**, UNIX displays the help information on the **grep** command. (The | **more** part of the command tells UNIX to display the information one page at a time. Press **Spacebar** to see the next page; press **Enter** to move a line at a time.)

Did You Leave Something Running?

It's easy in UNIX to make a mistake and leave a program stalled or running in the background. You might try to run a program and get a message such as **There are stopped jobs** or **You seem to have left a rn running, process 13178**. This is not always your mistake, of course; sometimes the system just locks. So you end the session—leaving a program running in the background. Try typing **fg** and pressing **Enter** to run the program in the foreground. Or you can try to "kill" the process. First, find the *PID* (process ID) by typing **ps -u** (or, if this doesn't work, try **ps -e** or **ps -a**) and pressing **Enter**. You'll see something like this:

```
USER     PID    %CPU   %MEM   SZ    RSS   TT   STAT   START TIME   COMMAND
peterk   13178  0.0    0.2    384   112   p2   D      12:03 0:02    rn
```

Then type **kill %PID** and press **Enter**.

There's Plenty More

No doubt this introduction to UNIX has left you eager for more. There's plenty more you can do in UNIX, but I'm not going to explain it here (except specifics, such as using xmodem and zmodem for transferring files, which is in Chapter 19). I've got enough on my hands with the Internet. If you'd really like to find out more about UNIX and how it can improve your life, pick up a good book on the subject and settle in for some good times. (Try *The First Book of UNIX*, published by Alpha Books!)

The Least You Need to Know

> ➤ The UNIX shell prompt (% or $) tells you that you can enter a command.

> ➤ Type **cd** and press **Enter** to return to your home directory. Type **cd** *directoryname* to go directly to a particular directory.

> ➤ Type **cd ..** and press **Enter** to go back one directory (but remember to leave a space between cd and ..). If you are not sure where you are, type **pwd** and press **Enter**.

> ➤ Type **ls -l | more** to see a full-information listing of a directory, page by page.

> ➤ Use **rm** *filename* to delete a file; use **mv** *filename directoryname* to move a file.

> ➤ Use **more** *filename* to view a text file page by page.

> ➤ Cancel commands using **Ctrl-c**, **Ctrl-x**, or **q**.

Part II
An E-Mail Extravaganza

Is there anyone out there? Yes, indeed there is. There are millions of people hooked up to the Internet in one way or another, and you can send electronic mail (e-mail) to almost any of them. Pretty staggering, huh? Internet's e-mail system gives you a rapid, cheap link to literally millions of other computer users. In fact, e-mail is the only reason most Internet users ever log on.

Like everything else on the Internet, though, e-mail is not as straightforward as it could be. Addressing messages is a pain, and so is having them returned to you because you typed a period in the wrong place. But don't worry; in Part II I teach you how to address messages, how to use the different mail readers and writers available, and even how to send computer files as mail messages. And if you can't find someone's mail address, I'll give you some tips for tracking it down.

MODEM PROBLEMS

## Chapter 10

Please Mr. Postman: An Intro to E-Mail

In This Chapter

➤ The e-mail advantage

➤ Making yourself understood

➤ Addressing the envelope

➤ Sending mail to another network

➤ Easy living with mail programs

➤ E-mail etiquette

The Internet's most popular feature is its e-mail system. Few Internet users use even a small fraction of the vast information resources available to them. Instead, they use the Internet as a cheap and convenient way to send messages to friends across town or to colleagues across the world.

E-mail (from the term *electronic mail*), is the process by which you send messages across a computer network. Instead of writing a message, placing it in an envelope, and dropping it in a mailbox, you can send the message across the Internet to any user anywhere.

Why Use E-Mail?

The advantages of e-mail are obvious. It's cheap—often cheaper than sending a message by mail and almost always cheaper than making a phone call. It's fast. Messages can be delivered in seconds. There's no waiting a week or two for your letter to be delivered to France, and no waiting on hold while the receptionist finds the person you need to contact.

The last time I e-mailed my buddy Al Gore, he received the message and responded within ten seconds. (Well, admittedly, he didn't respond personally, but he's been busy. Because his and Bill's Internet mailboxes receive around 30,000 messages a month (though some of them are addressed to Socks, Chelsea's cat), they respond automatically with a polite message, saying "thanks very much, but I've been busy," or something similar. If you have something special to say, you can contact Al at **vicepresident@whitehouse.gov**. If you'd prefer to chat with Bill, try **president@whitehouse.gov**.)

E-mail is also convenient. A friend told me he uses e-mail to contact a colleague in Japan. He doesn't need to worry about time zones, figure out exactly when his Japanese colleague gets up, or find the overlap between an American day and a Japanese day. Nor does he need to worry about explaining to a Japanese receptionist what he wants. He just sends a message over the Internet, and reads the reply the next day. (Nothing's 100%, however. Sometimes messages take hours to get through, and sometimes—though not often—they get lost.)

You can also use e-mail to send the same message to several people at a time. You can create mailing groups, which make it possible for you to write one message and then tell your e-mail program to ship it out to everyone in a particular group. Or, simply write a message addressed to one person and "CC" (carbon copy) it to other e-mail users.

Two E-Mail Caveats

Of course, e-mail is not the solution to all the world's ills, and it can't replace a nicely formatted report or a face-to-face meeting. By its very nature, e-mail has some limitations; you should be aware of them.

None of That Fancy Stuff...

Although e-mail can get your message across, it's no substitute for a word processing program's output. When you send text messages with Internet e-mail, they're just that: text. No special formatting is allowed: you can't use bold or italic text, for instance. You can enter carriage returns to format paragraphs and lines, but that's about it.

E-mail of the near future, however, will probably overcome this limitation. It's already possible to send messages over CompuServe using bold and italic text and a number of different fonts (if the user has a special *navigator* program, that is). No doubt that feature will eventually reach the Internet as well.

...And They Can't See Your Face

Many people regard e-mail messages as a form of conversation. Sure, we're using written messages, but somehow they're less formal than if they were written on paper. So people often write in a very informal manner as if they were chatting to the recipient. The problem with this is that the recipient can't see your face and can't hear the inflection in your voice. Consequently, what you regard as a flippant or sarcastic remark may be regarded as deadly serious when the person to whom you sent the message reads it.

This is both an individual and a cultural problem. Some people (and some cultures) are simply more serious than others. What you feel is "obviously" a joke may not be so obvious to the other person. My compatriots, the British, have a very dry sense of humor, so you can probably get away with using sarcasm in messages to British friends and colleagues without worry. But you may want to be more careful with messages to others.

Face-Time Substitutes

Over the past few years, e-mail users have developed a number of ways to clarify the meaning of messages. You might see <g> at the end of the line, for example. This means "grin" and is shorthand for saying, "You know, of course, that what I just said was a joke, right?" You may also see :-) in the message. Turn this book sideways, so that the left column of this page is up and the right column is down, and you'll see that this is a small smiley face. It means the same as <g>, of course: "That was a joke, okay?"

Emoticons Galore

The smiley face is just one of many available symbols, though by far the most common. You might see some of the following, and you may want to use them yourself. Perhaps you can create a few of your own.

Many people simply call these character faces "smiley faces," but if you'd like to impress your friends with a bit of technobabble, you can call them **emoticons**. And if you really want to impress your colleagues, get hold of *The Smiley Dictionary* (Seth Godin). It contains hundreds of these things. You wouldn't have thought there were that many possible combinations that made sense, would you?

: - (	Sadness, disappointment
8 -)	Kinda goofy-looking smile, or wearing glasses
: - >	A smile
; -)	A wink
*<¦:-)	Santa Claus
: - &	Tongue-tied
: - o	A look of shock
: - p	Tongue stuck out
,:-) or 7:^]	Ronald Reagan

You might even try really weird stuff, like this smiley cow I found in the alt.ascii newsgroup (more about newsgroups in Chapter 15).

```
]:o_
¦0 =
¦_o=
```

Or you can get really artistic with something like this (don't turn your head sideways for this one).

```
 ;~; ,      .~.
._#_.)   [ _#_ ]
( @ @    '^. .^'
' ).(       \./
 ( v )      /q\
  \¦/       \¦/
  (¦)       (¦)
   ~ ~      ~ ~
```

And lots of people put smiley art in their signature files so it goes out with every message they send (there's more about signature files in Chapter 11).

```
      _   .                  - ,,           .
    /# /_\_    ¦   Speed limit????  69 Dude!!!  ¦   ¦\_¦/__/¦
    ¦  ¦/o\o\  ¦                                 ¦   / / \/ \  \
    ¦   \\_/_/ ¦      'Kacagolan of XYZ'         ¦  /__¦0¦¦0¦__ \
  / ¦_   ¦     ¦                                 ¦  ¦/_ \_/\_/ _\ ¦
  ¦  ¦¦\_ ~¦   ¦     Mt. Ararat,  /\   Armenia   ¦  ¦ ¦ (___) ¦ ¦¦
  ¦  ¦¦¦ \/    ¦               /     \           ¦   \/\___/\_/
  ¦  ¦¦¦_      ¦       /\   ////¦ /\/\\           ¦  (_/          ¦¦
   \//  ¦      ¦     ///¦\\\¦////////\\\\\        ¦    ¦          ¦¦
    ¦¦  ¦      ¦___/////\\\\\////////\\\\\\\\\___¦    ¦          ¦¦\
    ¦¦_  \     ¦ RAFFI RAZMIG KOJIAN  ¦  HAPPY  ¦     \         //_/
    \_¦  o¦    ¦ raffi@watserv.ucr.edu¦  HAPPY  ¦      _____//
    /\___/     ¦ raffik@aol.com       ¦ JOY JOY¦     _ ¦¦ _¦¦
   / ¦¦¦¦_  ¦¦   (____(____)                          ¦¦
    (___)_)  ¦   -Picture by Norman Sippel-  ¦   /***********\
```

Message Shorthand

There are a couple of other ways people try to liven up their messages. One is to use obscure abbreviations, such as these:

BTW	By the way
FWIW	For what it's worth
FYI	For your information
IMHO	In my humble opinion
IMO	In my opinion
LOL	Laughing out loud (used as an aside to show your disbelief)
OTF	On the floor (laughing) (used as an aside)
PMFBI	Pardon me for butting in
PMFJI	Pardon me for jumping in
RTFM	Read the &*^%# manual

ROTFL or ROFL	Rolling on the floor laughing (used as an aside)
ROTFLMAO	Same as above, except with "laughing my a** off" added on the end. (You didn't expect me to say it, did you? This is a family book.)
TIA	Thanks in advance
YMMV	Your mileage may vary

The real benefit of these abbreviations is that they confuse the average neophyte. They certainly don't save any money; e-mail is so cheap that cutting a message by 15 or 20 characters won't have much effect on the "bottom line."

You'll also see different ways to stress particular words (you can't use bold and italic, remember). You can emphasize a word by using underscores (_now!_) or, less frequently, asterisks (*now!*).

Now, Where's That Address?

You might imagine that addressing a message would be simple. However, because the Internet is a conglomeration of so many different networks and provides access to so many different e-mail systems, addressing a message may not be straightforward. Let's take a quick look at a few rules.

The Internet uses the Domain Name System (DNS) to look up names. The local server (computer) starts by contacting a root server, a computer that knows the number associated with the highest-level domain in your domain name. For instance, if you are sending a message to **joebloe@apotpeel.com** the root server tells your local server which computer is responsible for the **.com** domain. The local server then contacts the **.com** computer and asks where **apotpeel** is. Then, with the complete domain number it needs, the local server addresses the message and sends it off.

Remember that your Internet address is made up of two parts: your login name and your domain name. These two parts are separated by an @ sign: the text to the left of the sign is your login name, and the text to the right is your domain name. Take, for instance,

peterk@csn.org. The first part, **peterk**, is the login name, and **csn.org** is the domain name. The domain name is used to describe where you can be found on the network; you are given this name when you first open an account. (We looked at this in detail in Chapter 6, so if you skipped that chapter you might want to backtrack for a moment.) The Internet looks up your domain name, finds the associated number (the address of the computer that is handling your mail), and uses the number to direct your message to the correct place.

Addressing E-Mail to Your CompuServe Friends

After the Internet, one of the most popular e-mail systems is that run by CompuServe. Eventually, you'll probably want to send an e-mail message to a CompuServe user or have a CompuServe user send you something. Because CompuServe is linked to the Internet, you can send and receive CompuServe messages.

To send a message, all you need is the CompuServe ID (identification number) of the person to whom you want to send the message. CompuServe IDs are generally five-digit numbers, followed by a comma, followed by two or more numbers, such as 71601,1266. However, since you can't put a comma in an Internet address, you have to replace the comma with a period. So to send a message to this person, you would enter the address as: **71601.1266@compuserve.com**.

To send a message from CompuServe to your Internet account, a user would precede your Internet address with **INTERNET:**. For instance, to send a message from CompuServe to **joebloe@thiscompany.com**, a CompuServe user would enter the following as the address: **INTERNET:joebloe@thiscompany.com**. People frequently send messages between CompuServe and the Internet, and it works quite well.

There are other rare CompuServe address formats. For example, some organizations have private CompuServe mail areas, in which case you would use: *user@department.organization*.**compuserve.com**.

If you'd like to find more information about addressing mail to different networks, get hold of the MAILGUIDE.TXT. You can find this at the Macmillan Publishing Internet site (**ftp.mcp.com**) or by anonymously ftping to **csd4.csd.uwm.edu**, changing to the **/pub** directory, and then getting the file named **internetwork-mail-guide**. (See Chapters 18 and 19 for information on how to use FTP.)

Even More E-mail Links

There are a number of other e-mail systems that you can send messages to through the Internet, such as Bitnet, Fidonet, Sprintmail, MCImail, and UUCP. But the system is not perfect, and what may work in one area may not work in another. You may have to try a couple of different forms of the address to get a message through. (Once you've found the form that works for that network, you'll be able to use that format for future messages.)

PRODIGY

To send a message to a PRODIGY information service user, add **@prodigy.com** to the end of the user's PRODIGY address.

America Online

To send a message to an America Online information service user, add **@aol.com** to the end of the America Online user's normal address. To send you a message, an America Online user simply uses a normal Internet address without modification.

GEnie

To send a message to the GEnie information service, format the address like this: *recipient*@**genie.geis.com**. To send you a message, a GEnie user would tag @INET# onto the end of the normal Internet address (for instance **peterk@csn.org@INET#**).

Bitnet

Bitnet addresses look very similar to Internet addresses: they are in the form *name@host*. You then add **bitnet** to the end, so the highest-level domain is called bitnet. For example, if the address is something like **jblow@golden**, try **jblow@golden.bitnet**. If that doesn't work, ask your system administrator or service provider for an Internet-Bitnet gateway name (a *gateway*, in this context, is a computer that links one network to another). Replace the @ with %, throw away the .bitnet (**jblow%golden**), and add an @ followed by the name of the Internet-Bitnet gateway. The Bitnet address ends up looking like this: **jblow%golden@cunyvm.cuny.edu**.

Fidonet

Fidonet addresses look something like this: **Joe Blow 1:6/1.2**. Replace the space between the names with a period, and replace the space between the last name and first number with an @ (**Joe.Blow@1:6/1.2**), and then add the letters **p**, **f**, **n**, and **z** in front of the numbers (**Joe.Blow@p1:f6/n1.z2**). Replace the colon and backslash with periods and add **.fidonet.org** (**Joe.Blow@p1.f6.n1.z2.fidonet.org**). (Is this fun, or what?)

However, the message still might not go through. If it doesn't, replace the @ with % and add **@zeus.ieee.org** at the end (**Joe.Blow%p1.f6.n1.z2.fidonet.org@zeus.ieee.org**).

MCImail

Sending messages to MCImail is similar to sending messages to CompuServe. Simply add **@mcimail.com** to the end of an MCImail address. MCImail addresses can be numbers (**1111111@mcimail.com**) or names (**joe_blow@mcimail.com**).

Sprintmail

If you are given a Sprintmail address, you will probably get only two parts: a name and an organization (such as **Joe Blow/APOTPEEL**). You will have to drop these items into the following address, using a period between the first and last name:

> /PN=Joe.Blow/O=APOTPEEL/ADMD=TELEMAIL/C=US/ @sprint.com

UUNET

UUNET addresses look like Internet addresses: **joebloe@golden.uucp**. Remove the .uucp, replace the @ with %, and put an @ at the end (**joebloe%golden@**). Ask your system administrator or service provider for a UUNET-Internet gateway, and add that to the end. For instance, **joebloe%golden@uu.psi.com**.

You may be given a UUNET path that looks like this:

...!uunet!*host*!*name*

This isn't really an address; instead it shows the route a message takes to reach its destination. Once you get the message to UUNET, it will send it on to *host*, which will send it on to the person. Therefore, you have to reverse this: ***name%host@gateway***.

No, it's not just your imagination. All these different mailing-label schemes really are a royal pain in the derriere.

And More!

The networks we have mentioned aren't the only ones; they're just the most common. Here are a few more you may run into:

➤ GEONET (GeoNet Mailbox Systems)

➤ NASAMAIL

➤ ENVOY (Telecom Canada)

➤ BIX (Byte Information eXchange; *Byte* magazine)

➤ ATT (AT&T)

➤ MFNET (Magnetic Fusion Energy Network)

➤ and a couple of dozen more

There's no way I'm going to describe all of these, so if you'd like to see a detailed description of how to work with all these networks, take a look at the MAILGUID.TXT document that I mentioned earlier.

Don't Lose Those Addresses!

If someone gives you an e-mail address, don't lose it! Add to your address book all those e-mail addresses you have noted on business cards, letters, e-mail you receive, or other people's address books. Losing an Internet e-mail address is not like losing a telephone number. If you lose a phone number, you can look in the phone book or call information; getting an e-mail address can be much more difficult. We'll discuss some of your alternatives in Chapter 13, but none are perfect. So if you ever come across an address you think you might need, save it!

E-Mail Helpers: Just Add Addresses

You probably have a choice of e-mail programs you can use. These are simply *interfaces* or *front ends* (programs that sit between you and the Internet).

Your service provider probably provides a couple of different programs from which you can choose. They vary from the arcane and irritating to the reasonably good. But remember that this is the Internet; don't expect anything wonderful. Take a look at what's available, and pick the one you find easiest to use. If you've got the time and inclination, you can search for other mail programs on the Internet and experiment with them.

There are a couple of dozen programs available (several for each type of computer system you are using), so it's not possible for me to tell you exactly how your system will work. However, in Chapter 11, we'll take a look at a couple of different programs. And because all programs have a variety of common features, if you understand a feature in one program, you'll be able to use it in the others.

Internet Etiquette

There's an etiquette to the Internet (sometimes called *Internetiquette*). Follow these rules (which apply to e-mail and the newsgroups covered in Chapter 15) to avoid upsetting people and embarrassing yourself.

Don't write something you will regret later. There have been lawsuits based on the contents of electronic messages, so consider what you are writing and whether you would want it to be read by someone other than the recipient. For example, you never know when the recipient might forward a message or print it out and pass it around, or when someone else might read it over the recipient's shoulder. You don't have to use the Internet; there's always the telephone. (Oliver North has already learned *his* lesson!)

Consider the tone of your message. It's easy to try to be flippant and come out as arrogant, or try to be funny and come out as sarcastic. When you write, think about how the recipient might interpret your words.

Give the sender the benefit of the doubt. If you receive a message that sounds arrogant or sarcastic, remember that the sender may be trying to be flippant or funny! If you are not sure what he is saying, ask him to explain.

TURN YOUR CAPS LOCK KEY OFF. MESSAGES THAT ARE ALL CAPS ARE DIFFICULT TO READ. YOU ARE NOT USING A TELEX MACHINE, SO WRITE LIKE A NORMAL HUMAN BEING.

Don't use lines over 60 characters long. Some mail systems let you enter lines as long as you wish. Keep them to about 60 characters, so that even if the lines are indented a few characters, they are still short enough to fit on a screen. (When you forward or reply to a message, the existing text is usually indented a little.)

Read before you send. This gives you a chance to fix embarrassing spelling and grammatical errors or to reconsider what you've just said.

Be nice. Hey, there's no need for vulgarity or rudeness (except in certain newsgroups, where it seems to be a requirement for entrance). However, you can get away with a lot more on the Internet than you can on CompuServe, America Online, PRODIGY, or any other commercial service.

The Least You Need to Know

➤ E-mail can be a quick and inexpensive way to keep in touch with friends and colleagues.

➤ <g> means "grin." So does :-).

➤ You can use dozens of different smileys, or emoticons, but don't expect anyone to understand them all.

➤ Addressing most e-mail messages is no problem. If you do run into problems now and again, you can find detailed information about addresses in the MAILGUID.TXT file.

➤ Experiment with the mail readers available to you and find the easiest to use.

## Chapter 11

UNIX Mail: Down to the Nitty Gritty

In This Chapter

➤ Starting UNIX Mail

➤ Viewing, reading, saving, and deleting

➤ Replying to a message

➤ Sending your own messages

➤ Inserting text files into messages

➤ Using vi, a UNIX text editor

If you are lucky, your service provider will have some kind of improved e-mail system that you can use, such as Pine or Elm. If you are unlucky, you'll only have a standard UNIX mail interface.

In this chapter, I'm going to explain how to use the UNIX mail system because almost all service providers supply it. In Chapter 12, I'll describe Pine as an example of what a mail program does, and get into some more advanced mail stuff, such as sending computer files as mail and using a mail signature. Whatever system you have, you'll be able to do many or most of the same things you see in these chapters—though perhaps in a slightly different manner.

Getting Your Mail

If you don't have a mail system such as Pine available, you have to use the basic UNIX mail system. It's not the best system available, but it's usable. We'll assume you are at the UNIX shell's prompt. To get to the mail system, type **mail** and press **Enter**. (On some systems, you may have to type a different command—**mailx**, for example—if **mail** doesn't work. Talk to your system administrator.) You'll see another prompt, probably &. For instance:

```
teal% mail
&
```

With Mail's commands, you can view a list of messages, read messages, and reply to and compose messages.

When you first enter Mail, the first message in the list (the oldest one) is the *current message*. As you'll see, certain commands work on the current message. For instance, if you press **Enter** at the & prompt, Mail displays the current message. But the current message changes depending on various actions you take. Once you've read the first message, for instance, message number 2 becomes the current message. (Sounds confusing, but you'll catch on quickly.)

 Even if you are using a Mac or a PC, once you've dialed into your service provider's computer, you are probably working in UNIX. Your computer is simply functioning as a terminal connected to the UNIX computer. Although not all Internet host computers are UNIX machines, the majority are. Thus, most users will be able to use the UNIX mail system.

Looking A-Head(er)

When you look at a list of mail messages, you're actually looking at the message *headers*, brief descriptions of the message size, date, recipient, sender, and so on. You can view a list of your mail messages using these commands:

h	Displays the first 20 message headers.
z	Displays a screenful of message headers; each time you use the command, you see the next

screenful. Use **z-** for the *previous* screenful. (These won't do anything if you have less than one screenful of message headers!)

top *numbers* Shows the top few lines of the messages, including where the message comes from and when it was sent (plus some information you won't want, such as what route it took to get to you). For instance, **top 1–5** shows the top information for messages 1 through 5; **top 5–$** shows the information for messages 5 through the end of the list.

f Displays the header for the current message.

f *numbers* Displays the headers for the specified messages; **f 5–$** shows the headers for message 5 through the end of the list.

Here's what a header list looks like:

```
>  1 aesmoot@aescon.com Thu Oct  7 18:06   36/1350  Re: More on SLIP
   2 Markus.Sadeniemi@osteri.funet.fi Fri Oct 8 05:45 45/1709 Re:Internet Book
   3 pgold@copper.Denver.Colorado.EDU Fri Oct 8 12:50 19/614 Re: Do a favor?
U  4 root   Sun Oct 10 01:43  157/5019  teal:/homeclients4 is ful
P  5 aesmoot@aescon.com Sun Oct 10 03:54 46/1905  Re: More on SLIP
   6 tpowell@cerf.net Sun Oct 10 23:18 62/2372  Internet Book (fwd)
   7 Melisa_Parker@qm1.psi.com Mon Oct 11 15:13   35/1198  Internet Book
   8 root      Tue Oct 12 01:41  144/4630  teal:/homeclients4 is ful
   9 hfunk@CNRI.Reston.VA.US Tue Oct 12 12:49  27/935  INET-Connect
N 10 tpowell@cerf.net  Thu Oct 14 09:46  50/1741  Re: Internet Book(fwd)
N 11 aesmoot@aescon.com Thu Oct 14 09:54  34/1182  Re: More on SLIP
```

You're right, this is a mess, but it's UNIX. What does this information tell us? Some of the messages have a letter in the left column. A **U** means the message hasn't been read, a **P** means you've just used the **pre** command to "preserve" the message in the mailbox instead of moving it out of the box (more on this later), and an **N** means the message is new (it has arrived since the last time you checked your mail).

The rest of the header contains the following information: a message number, the address from which it was received, the date and

107

time it was received, the size of the message (the number of lines and characters), and the message subject. One of the messages is also preceded by >. This is the current message—the one that will be affected by any commands you issue, unless you select another message as the current one. (You'll see how to do that in a moment.)

Read It and Smile

When you're ready to read a message, you may prefer to read it in a text editor, or to save it in a text file and read it later, as we'll see in a moment. Alternatively, you can use one of these commands (you probably won't very often, but you could):

p	Displays the current message.
p $** or simply **$	Displays the most recent message.
number	Displays the message assigned that number. For instance, type **5** and press **Enter** to view message 5.
p *numbers* or simply *numbers*	Displays a particular message. For instance, **p 9** displays message 9; **p 9–15** displays messages 9 through 15; **p 9–$** displays messages 9 through the most recent. Or, use any of these commands without the **p**, that is, just type the numbers you want.
t	The **t** command works in the same way as the **p** command.
Enter or **n**	If you've just entered Mail, this displays the first message in the list. Otherwise it displays the message following the current message.
–	Displays the message immediately before the current message.
Ctrl-c	If you want to stop a message from scrolling across the screen, use **Ctrl-c** (or maybe **Ctrl-x**).

The problem with all these commands is that unless a message is short, it's going to scroll by so fast you won't be able to read it. And if you use **Ctrl-c**, UNIX stops the message completely. You can't stop and start it.

There are several things you can try to avoid this problem. You can use an editor to view the message, you can let the mail save the message in mbox (the saved-message file), or you can save the message in a file that you create. You'll learn to do all these things in the following sections.

Viewing Mail with an Editor

Every UNIX shell has an *editor* available, in which you can view, create, and edit text files. In fact, you may have several editors available to you. Find out from your system administrator or service provider which editors are available, and try them out.

To put a mail message into an editor, use **e** *number* or **v** *number*. For instance, typing **e 5** and pressing **Enter** places message 5 in the editor. In the editor, you can scroll through the message at leisure, probably by pressing the arrow keys. (The **e** command puts the message in the editor chosen with the **setenv** command. The **v** command puts it in the vi text editor.)

To change your default editor, go to the UNIX shell prompt (not the mail prompt), type **setenv EDITOR** *editorname*, and press **Enter**. For instance, type **setenv EDITOR vi** to tell your system that whenever you call the editor, you want to use vi.

Later in this chapter, we'll look at vi, a text editor to which almost everyone has access. If you are using the vi text editor, press **Esc** three times to exit it, type **:q!**, and press **Enter**. (To exit any other text editor, check your documentation for instructions.)

Stick It in a File

If you want to, you can copy your messages into a text file and then read them at your leisure later. To do so, use one of these commands:

s *numbers filename*   This will save the entire message (or messages) in the named text file. For instance, **s 4–$ msg.txt** saves all of the messages from number four to the last one in a file called msg.txt.

w *numbers filename* This works in the same way as the **s** command, except that it won't include the "From" line. (Since you still get all the other header rubbish, you might as well forget this command.)

Use this file-saving method to organize your messages into folders. You could create a file called personal, one called hobbies, one called business, and so on, and copy messages into the appropriate file.

Once you've got the messages in a text file, you'll have to leave the mail system to read them. You can use the UNIX **more** or **cat** commands to read them (see Chapter 9), or you can copy them back to your computer (if you have a dial-in terminal connection) and read them in a word processor there.

When you use the **q** or **quit** command to close the mail system, the mail you have just read is removed from the mailbox and saved in a file called mbox. You can use the same methods (**more** or **cat**) to read this file. If you don't want a message to be removed and placed in the mbox file, use the **pre** *number* command before you exit ("pre" stands for "preserve," and that's exactly what it does to the message you specify).

ZAP! Deleting Messages

Tired of that dull old message? Delete it. This not only removes it from the mailbox, but makes sure it is not copied into the mbox file. Use the **d** *number* command. For instance, type **d 3–7** to delete messages 3 through 7. Although you won't see the messages in any lists, they are still there (for the moment at least). If you want to retrieve (undelete) the messages, use the **u** *number* command. For example, type **u 3–7** to bring those messages back.

Replying (Politely) to Messages

If you want to reply to a message, use one of the **r** commands. Use **r** *number* to reply to the sender of the message; use **R** *number* (capital R) to reply to the sender and send a copy of the reply to everyone who

received the original message. You'll see
something like this:

```
& r 1
To: joebloe@apotpeel.com
Subject: Re: New model
```

There may be times when your mail program can not figure out the From address, and is unable to create the To address. If this happens, the message is returned to you, and you have to re-enter the correct address manually.

The mail system automatically entered
the new message's To: line and Subject: line
for you, so you can now write a message. (If
you want to cancel a reply, press **Ctrl-c**
twice.) But let's step back a bit and look at
how to send a message from scratch.

Quoting or Forwarding the Original

You'll soon notice that it's common for people in the e-mail crowd to
include the original message in the reply. That's simply a way of re-
minding the recipient (the author of the original message) of what he
or she said. Most mail programs have some simple way to do this. In
UNIX Mail, you use the **~f** *number* command. For instance:

```
& r 1
To: joebloe@apotpeel.com
Subject: Re: New model
~f 1
```

You used the **r 1** command to reply to message 1, and you used
the **~f 1** command to include the original message in the reply. You
can then use a text editor (use the **~v** or **~e** command) to insert your
message within the body of the original message. By doing so, you can
answer the points of the original message one by one, by following the
original text with your replies.

Of course, this command also provides you with a simple way to
forward a message (to send it on to someone else). Simply start writing
a message; then use the **~f** *number* command to include another
message.

A variation of this command, the **~m** *number* command, includes
the file in the same way that **~f** *number* does, but it also places a tab

before each line so the recipient can quickly identify which lines he wrote. (More advanced mail programs use a character such as > instead of the tab or in conjunction with it to make this even clearer.)

Starting from Scratch: Composing Your Own Messages

You don't even have to start the mail system to begin sending a mail message. Whether you are inside the mail system or still at the UNIX-shell prompt, use the **mail** *address* command (remember, we discussed addresses in Chapter 10). If you are inside the mail system, you can abbreviate this **mail** command to simply **m**. An example might be **mail joebloe@apotpeel.com**. You can send the message to several people by separating addresses with a comma and a space. (As you'll see later, you can also use an *alias* or *mailing list* here in place of a single address.)

When you press **Enter**, the mail system prompts you for a subject. Type the message subject (something that succinctly describes what is in the message), press **Enter** again, and you see a blank line. Just start typing. Press the **Enter** key at the end of each line, and remember not to make the lines too long (don't go over about 60 characters).

When you've finished the message, press **Enter**, type a period (.) on the last line, and press **Enter** again. The mail system asks you for a Cc: (the address of the person to whom you want to send a copy of the message). You'll enter the Cc addresses, if there are any, in the same way you entered the original address. Then press **Enter** to send the message. Here's what it all looks like:

```
& mail joebloe@apotpeel.com
Subject: Your new potato peeler
Mr. Bloe.
I've just seen an ad about your new super duper
potato peeler. I wonder if you could send me information
about this, with details on how to order 10,000.
Thanks v. much.
.
Cc: fred@ourplace.org
&
```

If you were in the mail system when you started to send the message, you will still be at the & prompt. If you were at the UNIX-shell prompt (probably the % prompt) when you started, you'll find yourself back there, so you can write messages from the UNIX shell without really going into the mail system.

You can also send a Cc: using the ~c *address* command anywhere in the message. You can send a "blind" carbon copy with the ~b *address* command. When you use a blind carbon copy, the system sends a copy of the message to each of the people to whom you sent "blind" copies, but the original message shows no indication of these other copies.

Adding a Text File to a Message

Sticking a text file into a message is useful in three cases. The most common one is when you're sending a long message. You can type the message in a word processor, save it as a text file, begin your mail message, and plop down the saved file into the message at the right spot. This is much easier than trying to write the whole long thing using a clunky UNIX editor.

The second use for this procedure is that it enables you to transmit non-text files as text. For example, let's say you want to send a database file, spreadsheet file, picture, sound, or some other kind of non-text file. Internet's mail programs don't generally handle such files; they usually permit you to transmit only text messages. However, there is a way around the problem. Convert the file into text first, transmit it, and then convert it back to its original format at the other end. (We'll look at this procedure in the next chapter.)

To cancel the message at any time while writing it, press **Ctrl-c** twice.

The third common use is to add a signature to a message. This is usually four or five lines of text telling the recipient something about the sender (usually the sender's name and address) and looks something like this:

```
=======================================================
¦  Joe Bloe              ¦Internet: Joeblo@this.here ¦
¦  2291 N. Coors Drive ¦   CompuServe: 11601,12666 ¦
¦  Podunk, CO, 80000     ¦     Phone:  303-555-4321 ¦
=======================================================
```

The signature is often something else—perhaps something weird. I recently received a message with the signature, "Barney eats children!" (My two-year-old vehemently disagrees, claiming that Barney eats only food.) You might also see quotes from famous people, pieces of poetry, or pictures created with the text characters. Some users go to such degrees that various newsgroups (which you'll learn about in Chapter 15) have taken to rejecting messages with long signatures.

In Chapter 12, you'll learn about a mail program you can use for writing mail messages. But you can use this ~r command only while in UNIX mail itself, not while in most other mail programs. Many editors have their own (usually superior) methods of including text files. Check your system's documentation.

If you want to use a signature file, create the file, place it in your home directory, and give it a simple name, such as "s." When you want to insert your signature file in your message—or in any other kind of text file— type ~r *filename* on a new line (make sure the ~ is the first character on the line) and press **Enter**. (That's why you want a nice simple file name, so it's easy to type each time.) You can then continue with the message if you'd like. When you send the message, the text file is inserted at the ~r point. Other mail programs let you add signature files to messages automatically: you tell the program where the file is, and it adds it for you each time you write a message. With UNIX Mail, however, you must use the ~r command.

Using vi—An Exercise in Futility?

Most UNIX systems come with an amazing text editor called vi. This editor is to most modern word processors what a horse and cart are to a Chevy truck: it'll get the job done (with a little effort), but you won't use it if you've got the Chevy available. Still, in case you don't have a Chevy, let's take a look.

Once you've used vi a few times, you might even come to like it. To be fair to UNIX freaks, if you know what you are doing, vi can be quick and easy to use (as EDLIN is for old-time DOS users). Just don't admit it to your friends.

When you've started your mail message, place the cursor on a new line (you can start on the first line if you want, or you can type some of the message and then start vi), type ~v, and press **Enter**. You'll see something like this:

```
~
~
~
~
~
~
~
~
~
"/tmp/Re26352" 0 lines, 0 characters
```

This, believe it or not, is vi's text editor screen, the equivalent of being inside a word processor's screen or window.

vi has two modes: a *command mode* (in which you enter commands such as moving the cursor) and an *input mode* (in which you type). When you first start vi you are in command mode. Press **a** to change to input mode (we'll come back to that in a moment). Now you can type. You have to enter carriage returns (press **Enter**) at the end of each line because vi won't do it for you. Don't make the lines too long; limit them to about 60 characters.

In some versions of vi, you may be able to use the cursor keys to move the cursor around. Other versions don't like it and do strange things (like adding a line). In such a version, you'll have to use command mode to move the cursor. You may find that you can use Backspace in vi to move the cursor back a few spaces so you can type over something.

Jumping into Command Mode

When you are ready to move the cursor back to fix something, you'll need to enter command mode. Press **Esc** once. Then use one of these wonderful commands (remember, they're case-sensitive):

To move the cursor   Use the arrow keys. If they don't work, try pressing **h**, **i**, **j**, and **k**. You can also press + to move to the beginning of the next line, – to move to the beginning of the preceding line (use the hyphen and + sign on the keyboard, not the numeric keypad), **G** to move to the end of the file, and **1G** to move to the beginning of the file (isn't this great?). **Ctrl-f** moves you down one screen at a time, and **Ctrl-b** moves you back one screen at a time.

Adding text   When you've got the cursor in position and are ready to add new text, you have a few options, each of which returns you to input mode. Press **R** to replace text, **i** to insert text before the cursor position, **a** to insert text after the cursor position, **A** to add text at the end of the current line, or **O** (the capital letter O, not zero) to add text on a new line in front of the cursor position.

Deleting text   To delete text, press **dd** to remove an entire line, **D** to delete from the cursor to the end of the line, or **x** to delete a single character. You can press and hold the **d** key to delete line after line.

Undo   To undo changes, press **u** to undo the previous change, or press **U** to undo changes to the current line.

Save   To save your changes but continue working in vi, type **:w** and press **Enter**.

You opened vi using the ~v command. If you use ~e instead of ~v, you'll probably see another text editor, perhaps emacs or pico. (You'll see the text editor that was set using the **setenv EDITOR** command at the UNIX prompt. For instance, **setenv EDITOR pico** or **setenv EDITOR emacs**.) You may find one of these editors easier to use than vi. Try pico if your system has it. I think it's easier to use than vi or emacs.

Closing vi

To close vi, press **Esc** three times. Your computer beeps. Type **ZZ** (uppercase) and press **Enter** to save the work you have done. Alternatively, you can type **:q!** and press **Enter** to abandon all the work you have done and close vi. Either way, you will see (**continue**). You can now continue working in your e-mail message. Although you can add more text, you cannot go back and make changes to the previous stuff (unless you reopen vi, of course). Finish the message in the usual way: type a period (.) on a blank line and press **Enter**. Enter a Cc name (if necessary) and press **Enter** again.

Closing the Mail System

How do you get out of the mail system? There are a couple of ways. Type **x** and press **Enter** to leave all the read mail in your mailbox. Type **quit** (or simply **q**) and press **Enter** to leave the system and move the messages you have just read into the text file called mbox, which you will be able to read later. Deleted messages are removed, and unread messages remain. Messages you send are not placed anywhere; you've got no record of them. (One advantage of the more advanced Internet mail systems is that they save a copy of your sent mail.)

The Least You Need to Know

➤ Start UNIX mail by typing **mail** and pressing **Enter**.

➤ View a list of messages by typing **h**, **z**, or **z–** and pressing **Enter**.

➤ Read a message by typing its message number and pressing **Enter**.

➤ Reply to a message by typing **r** and the message number and pressing **Enter**.

➤ Use the **~f** *number* command or **~m** *number* command to include the original message in the reply or in a new message.

➤ Start a mail message (from the UNIX prompt or the Mail prompt) by typing **mail** *address* and pressing **Enter**.

➤ To use a text editor while writing a message, type ~v or ~e on the beginning of a line and press **Enter**.

➤ Cancel a message by pressing **Ctrl-c** twice.

➤ Close Mail with the **q** or **x** command. The **x** command tells Mail not to remove messages you've read.

## Chapter 12

Still More on Mail

In This Chapter

➤ Mailing with aliases

➤ Mail reflectors: public mailing lists

➤ Getting an automatic response

➤ Sending files by converting them to ASCII

➤ Reading and writing messages in Pine

➤ Signature files revisited

In Chapter 11, you saw how poor unfortunate souls using the UNIX mail program send mail. Although you might not realize it from gazing at the UNIX prompt, there are many cool things you can do with mail, and I'll tell you about a few of them in this chapter. We'll also take a look at Pine, a popular mail program that you might have available.

Psst! Use an Alias!

As you have no doubt noticed, some Internet addresses are rather long and confusing. You'll save yourself a lot of time if you create a nick-name or *alias* list that speeds up sending messages to people you mail to frequently. This information is stored in the .mailrc text file along with other information about your mail system; the .mailrc file may be in your home directory.

Files with a period before the name are hidden files. They won't appear when you use the **ls** command at the UNIX prompt to list your files. If you want to see all the hidden files, use the **ls -a** or **ls -al** command.

If you are using UNIX mail, you'll have to edit the .mailrc file using a text editor. For example, if you want to use vi to edit the file, type **vi .mailrc** and press **Enter**. Add the aliases you want to use in the format **alias *nickname address***, such as **alias joeb joebloe@apotpeel.com**. Then, instead of writing the entire address each time you want to send a message to this person, you can just type **joeb**.

You can create mailing lists in the same way. Let's say you want to create a mailing list containing members of your sales staff. We'll call the list **staff**. Enter each address in the format **alias staff *address***. You can put several addresses on one line by separating them with a comma and space, as in this example:

```
alias staff address, address, address
```

When you are ready to send a message to everyone on the list, simply type **staff** in the address field, and the mail system will pick out all the individual addresses for you.

Some mail programs let you create aliases and mailing lists without messing with the .mailrc file. See your program's documentation.

Reflective Mail? Using Mail Reflectors

There's another kind of mailing list called a *mail reflector*. This is a kind of public mailing list: when a message is sent to a reflector's address, that message is automatically sent out to all the people in the reflector's mailing list. This is a convenient way to centrally control a mailing list used by a group of people (everyone in the sales department, the history department, etc.).

If you want to create your own mailing list, talk with your service provider (or see *The Complete Idiot's Next Step with the Internet*, in which I discuss this subject). For more information about mailing lists, see Chapter 16.

Automatic Mail Responses

You may have noticed that some e-mail addresses send a response back to you automatically. For example, if you send a message to **info@***hostname*, and what you write in the message is ignored, the system simply sends back to you a "form letter," describing its services. Lots of people and organizations (even the President of the United States) use this automatic-response system.

It's pretty simple to set up your own automatic response. Because you're most likely to want to do this when you go on vacation, there's a UNIX command called (not surprisingly) **vacation**. At the UNIX prompt, type **vacation** and press **Enter**.

```
teal% vacation
```

Then you'll see a text editor that looks something like this:

```
This program can be used to answer your mail automatically
when you go away on vacation.
You need to create a message file in /home/clients4/peterk/.vacation.msg
first.
PICO 1.7    File: /home/clients4/peterk/.vacation.msg    Modified
```

Type your message. Notice that you can type **$SUBJECT** to make the vacation program grab the incoming message's subject line and drop it into the message.

```
From: peterk (via the vacation program)
Subject: away from my mail

I will not be reading my mail for a while. I'm going to Disneyland!
(Well, okay, I'm going on a sales trip.) Your mail regarding "$SUBJECT"
will be read when I return.

^G Get Help ^O WriteOut ^R Read File^Y Prev Pg  ^K Del Line ^C Cur Pos
^X Exit     ^J Justify  ^W Where is ^V Next Pg  ^U UnDel Lin^T To Spell
```

When you are finished, close the text editor (in this case, by pressing **Ctrl-x**). The program will ask you some simple questions (such as "Would you like to see the message now?") and then send you on your way.

That's it. Each time a message comes in, your message goes out automatically. When you come back and want to stop this, use the vacation command again.

```
teal% vacation
```

The vacation program will show you your messages and give you the option to discontinue or continue the auto-response.

Sending Computer Files by Internet Mail

The Internet's mail system transmits text. That is, the only things transmitted are text characters; the Internet doesn't transmit a file. Rather, it just sends characters, which are then placed in a file at the other end. That means you can't send computer files containing programs, sounds, desktop-publishing or word-processing pages, spreadsheets, graphics, smells, or anything else programmers have figured out they can store in a computer.

However, there is a way around this problem. You can convert a file to text, send the text file (which could be huge) across the Internet, and then have the recipient convert it back to its original format. There are various programs for doing this: uuencode and btoa for UNIX, BinHex and UUTool 232 for Macintosh, for example. There's also a UUENCODE program for DOS computers, and one for Windows computers called Wincode. There are others available, as it's a relatively simple programming task. (You should be able to find these on your service provider's system. You'll also find them at the Macmillan Publishing Internet site, which you can reach at **ftp.mcp.com** for FTP, gopher.mcp.com for Gopher, and **http://www/mcp/com** for World Wide Web.)

Let's say you want to use the Internet to send a colleague a photograph or a small program you have written. The file is called ORIGINAL.TIF. You can encode it on your computer or on your service provider's computer. We'll look at the latter case first.

Okay, I lied. You *can* send computer files by Internet. It's just not easy. You can use a system called MIME (Multipurpose Internet Mail Extensions) to do so. But you're going to have to do so without my help, because MIME is in its infancy, is not widely used, and is difficult to work with. However, the Pine mail program has MIME, so you might want to play with it. To quote the authors, it's "an early implementation of MIME so we undoubtedly have made some mistakes."

Converting the File in UNIX

Let's assume the ORIGINAL.TIF file is on the service provider's computer, ready to be sent with mail. First, let's convert it to ASCII. Type this command at the UNIX shell:

```
uuencode ORIGINAL.TIF OUR.TIF >1.uue
```

This will use the ORIGINAL.TIF file to create an ASCII file called 1.uue. It also puts the name *OUR.TIF* inside the ASCII file.

Include the encoded file in your mail message. You'll start a message, write a line or two, if you want, explaining to your colleague what the file is, and perhaps even providing instructions on how to decode it. Then you'll send the message. When the file gets to the other end, your colleague will see the beginning of the message and realize it's an encoded file. The next step at that end is to save the message in a file using whatever command the recipient's mail program uses to do so (UNIX mail, for example, uses the **s** *filename* command).

Your friend will then decode the message using a command such as **uudecode** *savefilename*, which will decode the saved file (*savefilename*). It will then save the converted file in a file that bears the name you included in the original command (in this case, **our.tif**). Once the file is decoded, your colleague can use it or do a file transfer to get it back to his or her computer. We'll look at file transfers in depth in Chapter 19.

Encoding and Decoding on Your Computer

You can also encode and decode files on your own computer, transferring them to and from the service provider's computer as needed. The PC and Macintosh programs are generally easier to use and may have more features than the UNIX programs. For example, you can sometimes decode a file and give it a different name at the same time (i.e., when your colleague decodes the file you send, he might change the name to MY.TIF instead of OUR.TIF).

123

Your colleague shouldn't even have to worry about removing the actual message text and header from the file before converting. The uudecode program can figure out where the encoded text begins and ends.

You are likely to face one significant problem with the uuencode program on your service provider's computer. If you convert a file to ASCII and then send it in e-mail to another network (such as CompuServe), the recipient may be unable to decode the file because some of the characters may have been corrupted. In some cases, the recipient will be able to decode the file, but generally he won't. The latest version of Richard Marks' DOS version of UUENCODE and UUDECODE (originally written to coincide with this book), gets around this problem, as do some other Mac and PC programs. You can find this at the Macmillan FTP site (**ftp.mcp.com**).

Requesting Files with E-mail

In Chapter 18, you'll learn about FTP, a method by which you can "travel" to computers all over the world and grab files of all kinds: programs, graphics, sounds, text and word processing documents, and so on. There are also a few methods for using the Internet's mail system to grab files automatically. As this isn't, strictly speaking, e-mail (but simply a way to use e-mail to automate file transfers), I'm not going to cover it here, but I'll explain how it works in Chapter 19.

Back to the Real World: Using a Mail Program

If you are lucky, you have a mail program other than UNIX mail. The service provider I'm working with uses Pine, a mail interface that is relatively easy to use. (No, it's probably not as good as the e-mail system you use on your company's network or as good as the one that comes with the CompuServe navigator you use, but it sure beats the plain old UNIX mail interface.) Let's take a look at how Pine works. Even if you don't have Pine, you may want to scan the list of commands to get an idea of what your program should be able to do.

Using Pine

To get to Pine, I select the **11. Mail** option from my service provider's Main Menu; then I select **1. Read or Send Mail**. You can also run it directly from the UNIX shell by typing **pine** and pressing **Enter**.

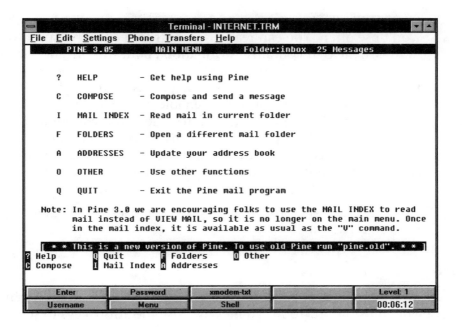

The Pine Main Menu is your starting point for the mail system.

You then see another menu with several options, as shown in the preceding figure. You can choose from the options (listed below) by typing the letter that precedes the one you want.

?–HELP   View the Pine user's manual.

C–COMPOSE   Write a message.

I–MAIL INDEX   Read the mail in the current folder. You can select the folder you want to use with the **F** command, but by default the current folder is the inbox.

F–FOLDERS   This shows you a list of mail folders (each of which is actually a text file that holds the messages). My folders include inbox, sent-mail, saved-messages (a file that holds messages sent to me that I've read), sent-mail-dec-94, sent-mail-nov-94, and so on. You can use the arrow keys to select the one you want.

A–ADDRESSES   A file in which you can save addresses. When you're writing a message, you can quickly view the address book and drop the correct address into place. The address book also enables you to set up mailing lists and aliases (*nicknames*).

125

O–OTHER   This gives you access to a few commands you probably won't use often. You can read a "news" file about Pine (a sort of README file that contains information about the current release). If you need to leave your terminal for a while, you can lock your keyboard (you'll have to type your login password to get working again). There are commands that enable you to enter a new login password or select a printer (if you're lucky, your communications program will let Pine print a document on your computer's printer). There's even a command that enables you to view the amount of space used by your mail folders (which I find very useful because if I use too much disk space, I have to pay an extra fee).

Q-QUIT   Exits the program and takes you back to the menu system or to the UNIX shell.

Using the Mail List

To read your mail, type **I**, which displays a list like the one shown in the following illustration. To read a message, use the arrow keys to select it; then press **Enter**. To see the next page of the index, press **Spacebar**.

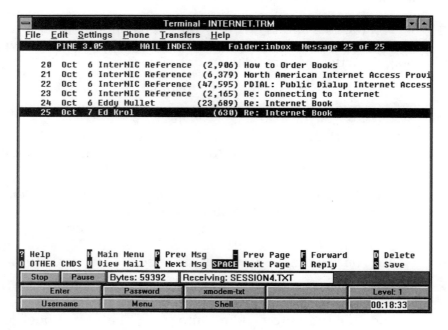

Pine's mail index is a lot easier to use than UNIX Mail is!

As you can see from the two lines at the bottom of the screen, there are a number of other commands:

? Help   Displays more help information.

M Main Menu   Takes you back to Pine's Main Menu.

P Prev Msg   Moves the highlight up the list of messages.

- Prev Page   Displays the previous page in the list.

F Forward   Enables you to create a new message, and puts the selected text in the message so you can forward it.

D Delete   Marks the message as deleted (puts a **D** in the left column). When you quit Pine, you'll be asked to confirm deletion of the message. (Alternatively, you could use the X command to remove it immediately.)

V View Mail   Displays the selected message. This is the same as pressing Enter.

N Next Msg   Moves the highlight down the list of messages.

SPACE Next Page   Press **Spacebar** to see the next page in the list.

R Reply   Lets you send a reply to the selected message. You'll be asked if you want to include the original message in the reply; if you say yes, Pine will indicate each line of the original with a > so the person you are replying to can see the original text easily. And if the original message went to other recipients, you'll be asked if you want to reply to all recipients.

S Save   Lets you save a message in a particular folder. You can also create a new folder with this command. This is similar to UNIX mail's **s** command (though UNIX mail doesn't think of the file as a folder).

If you type **O**, you'll see a few more commands, such as:

E Export Msg   Lets you save the selected message. (The same as UNIX mail's **s** command.)

C Compose   Lets you begin writing a new message.

U Undelete   Undeletes a message.

T Take Addr   Grabs the address from the selected message and drops it into the address book.

These commands are not case-sensitive, by the way. **D** is the same as **d**.

G Go to Fldr Lets you go directly to one of the other mail folders, such as sent-mail.

O OTHER CMDS Displays more commands (which we'll look at in a moment).

Z Sort Folder The folder is initially sorted by the order in which the messages were received, but you can use this command to change the order so that they are sorted by the subject, the From name, the date sent, the size, or in reverse arrival order (with the most recent at the top of the list).

L Print This may print the message on your printer (if your communications software allows it).

X eXpunge If you use the **D** command to delete a message, the message is marked with a **D** in the left column. The X command actually removes it from the list.

J Jump Lets you jump to a particular message number (which can be quite useful if you have a huge list of messages).

W Where is Searches the message Number, Date, From, and Subject for text you specify.

Q Quit Closes Pine.

Reading Mail

If you select a message and press **v** or **Enter**, you can read the message. You'll see most of the commands that we've just looked at, with a few variations. The - and **Spacebar** commands now move you through the message itself (- moves you up; **Spacebar** moves you down).

There's an **I** (Mail Index) command to take you back to the message list, and there's an **A** (Attachments) command, which is intended for use with the MIME (Multipurpose Internet Mail Extensions) system we mentioned earlier. The A command enables you to extract the non-ASCII attachments or, if the attachment is a GIF file, to view the picture (maybe—it depends on your terminal). However, even if you are not using MIME (and you probably won't be), you can still use the **A** command to strip out all the header garbage, extract the body of the message, and drop it into a file.

128

Writing Messages with Pine

As you've seen, you can begin writing a message several ways with Pine. The **C** command starts a brand new message; **R** replies to the selected message (and, if you want, includes the original message in the new one); and **F** forwards a message, putting the original into a new one. In the following illustration, we've got a brand new message.

Let's take a look at what you can do here. The commands that are available vary, depending on which line contains the highlight. For example, while you're on the **To:** line, you can use the **Ctrl-T** command to go to the address book. In the address book, select an address and press **M** to copy it into the **To:** line.

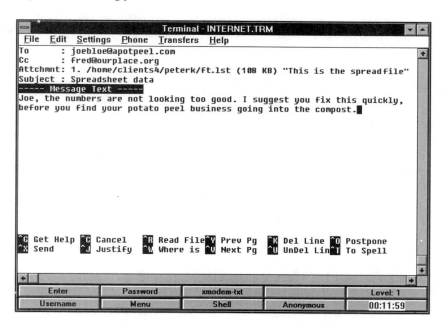

Entering a mail message into Pine. Notice that this one has an attachment.

You can use a similar method with the **Attchmnt** line. (Again, this is for MIME attachments, non-text files that you want to send with the file. MIME is in its infancy, and even the authors of Pine say it may not work correctly. You can experiment with it if you want, but remember that the recipient will also need "MIME-enabled" software to be able to read the file.) If you place the highlight on the **Attchmnt** line and press **Ctrl-T**, you'll see all the files in your home directory. You'll be able to select a file, and even move to other directories. When you've got the one you want, press **S** to select it. You'll be asked to enter a comment line to go with it.

The **Ctrl-R** command, available as long as the highlight is in any of the header lines, adds two new header lines: **Bcc** (Blind carbon copy) and **Fcc** (File carbon copy). We discussed blind carbon copies in Chapter 11; it's a message that is sent to other people, without any indication of that in the original message. The Fcc is a method of automatically keeping a copy of outgoing mail. By default, the system puts all messages in the sent-mail file.

Here are some other commands you can use while writing the message:

Ctrl-G Get Help   Displays help information about composing messages.

Ctrl-C Cancel   Cancels the message without saving or sending.

Ctrl-R Read File   Inserts a text file. This is the same as UNIX mail's ~r command. You'll be able to select from a list of files in your home directory and move around into other directories.

Ctrl-Y Prev Pg   Moves up the message to see what you've already written.

Ctrl-K Del Line   Deletes the current line.

Ctrl-O Postpone   Lets you save the message without sending it. The next time you try to compose a message, you'll be asked if you want to continue with the postponed message.

Ctrl-X Send   Sends the message.

Ctrl-J Justify   This reformats the paragraph the cursor is in. Pine assumes that a paragraph ends with a blank line. Any contiguous lines not separated by a blank will be reformatted to clean up ragged edges (which is useful if you've been editing the text).

Ctrl-W Where is   Searches your message for what you've written or for text from other sources (inserted using the Ctrl-R command or from a message you are replying to or forwarding).

Ctrl-V Next Pg   Moves down the message.

Ctrl-U UnDel Lin   Undeletes the last lines you deleted. You can combine this with Ctrl-K to move blocks of text in a message.

Ctrl-T To Spell   Checks your spelling. Although this feature is not as sophisticated as most word processors' spell checkers, it is useful nonetheless.

Signature Files

In Chapter 11, we looked at how you can insert a signature file into an e-mail message using UNIX mail's ~**r** command. With Pine (and many other mail programs), you can get the program to remember to place the signature file for you. All you need is a text file called .signature in your home directory. The period before the name means it's a hidden file—but don't worry about that. Simply create the file and give it the name. Hidden files in UNIX don't have the same significance that they do in DOS.

Yes, There's More

Okay, so I haven't described everything that Pine can do. Pine's help system is actually quite good, so if you have this program, spend a little time looking around. That goes for whatever program you happen to be using. Find out how the program can help you deal with your mail—it could save you lots of time and hassle in the long run.

Some mail programs have other useful features, but you may not be able to use them! For example, you may be able to request a notification of receipt (a message sent back to you when the message you sent arrives, so you know for sure it got where it was supposed to go). You may also be able to get a notification of reading, which tells you the user actually read the message, or at least opened it.

The message cancel feature enables you to retrieve a message you've sent—assuming it's retrievable, which it may not be (depending on where it has reached when you decide to cancel it). There are also systems such as MIME (Multipurpose Internet Mail Extensions), a little-used system that lets you send computer files as e-mail.

These features are seldom used by dial-in terminal users and are dependent on both sides—the sender and the recipient—using software that matches. However, people working with fancier systems (see Chapter 25) will have fancier features, such as automatic uuencoding and decoding of files.

The Least You Need to Know

➤ Using aliases and mailing lists on the Internet is important: it helps you avoid having to type funky e-mail addresses.

➤ If you are using UNIX mail, you'll have to edit the .mailrc file to create aliases. If you have another program, you may be able to create aliases and mailing lists from within the program.

➤ To request to be added to a mail reflector, send a message to *username*-request@*hostname*.

➤ To convert a file using uuencode on UNIX, type **uuencode** *originalfilename encodedfilename* >*filename*.uue; then include the encoded file in a mail message.

➤ To convert an encoded file, type **uudecode** *filename*. The decoded file will be placed in a file with the original name.

➤ If you have the Pine mail program, read this chapter for more information. If you don't have Pine, read this chapter to see what your mail program should be able to do.

## Chapter 13

Return to Sender, Address Unknown

In This Chapter

➤ Why e-mail gets returned and what to do about it

➤ Where to look for e-mail addresses

➤ Using finger to find login information

➤ Searching for newsgroup users

➤ Use a Knowbot to automate searches

➤ Using Netfind

Nothing's simple on the Internet. You might be sure that you've entered the correct e-mail address—you might have even used your mail program to "grab" an address from a message you received—but just when you think you've finished with an e-mail message, it comes back. You look in your inbox and find something like this:

```
22  Nov  8 Mail Delivery Subs  (1,274) Returned mail: Host unknown
```

You view the message, and find a horrendous mess of header lines with comments like:

```
Host unknown (Authoritative answer from nameserver).
```

Your message has gone out onto the Internet, but nobody knows what to do with it. There may even be occasions when you have used a correct address, and the Internet still can't deliver it.

What's Up?

There are four reasons, with some variations, why your mail may not be delivered:

Host unknown   The Internet can't find the host that you used in the e-mail address. Remember that e-mail addresses are in the format *user@host*. For some reason the Internet can't get through to the host.

User unknown   The Internet can get your mail to the host, but the host claims it doesn't recognize the user and sends the mail back.

Service unavailable   The address is fine, but the host computer is not accepting mail at the moment. The mail system may be shut down due to hardware or virus problems. Or maybe the message was sent at a time when the host simply doesn't accept mail; some systems refuse mail during certain times.

Can't send   The specified host is correct, and the host might be inclined to accept the mail, but the Internet can't get through to the host. Maybe the network is damaged, maybe the host itself is out of business due to hardware problems, or maybe the host has changed its mail configuration and the information hasn't been passed on to the right people.

Look carefully at your returned mail, and you'll see one of these reasons (or something like it) somewhere in the header. It's usually, but not always, on the Subject line near the top.

Who Didn't Get It?

If you sent a message to several people, you should check carefully to see who didn't receive it. For instance, if you used a mailing list or sent carbon copies to other people, the message could have been delivered to all but one person. So look carefully at the **Transcript of session follows** section of the header (as shown here) to see who didn't get it.

```
— —Transcript of session follows— —
550 apotpeel.com (TCP)... 550 Host unknown
554 <joebloe@apotpeel.com>... 550 Host unknown (Authoritative
answer from name
server)
550 ourplace.org (TCP)... 550 Host unknown
554 <fred@ourplace.org>... 550 Host unknown (Authoritative
answer from name server)
```

You can see that this message was sent back from two addresses, in both cases because the Internet couldn't find the host. The message may have gone through to other recipients.

So What's the Problem?

Why is your mail coming back? There are a number of possible reasons:

You typed the address incorrectly. You could have made a mistake when typing the address. Take a look at the address in the returned message to confirm that you got it right. See if you typed a zero instead of an o, or a one instead of an l, for example.

A mailer incorrectly modified the domain. A mail server somewhere saw the address, misunderstood it, and added its own domain. If the returned message shows the address you entered, and some higher-level domain stuff that you didn't include in the address, this is what has happened.

You've been given an incomplete address. Some people assume too much when they hand out their addresses: they give you part of it and assume you know where they are and understand how to complete the highest level of their domain. In many cases, a complete address is needed only if the mail is leaving your host. Therefore, if your host sees an incomplete address, without the higher-level domain, it may assume the mail goes to someone in the same domain. (And if a user gets used to giving his address to other local users, he may forget about the higher-level domain part when giving his address to non-local users.)

You used a correct address, but the mailer doesn't know it's correct. There's not much you can do about this except complain. Some mail servers may not have the latest domain information.

The mail program that sent you a message didn't fill out the From name correctly. Not all mail programs fill out the From name correctly. They often abbreviate it, stripping out the higher levels of the domain name. The From name is for reference only; it's not used to actually deliver the mail. However, if you use your mail program to "grab" the From name and put it into your address book (or to reply directly to this message), you're going to have an incorrectly addressed message. If you know the From address is wrong, you should correct it before you use it, of course. Check the body of the message to see if the sender included a signature with his full mail address.

Who Ya Gonna Call?

What do you do about these problems? If it's a system problem, in which a mail server does not recognize an address or modifies it incorrectly, there's not much you can do except talk to your service provider. If you can see what the problem is, simply correct the address, strip out all the header garbage you don't need, and send the message again. (You could use your mail program's Forward command to do all this.)

You might also have to try to contact the person some other way (the telephone, remember?) and get the correct address. However, there will be times when you are stuck with a bad address and no other way to find the person. That's when things might get tough.

The Internet Directory? There Isn't One

There is no single directory in which you can look up an Internet user's mail address. Finding an address takes a little more work than that. One problem is that the Internet is an amorphous blob that seems unrelated to geography. Although there's no single directory of Internet users, there are many different directories. The problem is, if you've no idea where the person is, which directory do you use?

While researching this book, for example, I came across the names of two people I wanted to talk to about a particular program. I'd seen their names in a couple of documents, but no addresses were included.

Where were these people? It turned out that one was in England, and the other was in California. There are a number of different techniques you can employ for finding people.

Talk to the Postmaster

If you are sure a user is at a particular host, you could ask the host's "postmaster." Write an e-mail message to **postmaster@***hostname*. Provide as much information about the person as you can, and maybe the postmaster will be able to send you the correct mail address.

Ask Someone Else

Think about who else the person might know: other people the person has worked with or with whom you know the person has communicated. Then e-mail that person and ask if he knows where the first person is.

finger Him

UNIX has a command called **finger** that lets you ask a host about someone with a name that you know. You enter the command in this format: **finger** *name@host*. If you were looking for someone named **Smith** at the host named **apotpeel.com**, you might go through the following:

```
teal% finger smith@apotpeel.com
[apotpeel.com]
Login name: bsmith                     In real life: Bert Smith
Directory: /ftp/./                     Shell: /bin/true
Never logged in.
No unread mail
No Plan.


Login name: gsmith                     In real life: George Smith
Directory: /ftp/./                     Shell: /bin/true
Mail last read Tue Nov  9 10:18:03 1993
No Plan.
```

You've found two Smiths: Bert and George. Bert has never used his account (see the **Never logged in** line). Sometimes you'll see a **Last login** line with a date or a **Mail last read** line; these give you an idea of how often the account is used.

137

What name are you going to enter with the **finger** command? You can enter a complete first name, complete last name, or complete login name. (If you enter a login name, you'd better get the capitalization correct; for first and last names it doesn't matter.) You can enter **finger** *@host* with no name to see a list of all the people currently logged onto that domain. (You can even enter **finger** by itself to see a list of all the people currently logged onto your domain.)

Notice the **No Plan** line in the earlier example. This refers to the user's plan file, a hidden file in his home directory. It's simply a text file that includes any information the user wants to give people who finger him. Take a look at this example:

```
teal% finger bloe
Login name: joeb                      In real life: Joe Bloe
Directory: /home/clients4/joeb           Shell: /bin/csh
On since Nov  9 09:32:01 on ttyra from ucb-annex.csn.or
Mail last read Tue Nov  9 10:18:03 1993
Plan:
     =====================================================
     ¦  Joe Bloe           ¦Internet:joeb@apotpeel.com ¦
     ¦  2291 S. Coors St.  ¦   CompuServe: 79999,9999  ¦
     ¦  Podunk, CO  80228  ¦   Phone:   303-555-1869   ¦
     =====================================================
```

Joe Bloe has created a text file containing his address, Internet address, CompuServe address, and phone number. You can really track this guy down now. He could also have included a mini résumé if he'd wanted, telling you what he does.

The **finger** command also displays the contents of the first line of the .project file (another text file the user may have created to provide more information). The .project file is likely to be updated periodically, while the .plan file contains more permanent information. The **finger** command won't always work. Some hosts don't allow it, and many Internet system administrators believe that it provides too much information and poses a security risk. In some cases, a system lets you finger someone only if you know the person's user name. (It won't let you get a list of all the people named Smith, for instance.) All of these things depend on how each system administrator set up his or her system.

Search for Newsgroup Users

In Chapter 15, you will learn about newsgroups, areas in which you can post and read public messages on thousands of different subjects. In order for you to be able to read these newsgroups, your service provider must subscribe to them.

A quick way to create a .plan file is to make a copy of your e-mail signature file. Some mail programs automatically pull text out of a file called .signature and drop it into the end of your messages. You could use this UNIX command to copy the signature file to your .plan file: **cp .signature .plan**. Press **Enter**, and you're finished.

MIT subscribes to most of the newsgroups, and each time a newsgroup message comes into MIT, the system grabs the From: line and saves it. If you think the person you are trying to track down might have used the newsgroups, you might want to search MIT's database by sending an e-mail message to **mail-server@rtfm.mit.edu**. For instance:

```
CNS> mail mail-server@rtfm.mit.edu
Subject:
send usenet-addresses/name

.
CNS>
```

In place of *name* in this example, substitute the name for which you are searching. An hour or two after you send the message, you'll probably receive an e-mail message containing a list of the matches. You can send the message **send usenet-addresses/help** to get more information about using this system.

There are a few problems with this method, of course. You have to have an exact match from the From: line. Likewise, you can't use a partial name (for example, entering only one name with no spaces). In addition, many people use aliases (in the sense of "fake names") when they post messages in the newsgroups.

You'll sometimes see messages telling you to finger someone for more information. When you use the **finger** command on their address, you'll see the contents of the .plan file. This is a quick and easy way to distribute information.

139

Using KIS

You can use the Knowbot Information Service (KIS) to search multiple directories at once. A *Knowbot* is a program that can search the Internet for requested information. We may be seeing more of these in the future (searching for more than just names), but for now they are in an experimental stage. That includes KIS, and although it is usually functioning, its scope is rather limited. At the time of this writing, KIS could search the whois directory at **nic.ddn.mil** and the X.500 directory that fred searches, and could use the UNIX **finger** command on a named host—all of which you can do for yourself. (We'll look at whois and X.500 in Chapter 14.) KIS can also search the MCImail directory (which may be useful if you know that the person you are trying to contact uses MCImail) and RIPE (a directory of European Internet users).

To begin using KIS, you'll have to use telnet:

```
CNS> telnet info.cnri.reston.va.us 185
Trying 132.151.1.15 ...
Connected to info.cnri.reston.va.us.
Escape character is '^]'.


                Knowbot Information Service
KIS Client (V2.0).    Copyright CNRI 1990.    All Rights Reserved.


KIS searches various Internet directory services
to find someone's street address, email address and phone number.


Type 'man' at the prompt for a complete reference with examples.
Type 'help' for a quick reference to commands.
Type 'news' for information about recent changes.


Backspace characters are '^H' or DEL


Please enter your email address in our guest book...
(Your email address?) > pkent@usa.net


> kent
Connected to KIS server (V1.0). Copyright CNRI 1990. All Rights
Reserved.
```

```
Trying whois at ds.internic.net...
[No name] (KENT)         KENT.ABBB.GOV.AU        137.157.45.204
Anderson, Kent (KB111)   kent@123.ITC.COM        (213) 555-2576
Grip, Kent (KG187)       kent@ISM.ITB.COM        (301) 555-1813
Kent County Constabulary (NET-KENTPOLICE) KENTPOLICE
151.129.0.0
(Press RETURN to continue)
Trying mcimail at cnri.reston.va.us...
Trying ripe at whois.ripe.net...
Name:          Kent Bergen
Phone:         +46 8 777 71 62
E-Mail:
Address:       Riksradio
               S-101115 10 Stockholm
               Sweden
Source:        RIPE
Last Updated:  05/20/92
```

As you can see, you may get different result formats because the system searches different sites.

If you'd like to use KIS, spend a few moments reading the user manual: at the > prompt, type **help** and press **Enter**. When you have finished reading that text, type **man** and press **Enter** to see some more. You can, for example, specify an organization name, use a first and last name, and so on. To search the RIPE directory for the name **Kent**, you would do this:

```
>service ripe
>kent
```

To search MCImail, you would type **service mcimail** as the first line. (To see a list of the service names, type **services** and press **Enter**.)

KIS has a lot to do when it carries out a search.

Because it has no directories of its own, it is sending requests out across the Internet for information—which means a search can be very slow. Be patient. I've also found that even when you are not searching (when you are just entering commands or reading the online manual), KIS can be sluggish.

As do some of the other directory services, KIS also lets you search using e-mail. Send a message to **netaddress@nri.reston.va.us** or **netaddress@sol>bucknell>edu**, and type the command (using the same commands you'd use if you were using KIS directly) in the body of the message. You might want to try this instead of sitting and waiting for KIS to do its work.

Using Netfind

There's another system, called Netfind, that you might want to try. You can use Netfind by telneting to any of these hosts:

archie.au (AARNet, Melbourne, Australia)

bruno.cs.colorado.edu (University of Colorado, Boulder)

dino.conicit.ve (Nat. Council for Techn. & Scien. Research, Venezuela)

ds.internic.net (InterNIC Directory and DB Services, S. Plainfield, NJ)

eis.calstate.edu (California State University, Fullerton, CA)

krnic.net (Korea Network Information Center, Taejon, Korea)

lincoln.technet.sg (Technet Unit, Singapore)

malloco.ing.puc.cl (Catholic University of Chile, Santiago)

monolith.cc.ic.ac.uk (Imperial College, London, England)

mudhoney.micro.umn.edu (University of Minnesota, Minneapolis)

netfind.ee.mcgill.ca (McGill University, Montreal, Quebec, Canada)

netfind.fnet.fr (Association FNET, Le Kremlin-Bicetre, France)

netfind.icm.edu.pl (Warsaw University, Warsaw, Poland)

netfind.if.usp.br (University of Sao Paulo, Sao Paulo, Brazil)

netfind.sjsu.edu (San Jose State University, San Jose, California)

netfind.vslib.cz (Liberec University of Technology, Czech Republic)

nic.uakom.sk (Academy of Sciences, Banska Bystrica, Slovakia)

For example, if you were to telnet the Association FNET, in France, it would look something like this:

```
CNS> telnet netfind.fnet.fr
Trying 192.134.192.10 ...
Connected to mississipi.fnet.fr.
Escape character is '^]'.


SunOS UNIX (mississipi)

login: netfind
Last login: Thu Oct  6 21:11:59 from mach1.wlu.ca
SunOS Release 4.1.3_U1 (MISSISSIPI) #1: Fri Mar 4 18:34:35 MET 1994


========================================================
Welcome to the Fnet France  Netfind server.
========================================================
I think that your terminal can display 24 lines.  If this is wrong,
please enter the "Options" menu and set the correct number of
lines.


Top level choices:
        1. Help
        2. Search
        3. Seed database lookup
        4. Options
        5. Quit (exit server)
```

You'll probably want to read the Help file to get a good idea of the different searches you can perform. When you are ready to search, use option **2**. If you'd like to search a list of host names, use option **3**. (You enter a portion of the host name, and Netfind searches for matches among a number of different host names.) Let's search for my name. I'll enter my last name and the city in which I live.

```
—> 2
Enter person and keys (blank to exit) —> kent lakewood
Please select at most 3 of the following domains to search:
 0. amc.org (amc cancer research center, lakewood, colorado)
 1. burner.com (the back burner bbs, lakewood, colorado)
 2. cobe.com (cobe laboratories, inc, lakewood, colorado)
```

```
   3. ecog.edu (eastern co-operative oncology group, lakewood, colorado)
   4. lakewood.com (lakewood microsystems, lakewood, new jersey)
```

Unfortunately, Netfind didn't find me. (Notice that it searched for Lakewood in both the host name and the host description.) The next step is to pick up to three of these to search again; you'll be prompted to enter up to three numbers. If those domains have "nameservers," you'll be able to see more information—perhaps information on the person you are looking for. However, there's a good chance that the one you select won't have more information.

This search didn't do me any good; none of the hosts were mine. Let's try another search method, in which I'll enter my name and the host name of one of the services I use.

```
Enter person and keys (blank to exit) —> kent csn
Please select at most 3 of the following domains to search:
   0. csn.com (colorado supernet, inc, colorado supernet, inc,
      colorado supernet, inc.)
   1. csn.es (consejo de seguridad nuclear, dpto. informatica,
      justo dorado, madrid, spain)
   2. csn.net (colorado supernet, inc, colorado school of mines,
      golden, colorado)
   3. csn.org (colorado supernet, inc)
   4. csn.duke.edu (duke university, durham, north carolina)
Enter selection (e.g., 2 0 1) —>0
```

The first entry is Colorado SuperNet, but it doesn't include the domain I'm using. Therefore, when I entered 0 and pressed Enter (on the last line of this example), Netfind was unable to find any information on me. Well. that's life. There's a good chance Netfind won't have what you're looking for—but it's worth a try.

The Least You Need to Know

➤ You may think you've got the right e-mail address, but you could be wrong.

➤ Check the header of the returned message carefully. It should tell you why the message was returned and who didn't receive it.

➤ The easiest way to get a person's e-mail address is to talk to him. Pick up the phone or get it from someone who knows the person.

➤ If you know the person is at the host that returned the e-mail, send e-mail to the postmaster and ask about the person. Address the message to **postmaster@***hostname*.

➤ The **finger** command is a useful way to track someone if you know the host name.

➤ If you know the user uses the newsgroups, try MIT's system. It might have the person's address.

➤ KIS can help you search for MCImail users and European users.

➤ Netfind is a good way to check host names. However, it may be difficult to find individuals.

## Chapter 14

Finding Folks with fred and whois

In This Chapter

➤ Using whois to find "Interneties"

➤ Using fred to simplify X.500

In Chapter 13, we looked at a number of ways to track people down on the Internet. This chapter is going to give you a couple more options: *fred* (which searches the X.500 system) and *whois*. Hold on tight!

Using Whois

If you are searching for a person you know to be involved in maintaining the Internet network or in network research, he may be listed in the whois directory on the InterNIC Registration Services host (run by the DDN Network Information Center). You can use the whois directory in several ways: using the **whois** command, using telnet, and using e-mail.

The Whois Command

The **whois** command is very easy to use. Simply type **whois** *name* at the UNIX shell prompt and press **Enter**. The *name* can be a first name, last name, or login name, and if you're not sure of the complete name, end it with a period. For example, **whois ken.** will find Ken, Kent, Kentworth, and so on. (You don't have to worry about capitalization.) Note that you can use only one name at a time; you can't enter a person's first and last name.

If you enter an unusual name, the system might find just one person and display all the information it has about that person. More likely, though, it'll find several people and will display a one-line entry for each one. You'll see listings like this:

```
Bloe, Joe (BJ31)    joebloe@apotpeel.com         (303) 555-1869
```

In Chapter 18, you'll learn how to use FTP to transfer files across the Internet. You can use FTP to get the latest list of whois servers. Go to **sipb.mit.edu**. Log in as **anonymous**. Then go to the **/pub/whois** directory and get the file called **whois-servers.list**.

The **BJ31** in parentheses is the person's *handle*. Once you know a person's handle, you can use the **whois** command with the handle to get full information. For example, if you enter **whois bj31**, the system displays the person's full information: his e-mail address, USPO address, telephone number, and the date the record was last updated. (In some cases this command may not work. Instead, try **whois \!***handle* or **whois !***handle*.)

There are currently a number of whois *servers*, directories that work in the same way as the InterNIC Registration Services directory. These include servers at Pacific Bell and GTE Laboratories, at many universities, several at NASA, and so on. If you want to search the directory on one of these servers, you must use a different format of the **whois** command: **whois -h** *hostname name*. For instance, if you type

```
whois -h wpi.wpi.edu kent
```

whois searches the server at the Worcester Polytechnic Institute (**wpi.wpi.edu**) for the name Kent. Unfortunately, not all systems will let you use the **whois** command to do this; they let only local users work with them.

By Telnet and Mail

If you find you can't search the whois directory from your system, you have two other options. You can telnet to the directory at **nic.ddn.mil** or to another whois server, but many won't let you in. When you get there, you'll find an @ prompt. Type the **whois** *name* command as usual. (Note: you won't need a login name or password to get into whois at this server. You'll learn more about telnet in Chapter 17, so check there for details.) Alternatively, you can use e-mail to use whois. Send a message to **whois@internic.net**, like this:

```
teal% whois@internic.net
Subject:
whois kent
.
Cc:
teal%
```

The body of the message is the **whois** command. After a while you'll get a report on your e-mail system, showing what whois found.

Using X.500 and fred

Some time ago, a group called the International Standards Organization came up with a standard called X.500, a method for letting computers search directories. X.500 uses a *hierarchical* system to track down system users: the computer (or you) provides the country, organization, and person, and X.500 follows this path down the directory to the exact person you are interested in. Unfortunately, it is difficult to use and, therefore, not widely used.

Okay, so what's fred? front end to dish, of course. Don't ask what it means.

You're in luck, though. There's a program called fred that makes X.500 easier for real people to use. First, you have to telnet to a fred server. (You'll learn about telnet in Chapter 17. In the meantime, I'll tell you all you need to know.) There are two fred servers: **wp.psi.com** and **wp2.psi.com**. (If you can't get one to work, try the other.) To get to fred, type **telnet** *server* and press **Enter**. When you are asked to log in, type **fred** and press **Enter**. Your screen should look something like this:

```
teal% telnet wp2.psi.com
Trying 38.146.90.2 ...
Connected to wp1.psi.net.
Escape character is '^]'.
SunOS UNIX (wp1.psi.net)
login: fred
Last login: Tue Nov  9 13:50:18 from teal.csn.org
SunOS Release 4.0.3c (WP_PSI_BOOTBOX) #3: Mon Mar 8 12:14:31 EST
1993
You have new mail.
Welcome to the PSI White Pages Pilot Project

Try  "help" for a list of commands
     "whois" for information on how to find people
     "manual" for detailed documentation
     "report" to send a report to the white pages manager

To find out about participating organizations, try
     "whois -org *"
accessing service, please wait...

fred>
```

Now you can search for people or organizations. Let's begin by searching for the organization of which the person is a member. Type **whois *partialname** organization -org ***. For example, **whois a* organization -org *** finds seven organizations, as you can see here.

```
fred> whois a* organization -org *
7 matches found.
  13. Advanced Decision Systems      +1 415-960-7300
  14. ALCOA                          +1 412-553-4545
  15. Anterior Technology            +1 415-328-5615
  16. Apple Computer, Inc.           +1 408/996-1010
  17. Argonne National Laboratory    +1 708-252-2000
  18. ATT                            +1 212-387-5400
  19. Auburn University              +1 205-844-4512
```

Notice that each entry has a number in the left column. fred assigns these numbers to each entry it finds for you during your session. (As you can see from this example, I've already done some searching—otherwise Advanced Decision Systems would have been number 1.) To find out more about one of these entries, you can type **whois** *number*. If you typed **whois 18**, you would see this:

```
fred> whois 18
ATT (18)                                    +1 212-387-5400
      aka: AT&T
      aka: American Telephone and Telegraph Company
ATT
   32 Avenue of the Americas
   New York
   New York 10013
   US
Comments about the ATT Directory should be sent to sri@qsun.att.com
Locality:   New York, New York
Name:       ATT, US (18)
Modified: Wed Jun 16 19:09:32 1993
        by: manager, att,
            US (21)
fred>
```

If it's a very long listing, it might stop in the middle. Press **Enter** to continue. Notice also the *aka* name. This is another name you can enter in a search that will find this organization ("aka" means "also known as"). Sometimes you'll find that the aka name is much shorter than the original. (Not all entries have an aka name.)

Assuming this is the one you want, you can ask about a particular person. In this case I'm going to search for names beginning with J.

```
fred> whois j* -org 18
3 matches found.
 20. Joe Bloe               joeb@att.comfred>
 21. Jay Harvey             jayh@qsun.att.com
 22. Andrew Josephson       Ajos@qsun.att.com
fred>
```

Now I can find more information about Joe Bloe:

```
fred> whois 20
Joe Bloe (20)                                    joeb@qsun.att.com
Member of Technical Staff
Bell Laboratories
Name:     Joe Bloe, Experimental Potato Division,
          ATT,
          US (20)
Modified: Tue Sep 29 14:13:54 1992
      by: Manager, ATT,
          US (21)
fred>
```

If you want to get fancy with fred, get hold of the fred manual. You can read the manual by typing **manual** and pressing **Enter**. You'll be able to move from page to page by pressing **Enter**, and stop the manual by pressing **Ctrl-c**.

I've just shown you the easiest way to use fred; there are many other ways. You could, for example, look for names that begin with a particular letter in every organization, or search phonetically.

When you are finished with fred, use the **quit** command to end the session. If your system seems to hang, press **Ctrl-]**. You'll find yourself back at the **telnet>** prompt. Type **quit** again to get back to the UNIX shell.

The Least You Need to Know

➤ Use the **whois** command if you know the person is involved with running the Internet or researching Internet issues.

➤ fred can help you search for users according to the organization of which they are a part.

➤ To save time (instead of waiting while whois or fred works), send the commands by e-mail.

Part III
Boldly Going Around the Internet

There's much more to the Internet than just sending messages to people. In Part III I teach you how to navigate the treacherous and poorly documented depths of the Internet. We start off looking at how to use the newsgroups and mailing lists — there are thousands of different subjects, and hundreds of thousands of different conversations going on over the Internet. Then I show you how you can get your hands on some of the millions of computer files publicly available on the Internet: books, magazine articles, programs, clip art, sounds, fonts, and so on.

But wait, there's more: there's telnet, which lets you run programs on other computers; Gopher, the Internet's menu system; WAIS, a database searching tool; and World Wide Web, a giant hypertext system spanning the continents.

THE HONESTY OF INTERNET

## Chapter 15

Newsgroups: The Source of All Wisdom

In This Chapter

➤ What you can find in the newsgroups

➤ About newsgroup subscriptions

➤ Finding out what newsgroups exist

➤ How USENET functions

➤ Using newsreaders

➤ Subscribing to newsgroups

➤ Reading messages

It would help if you knew what we were talking about, so let's start out this chapter with a few definitions. (Wait! Don't leave! It won't be boring, I promise.)

Are you familiar with bulletin board systems (BBSs)? They're computerized systems for leaving both public and private messages. Other computer users can read your messages, and you can read theirs. There are tens of thousands of small BBSs around the world, each of which has its own area of interest. Many computer companies have

BBSs through which their clients get technical support. Many professional associations have BBSs so their members can leave messages for each other and take part in discussions.

What, then, is an information service such as CompuServe? It's essentially a collection of many bulletin boards (called *forums*). CompuServe has about 1,000 such BBSs. Instead of having to remember 1,000 telephone numbers (one for each BBS), you can dial one phone number and access any number of BBSs in the series.

True to its UNIX heritage, the Internet uses the word **news** ambiguously. Often, when you see a reference to news in a menu or an Internet document, it refers to the messages left in newsgroups (not, as most real people would imagine, journalists' reports on current affairs).

So what is the Internet? As we've already seen, it's a collection of networks hooked together. Within these networks exist an enormous number of discussion groups. In Internet-speak, these are called *newsgroups*, and there are thousands of them on all conceivable subjects. My service provider subscribes to around 4,000 (more about subscribing in a moment), America Online subscribes to approximately 12,000, and there are many more scattered around.

If you've never used a newsgroup (or another system's forum or BBS, you may not be aware of the power of such communications. This sort of messaging system really brings computer networking to life, and it's not all computer nerds sitting around with nothing better to do. (Check out Internet's alt.sex newsgroup; these people are not your average introverted propeller-heads!) I've found work, made friends, found answers to research questions (much quicker and more cheaply than I could have by going to a library), and read people's "reviews" of tools I can use in my business. I've never found a lover or spouse online, but I know people who have (and anyway, I'm already married).

So What's Out There...

You can use newsgroups for fun or real work. You can use them to spend time "talking" with other people who share your interests—whether that happens to be "making and baking with sourdough" (see the **rec.food.sourdough** group), kites and kiting (**rec.kites**), or S/M (**alt.sex.bondage**). You can even do some serious work online, such as finding a job at a nuclear physics research site (**hepnet.jobs**), tracking down a piece of software for a biology project (**bionet.software**), or finding good stories about police work in the San Francisco area for an article you are writing (**clari.sfbay.police**).

The following newsgroups represent just a tiny fraction of what is available:

alt.ascii-art   Pictures (such as Spock and the Simpsons) created with ASCII text characters.

alt.comedy.british   Discussions on British comedy in all its wonderful forms.

alt.current-events.russia   News of what's going on in Russia right now. (Some messages are in broken English, and some are in Russian, but that just adds romance.)

alt.missing-kids   Information about missing kids.

alt.polyamory   A newsgroup for those with "multiple lovers."

alt.sex   Discussions on Hillary Clinton's sexual orientation, nude beaches, oral sex, and anything else marginally related to sex.

bit.listserv.down-syn   Discussions about Down's Syndrome.

comp.research.japan   Information about computer research in Japan.

misc.forsale   Lists of goods for sale.

rec.skydiving   A group for skydivers.

sci.anthropology   A group for people interested in anthropology.

sci.military   Discussions on science and the military.

soc.couples.intercultural   A group for interracial couples.

If you are looking for information on just about any subject, the question is not "I wonder if there's a newsgroup about this?" It's, "I wonder what the newsgroup's name is, and if my service provider subscribes to it?"

Can You Get to It?

There are so many newsgroups out there that they take up a lot of room. A service provider getting the messages of 3,000 newsgroups may have to set aside 500 MB of hard disk space to keep up with it all. So service providers have to decide which ones they will subscribe to. Nobody subscribes to all the world's newsgroups, because many are simply of no interest to most Internet users, and many are not widely distributed. (Some are of regional interest only; some are of interest only to a specific organization.) So system administrators have to pick the ones they want and omit the ones they don't want. Undoubtedly, some system administrators censor newsgroups, omitting those they believe have no place online.

 Okay, so you have a subject about which you want to start a news-group. Spend some time in the **news.groups** newsgroup to find out about starting a USENET newsgroup, or talk to your service provider about starting a local newsgroup.

I'll give you an idea of what is available, but I can't specify what is available to you. You'll have to check with your service provider to find out what they have. And if they don't have what you want, ask them to get it. They have no way of knowing what people want unless someone tells them.

Okay, Gimme a List!

You can go to the **news.announce.newusers** newsgroup to find messages containing various lists. (You'll find out how to get to a newsgroup in a moment.) Posted to this newsgroup are several messages listing both "official" USENET newsgroups and "alternative" newsgroups. In addition, you can use FTP to get lists from the **pit-manager.mit.edu** FTP site in the **/pub/usenet-by-group/ news.announce.newsgroup** directory. (See Chapter 18 for information about FTP.)

Where's It All Coming From?

Where do all these newsgroups come from? They are created on computers all over the world. Any host can create a newsgroup, and just about all do. Each host has newsgroups of local interest—about the service provider's services, local politics, local events, and so on.

A large number of newsgroups are part of a system called USENET. Like the Internet, USENET is intangible—a network of networks. It's not owned by anyone, and it doesn't own anything itself. It is independent of any network, including the Internet (in fact, it's older than the Internet). USENET is simply a series of voluntary agreements to swap information. Most widely available newsgroups go through USENET.

Some newsgroups are moderated, which means someone reads all the messages and decides which ones are actually posted. The purpose is to keep the newsgroup focused and prevent the discussions from "going astray." Of course, it may look a little like censorship—depending on what you want to say.

What's in a Name?

Let's take a quick look at how newsgroups are named. Newsgroup names look much like host addresses: a series of words separated by periods. This is because, like hosts, they are set up in a hierarchical system (though instead of going right-to-left, they go left-to-right). The first name is the top level. These are the top-level USENET groups:

comp   Computer-related subjects.

news   Information about newsgroups themselves, including software used to read newsgroup messages, and information about finding and using newsgroups.

rec   Recreational topics: hobbies, sports, the arts, and so on.

sci   Science: discussions about research in the "hard" sciences, as well as some social sciences.

soc   A wide range of social issues, such as different types of societies and subcultures, as well as sociopolitical subjects.

talk   Debate politics, religion, and anything else controversial.

misc   Stuff. Job searches, things for sale, a forum for paramedics. You know, *stuff*.

Not all newsgroups are true USENET groups. Many are local groups that are distributed internationally through USENET (don't worry about it, it doesn't matter). Such newsgroups are known as *Alternative Newsgroup Hierarchies*. So there are other top-level groups, such as these:

alt "Alternative" subjects: often subjects that many people would consider inappropriate, pornographic, or just weird. Sometimes it is interesting stuff, but the newsgroup has been created in an "unauthorized" manner to save time and hassle.

bionet Biological subjects.

bit A variety of newsgroups from the Bitnet network.

biz Business subjects, including advertisements.

clari Clarinet's newsgroups from "official" and commercial sources; mainly UPI news stories and various syndicated columns.

courts Related to law and lawyers.

de Various German-language newsgroups.

fj Various Japanese-language newsgroups.

gnu The Free Software Foundation's newsgroups.

hepnet Discussions about high energy and nuclear physics.

ieee The Institute of Electrical and Electronics Engineers' newsgroups.

info A collection of mailing lists formed into newsgroups at the University of Illinois.

k12 Discussions about K-through-12th-grade education.

relcom Russian-language newsgroups, mainly distributed in the former Soviet Union.

vmsnet Subjects of interest to VAX/VMS computer users.

You'll see other groups, too, such as the following:

brasil Groups from Brazil (it's spelled with an "s" in Portugese).

podunk A local interest newsgroup for the town of Podunk.

thisu This university's newsgroup.

(Okay, I made up the last two, but you get the idea.)

Reaching the Next Level

The groups listed in the previous section make up the top-level groups. Below each of those are groups on another level. For instance, there's **alt.3d**, a newsgroup about three-dimensional imaging. It's part of the alt hierarchy because, presumably, it was put together in an unauthorized way. The people who started it didn't want to go through the hassle of setting up a USENET group, so they created an alt group instead—where anything goes.

If you really care how this information ends up on your service provider's computer, here goes. Computers acting as news servers collect the newsgroups from various other places: other servers that are part of the USENET agreements, computers with local newsgroups, Clarinet (a commercial "real" news service that carries news from United Press International), gateways to other networks (such as Bitnet), and so on. The computers acting as news servers then make the information available to your system. Each server administrator has to make agreements with other administrators to transfer this data; it's usually (though not always) transferred across the Internet.

Another alt group is **alt.sex**, where anything really does go. This group serves as a good example of how newsgroups can have more levels. Because it's such a diverse subject, one newsgroup wasn't really enough. So instead of posting messages to the alt.sex group, you choose your particular pecadillo. The specific areas include:

alt.sex.bestiality.barney   Described as "for people with big purple newt fetishes."

alt.sex.fetish.feet   (Self-explanatory)

alt.sex.motss   Member of the same sex

alt.sex.pictures   Described as "Gigabytes of copyright violations."

And there are many more. If you're into it, chances are good that there's a newsgroup for it.

The same hierarchy is used in all areas. For example, there's **bionet.genome.arabidopsis** (information about the Arabidopsis genome project), **bionet.genome.chrom22** (a discussion of Chromosome 22), and for those of us interested in the eucaryote chromosomes **bionet.genome.chromosomes**.

Use a Newsreader!

Now that you know what newsgroups are, how are you going to use them? News messages are stored in text files. Lots of text files. The best way to read the messages you want to read is to use a *newsreader* to help you sort and filter your way through all the garbage.

You'll probably have several types of newsreaders available. For instance, I can use tin, nn, trn, and rn. (Remember, the Internet was developed by UNIX-types, and there's a UNIX law somewhere that says program names must not use recognizable and easily understood words.) These newsreaders vary in their ease of use, of course. However, chances are slim that you will run across a "user-friendly" newsreader anytime soon (except, of course, the SuperHighway Access newsreader—see Chapter 27).

You can also use the World Wide Web to read some newsgroups. If the ones you want are on the Web, you may prefer to read them there (see Chapter 23 for more information).

You may also have a menu system that helps you find your way to the newsgroups. To find the newsgroups on my service provider's menu, I select **12 News and Weather** and get this menu:

```
                    News and Weather


    —>  1.  Colorado Weather Underground/
        2.  National Weather Service Forecasts/
        3.  Post to Usenet Newsgroup*
        4.  Read Usenet News*
        5.  Select a Usenet Newsreader*
        6.  Select an Editor*
        7.  UPI News/
```

Remember that there's some confusion on the Internet as to the difference between personal messages and news. So this menu contains options through which you can access information about the weather (options 1 and 2) or actual news reports (7) and options related to the newsgroups (message forums).

If you don't want to use a newsreader, you can use the **grep** command to search for key words in the files in your service provider's /usr/spool/news directory. But if you do, you're on your own. Don't expect any help from me. (As you may remember, **grep** is a UNIX command used for searching text files. See Chapter 9.)

The other options let me select a text editor that I can use to write newsgroup messages, select the newsreader I want to use, write a message to a newsgroup, and read the newsgroup messages.

Using rn

I decided to describe the rn newsreader because it's probably the newsreader used most often, and it's similar to another popular reader, nn. However, it's by no means the best. You may have something better available. Ask your service provider, try several newsreaders, and pick the one you find easiest to use. Those of us who've been involved in the world of DOS and Windows for the past few years find that what Interneties describe as an "easy-to-use" newsreader may not actually be easy to use (though it's probably easier than the other choices). At least at this time, it's likely that

All these rn commands are difficult to remember, so I've put them on the tear-out reference card at the front of the book.

you'll have a rather clunky user interface that uses a multitude of special codes you have to type. However, other newsreaders are currently being developed, and things will get easier. (For a really great newsreader, you'd better install your SLIP or PPP connection and use the SuperHighway Access newsreader. See Chapters 26 and 27.)

The following sections will help you use rn (if that's what you have) or at least give you an idea of what the other systems can do.

Checking the Subscription List

Information about which newsgroups you are subscribed to is stored in a file called .newsrc. (The . before the name means it's a hidden file.) The file doesn't exist until you start your newsreader, so type **rn** and press **Enter**. When it starts, type **q** to quit.

First, you need to make sure the file was created in your home directory. At the UNIX prompt, type **cd** and press **Enter** to make sure you are in the home directory; then type **ls -a .newsrc** and press **Enter**. If the file is in your home directory, it is listed.

Now you can open the file in the text editor you use. If you use vi, for instance, type **vi .newsrc** and press **Enter**. You'll see something like this (although the entire file probably won't be in alphabetical order):

```
alt.clintons.health.care.plan.is.a.crock:
alt! 1-0
alt.1d! 1-795
alt.3d! 1-1421
alt.abortion.inequity! 1-2760
alt.activism! 1-11625,14909
alt.activism.d! 1-1400
alt.adoption! 1-2208
alt.aeffle.und.pferdle! 1-130
".newsrc" 4147 lines, 104462 characters
```

The .newsrc file lists all the newsgroups available to you. In this case you can see there are 4,147 lines in this file (a lot of groups). Any group that ends with ! is a group to which you are not subscribed (a group you won't automatically get). Any group ending with : is one to which you are subscribed (one you will get).

You can move through this list using the down arrow key or by pressing **Ctrl-f** in vi (we described vi in detail in Chapter 11). If you find you are subscribed to everything, you would be wise to change all the :'s to !'s so you aren't subscribed to any newsgroups. Then you can individually pick the ones to which you want to subscribe. (Even if your service provider has selected various newsgroups for you, you may want to deselect them and pick your own.)

Use your text editor to do a search and replace. In vi, you type %s/:/!/ and press **Enter**. Now you can select the groups to which you want to subscribe. You could scroll through one by one, and change each ! to a :, but that would take a long time. Instead, pick the groups you want to join (use the list on our disk, or ask your service provider for a list); then search for each one you want to join. In vi you type **:/*groupname*** and press **Enter**. When you find one you want, replace the ! with :. In vi, place the cursor over the ! and press **r:** to replace.

When you've finished subscribing to the groups you want, save your work and quit the editor. (In vi, press **Esc** three times and then type **ZZ**.)

Let's Get Started

Okay, let's start rn. You either select the newsreader from a menu, or start it from the UNIX shell. To start from the shell, simply type **rn** and press **Enter**. You'll probably see a short introduction. You'll learn three important facts from this introduction:

➤ To enter a command, just type the appropriate letter; you don't need to press **Enter**.

➤ To see a list of commands, type **h**. This shows the commands appropriate for your current location in the newsreader.

➤ Press **Spacebar** to tell rn to carry out the "default" command (the normal command, which is usually the "yes" response).

When you continue, rn may show you a list of new newsgroups. As it names each one, you can decide whether you want to subscribe to the group. For instance,

```
Newsgroup zer.z-netz.wissenschaft.physik not in .newsrc
subscribe? [ynYN]
```

tells you that your service provider has added the newsgroup **zer.z-netz.wissenschaft.physik**, and that it doesn't appear in the .newsrc file. Type one of these responses:

y to subscribe to the new group

Y to subscribe to all the new groups

n to not subscribe to the new group

N to not subscribe to any of the new groups

If you press N or n, the group is still added to the end of the .newsrc file, but it has an ! instead of a :. If you do decide to subscribe to a group, rn asks you where you want to put the group: at the top of the list (type ^), at the bottom of the list (**$**), before a specific newsgroup (-*name*), after a specific newsgroup (+*name*), or in a particular position (enter the position number). If you're not sure where to put it, you can type **L** to see a list of the newsgroups and their numbers. The position in which you add the new newsgroup will affect the sequence in which the newsgroups are presented to you when you start your newsreader.

When you've finished with the new groups, rn shows a list of your subscribed groups and tells you how many unread messages each one has. You'll see something like this:

```
Unread news in alt.sex.wizards                    1230 articles
Unread news in alt.silly.group.names.d               3 articles
Unread news in alt.society.revolution               55 articles
Unread news in bit.listserv.scuba-l               823 articles
Unread news in soc.culture.yugoslavia            1793 articles
etc.
******** 1230 unread articles in alt.sex.wizardsread now? [ynq]
```

The **etc.** means there are more newsgroups than are shown here. You'll see how to get to them in a moment.

So, what are your options now? You can type **y** or press **Spacebar** to begin reading the first unread article in the first newsgroup, **n** to have rn display the same question about the next newsgroup with unread messages, or **q** to leave rn.

There are lots of other options; I'll mention a few of the most useful: You can tell rn to unsubscribe (type **u**), or you can tell it to list the articles in the newsgroup (type =). You can type **N** for the next group, **n** for the next group with unread messages, **P** for the previous group, **p** for the previous group with unread messages, **$** for the last group, **1** for the first group, or ^ for the first group with unread messages. You can even subscribe to another group by typing **g** *groupname*.

Just Read It

Let's take a look at the first unread article in the first newsgroup. To do so, type **y**.

```
Article 3165 (187 more) in bit.listserv.scuba-1:
From: jpayne@NMSU.EDU (James S. Payne)
Subject: Sea of Cortez Dive Report
Date: 26 Oct 93 16:11:40 GMT
Lines: 30
Comments: Gated by NETNEWS@AUVM.AMERICAN.EDU
Return-Path: <@AUVM.AMERICAN.EDU,
             @BROWNVM.BROWN.EDU:owner-scuba-1@BROWNVM.BROWN.EDU>
Return-Path: <@BROWNVM.BROWN.EDU:jpayne@NMSU.EDU>
Mime-Version: 1.0
Content-Type: TEXT/PLAIN; charset=US-ASCII
In-Reply-To: <9310261549.AA03041@dante>


As I promised here is a dive report on conditions
around San Carlos, Sonora, Mexico.  We were there from Oct. 15-24.
Water temperature is currently running between 74-78 degrees.
Gary's Dive Shop has 85 degrees posted, but I don't think he ever
changes it.  During a dive to 110' we found temps of 71.  One day
at Isla San Pedro we had 80 degrees, but it didn't last long.
```

(So you thought we were going to take a look at alt.sex.wizards, did you? Sorry, you'll have to check it out yourself.)

As you can see, the first part of the message is the usual header stuff: you can see the article number, newsgroup name, address of the person who sent it, Subject title, and date. You can generally ignore the rest of the header. It shows how the message got to the newsgroup. What now? The following sections outline a few things you may want to do.

Unsubscribe

Although at first you weren't sure what the newsgroup was all about, now you've seen it and know you don't want it. Type **u** to unsubscribe so you won't come to this group next time.

Read the Rest of the Message

Press **Spacebar** to read the rest of the message (or press **Enter** to see the next line). If you're at the end of a message and press **Spacebar**, you'll move directly to the next message. You can move back one page by pressing **b**, or to the top of the message by pressing **Ctrl-r**.

Go to Another Article

Press **N** to go to the next article, or press **n** to go to the next unread article. (This is the same as when you first start. Your newsreader knows which messages you have seen and assumes you've actually read them.

To continue with the news analogy, messages posted to Internet newsgroups are called **articles**.

As you view each one, the newsreader marks it as read.) Press **Ctrl-N** to go to the next unread article with the same subject. To go the other way (backwards) substitute **P**. That is, press **P** for the previous article, press **p** for the previous unread article, or press **Ctrl-P** to go to the previous unread article with the same subject.

But there's more. You can also go to the last message you viewed by pressing **–**. If you know the number of a message you want to go to, simply type the message's number and press **Enter**. To go to the first unread message, press **^**; to go to the end of the newsgroup, press **$** (for example, press **$P** to display the last message).

As you move from message to message, your newsreader automatically marks the ones you have seen as read. That pulls them out of the way, so they won't appear when you move back up the list of messages using **p**.

View a List

You can save a lot of time by avoiding messages in which you have no interest. Instead, select the ones you want to see from a list. Press **=** to see a list of the unread articles:

```
3167 Re: New free dive record
3168 Re: Definition of Curmudgeon
3169 Re: catching tropical fish
3170 NED =
3171 Re: catching tropical fish
3172 Re: goodbye !!!
3173 Definition of Curmudgeon
3174 Re: Sea of Cortez Video
3175 NO SUBJECT
3176 The pros and cons of shrimpin
```

You'll see a screenful of subjects at a time. Press **Spacebar** to see more. Unfortunately, rn doesn't let you select directly from this list (though other newsreaders do). Still, it shows the message numbers, so you can type a number and press **Enter** to go right to a particular message.

Notice, by the way, that some message titles start with Re:. This means that they are replies to an original. It's these Re: messages that the Ctrl-N and Ctrl-P commands follow.

Mark Messages As Read

You can manually mark messages to indicate various conditions. If you decide you don't want to read a message right now but think you will want to come back to read it later, press **m** to mark it as unread. (If you go on to the next message by pressing Spacebar or N, for example, the message will be marked as read.) In your next rn session, the message will still be marked as unread. (If you don't do this, when you come back the next time the message won't be available.)

To temporarily mark a message as read, press **M**. This removes the message from the list of unread messages for the time being, but when you leave the newsgroup, the message is set back to unread. You can also use the **Y** command to "yank" the message back so that it's marked as unread again and appears in the listing.

You can mark as read all the messages related to a particular subject heading by pressing **k** (that moves them all out of the way when you are using the **n** command or **Spacebar** to move through the list). However, this process may take a little while because rn has to search all the messages (you can end the process by pressing **Ctrl-C**).

Go to Another Newsgroup

To leave this newsgroup, press **q** once to quit the message you're in, and press **q** again to return to the newsgroups list. rn shows you the name of the next group in sequence and asks whether you want to read its messages.

Use rot13

You'll sometimes find rot13 messages, messages that you can't read directly. If you are breezing through your messages and suddenly come across the text of a rot13 message, you can't read it because it has been *encrypted* (it just looks like garbage). If you want to read the message, you'll have to make a point of telling the newsreader to convert it. In rn, you press **Ctrl-x** to start the message in rot13 mode, or simply press x to display the next page of the message in rot13. To start the message over and turn rot13 off, press **Ctrl-R**.

 Rot13 is a very simple encryption method that stands for "rotation 13." The letters of the alphabet have been rotated 13 characters: a becomes n, b becomes o, c becomes p. If you had the time, you could convert a rot13 file yourself.

So what's the point of rot13? It's a way of saying "this message is probably offensive to some people, so if you are easily offended, don't read it." It ensures that nobody can claim they accidentally "stumbled" over an offensive message; they had to choose to read it.

The Least You Need to Know

➤ A newsgroup is an area in which people with similar interests leave public messages—a sort of online public debate or discussion.

➤ There's a newsgroup on just about any subject you can imagine. If there isn't, there probably will be soon.

➤ Newsgroup names use a hierarchical system, and each group may have subgroups within it.

➤ The NWSGROUP.EXE file on the disk you get with this book contains a text file that lists over 4,000 newsgroups.

➤ Your service provider probably offers several news-readers. Try them all and pick the best.

➤ The .newsrc file defines which newsgroups you are subscribed to.

➤ Take a look at Chapter 27 for information about the SuperHighway Access newsreader, a great incentive to install a SLIP or PPP connection.

More on Newsgroups— and Mailing Lists

In This Chapter

➤ Saving e-mail messages as text files

➤ Replying to messages

➤ Beginning a newsgroup discussion

➤ Working with mailing lists

➤ LISTSERV? What's that?

➤ Subscribing and unsubscribing to LISTSERV groups

In Chapter 15, you learned everything you need to know to get started with the Internet's newsgroups. But of course there's more. (There's *always* more!) How about saving messages in a text file? Replying to messages? And in the remote case that you can't find a newsgroup related to your interests, you may also want to know about mailing lists and the LISTSERV groups, thousands of groups that use e-mail to exchange information. That's right, thousands more—an additional 4,000 LISTSERV groups alone. Has it sunk in yet just how massive the Internet really is? The traffic volume is just staggering. That's why this book was such a great purchase: you'd never find your way around all alone.

Save That Message!

Sometimes you'll come across newsgroup messages that you want to save. For example, I recently found a long message containing lots of interesting quotes that I wanted to save. To save the message, type **s** *filename*, and you'll see something like this:

```
End of article 682 (of 683) — ]what next? [npq] s quote.txt
File /home/clients4/peterk/News/quote.txt doesn't exist —
        use mailbox format? [ynq] y
Saved to mailbox /home/clients4/peterk/News/quote.txt
```

The file is saved in the News directory. It doesn't much matter whether you type **y** or **n** here—either way you'll get a text file containing the message. (If you type **y**, you'll get an extra line of garbage showing you where the message is from).

You can also save a message with the **w** command. It's the same as **s**, but it strips out all the message header stuff that you probably don't want anyway. (You may want it if you are planning to contact the message's *poster*, the author, so think about it before you use this command.)

Replying to Messages

There are several ways to reply to a message you've just read. Press **f** to reply, or press **F** if you want to reply and include the original message in your reply (this is very common, as it reminds the recipient of what he said, and lets new readers see what you are replying to). If you want, you can type your message within the original message so you can break it down piece by piece and reply to each individual point. With a little thought, this allows you to make the original writer (now the recipient) look like a total fool—a common practice in the newsgroups. (Internet newsgroup members are often rude, mean-spirited, and childish, it seems, depending on the group. The messages in alt.current-events.usa are probably much more heated than in, say, rec.games.chess.)

If you are using a dial-in terminal connection, you might want to take advantage of your telecommunications program's capability to save incoming text to a file. Alternatively, if you are working in a program in which you can copy text using the mouse (such as Windows or the Macintosh), copy the text into another application, such as a text editor or word processor.

If you want to reply directly to the person who wrote the message using e-mail instead of the newsgroup, you can type **r**. Type **R** to include the original message in the response.

> **Flaming** is the act of writing an insulting message to or about another newsgroup member. Though you'll read that it's not polite, it's very common (and may be safer than saying it in person).

If you are working in rn, you will be leaving the "cbreak mode;" that is, you'll now have to press **Enter** after typing a command. You may also see a message such as this:

```
This program posts news to thousands of machines throughout the
entire civilized world. Your message will cost the net hundreds if
not thousands of dollars to send everywhere. Please be sure you
know what you are doing.
Are you absolutely sure that you want to do this? [ny]
```

Of course you are, so type **y** and press **Enter**. You'll see:

```
Prepared file to include [none]:
```

If you have a text file you want to include in the message, type the name here and press **Enter**. (If you don't, simply press **Enter**.) If you *did* include a file, you'll see this message:

```
Send, abort, edit, or list?
```

You can type **s** to send the included file, **a** to end the operation, **e** to go into the text editor, or **l** to display the message you've just created. (Remember to press **Enter** after the command.) If you didn't include a file, you'll simply go straight to the text editor.

> To define which text editor you want to use, you should use the command **setenv EDITOR** *editorname* before you open your newsreader. For instance, **setenv EDITOR pico** tells your system to use pico as the text editor.

Once you're in your editor, type the message, and then close the editor, saving your information. You'll see the same **Send, abort, edit, or list?** line. Type **s** and press **Enter** to send the message on its way, and return you to the newsreader.

Starting a Discussion

You can start your own newsgroup discussions, of course. Let's say you are searching for some information, or simply want to talk with "your own kind" (whatever or whoever that might be). First, you'll decide on the newsgroup to which you want to post the message. Of course, different systems use different methods to post news. (The rn newsreader doesn't have a direct way to post news.) On my system, I have to use the **Pnews** command, like this:

```
teal% Pnews
Newsgroup(s): alt.politics.usa.misc

Your local distribution prefixes are:
    Local organization:    local
    Organization:   csn
    City:     boulder
    State:    co
    Country: usa
    Continent:        na
    Everywhere:       world

Distribution (world): world
Title/Subject: GOP bought election in New Jersey?

This program posts news to thousands of machines throughout the
entire civilized world. Your message will cost the net hundreds if
not thousands of dollars to send everywhere. Please be sure you
know what you are doing. Are you absolutely sure that you want to
do this? [ny] y
Prepared file to include [none]:
```

Then it pops into the text editor, which looks something like this:

```
    PICO 1.7        File: /home/clients4/peterk/.article    Modified

Newsgroups: alt.politics.usa.misc
Subject: GOP bought election in New Jersey?
Summary:
Followup-To:
Distribution: world
Organization: Colorado SuperNet, Inc.
Keywords: GOP NEW JERSEY ELECTION
```

```
What's this talk this morning about the GOP buying an election?
Anyone out there heard about this? Anyone know where I can find
more information?


              [ line 11 of 13 (84), character 363 of 365 (99) ]
^G Get Help ^O WriteOut ^R Read File^Y Prev Pg  ^K Del Line
^C Cur Pos ^X Exit ^J Justify  ^W Where is ^V Next Pg  ^U UnDel
Lin^T To Spell
```

When I close my editor (using **Ctrl-x** in this case), I'm asked if I want to save the message, and if so in what file. (It's saved in a file before it's sent; just press **Enter** when you're asked if the file name is correct.) Then I'll see a message like this:

```
Send, abort, edit, or list?
```

I type **s** and press **Enter**, and it is on its way.

But Wait! There's More!

There are many more newsreader commands than we've looked at. You can operate on an entire range of messages at the same time, for instance, and create macros. In addition, other newsreaders may be more convenient or have other useful commands. Some let you scroll up and down the list of messages, marking the ones you want to read. What I've described here and in Chapter 15 will give you an idea of what a newsreader should be able to do as a minimum. To get an idea of what yours can do, read the manual of the newsreader you are using.

A Word of Warning

Newsgroups can be *very* addictive. You can find messages about anything that interests you, angers you, or turns you on. If you are not careful, you can spend half your life in the newsgroups. You sit down in the morning to check your favorite newsgroups, and the next thing you know you haven't bathed, haven't eaten, and forgot to pick up the kids from school.

Hang around the newsgroups and you'll find people who are obviously spending a significant amount of time writing messages. These people are usually independently wealthy (that is, they work for large corporations who don't mind paying for them to talk politics over the Internet or who don't know that they are paying for them to do so). If you have a job, a family, and a life, be careful.

Using Mailing Lists

Another form of discussion group you might want to take a look at is the mailing list: discussion groups based on the e-mail system.

Mailing lists work like this. Each discussion group has an e-mail address. You begin by subscribing to the group you are interested in (I'll explain how in a moment). The e-mail address then acts as a mail reflector. (You may remember we mentioned these in Chapter 12; they receive mail and then send it on to everyone on their lists.) So every time someone sends a message to a group of which you are a member, you get a copy of the mail. And every time you send a message to a group, everyone else on the list gets a copy.

There are thousands of mailing lists on the Internet. For a list of about 700 mailing lists, use FTP (see Chapter 18) to go to the **pit-manager.mit.edu FTP** site, change to the **/pub/usenet/news. announce.newsusers directory**, and find the **Publicly_Accessible_ Mailing_Lists,_Part_*n*** files.

Also, look for the document called "How to Find an Interesting Mailinglist," by Arno Wouters. You can get this by sending e-mail to **LISTSERV@vm1.nodak.edu** with the command **GET NEW-LIST WOUTERS** in the body of the message or by ftping to **vm1.nodak.edu**, changing to the **new-list** directory, and getting the **new-list.wouters** file.

Subscribing to Mailing Lists

There are two types of mailing lists: automated and manually administered. Some very small mailing lists are set up to be administered by a real person who will add your name to the list. Such lists are often private, and subscription is by invitation. Other lists use special programs (mailservers) to automatically add your name to the list when you subscribe. These are often, though not always, public lists that are open to anyone. (I explain more about this—and how you can easily set up your own simple mailing list—in *The Complete Idiot's Next Step with the Internet.*)

Subscribing to manually administered mailing lists is often as simple as sending a message to the administrator providing your e-mail address and asking to join the list. You can often reach an administrator by sending e-mail to *listname-request@hostname*.

To subscribe to an automated list, you often send e-mail to the mailserver program. In the body of the message enter **SUB** *firstname lastname* (that's your first and last name, of course). To unsubscribe, use the word **SIGNOFF** instead of SUB.

Note that the address of the list administrator and that of the list itself is usually different (in most cases, but not always). If the list is **biglist@bighost**, that's where you send your e-mail when you want to post messages to the list. But when you want to subscribe, unsubscribe, or do other administrative functions, you normally send e-mail to **biglist-request@bighost**. Although LISTSERV groups also have two e-mail addresses, working with them is a little different, as we'll see right now.

Using a LISTSERV Group

Many people think that mailing lists and LISTSERV groups are one and the same. Not quite. Although LISTSERV groups are a type of mailing list (perhaps the largest category), not all mailing lists are LISTSERV groups. The term "LISTSERV" refers to one popular mailserver program; so mailing lists administered by the LISTSERV program are known as LISTSERV groups, LISTSERV lists, or just LISTSERVs. LISTSERV originates on the Bitnet network. However, there are now many LISTSERV groups based on the Internet itself, on various UNIX hosts. There are well over 4,000 LISTSERV groups. For example, some LISTSERV groups include:

CHRISTIA@FINHUTC, a Christian discussion group

ISO8859@JHUVM, a group that discusses ASCII/EBCDIC-character set issues (what fun!)

L-HCAP@NDSUVM1, a group for people interested in issues related to handicapped people in education

PHILOSOP@YORKVM1, the Philosophy Discussion Forum

The subjects handled by the LISTSERV groups are often of a technical nature, related to networks and computer hardware and software. But there are plenty of nontechnical subjects as well, such as groups belonging to the African American Student Network, the American Association of Teachers of German, the Forum da Associacao Brasileira de Estatistica. There are also groups on Chinese music, Dungeons and Dragons, American dialects, aircraft, agriculture, and plenty more.

The LISTSERV Address

Let's take a look at the LISTSERV address. It's made up of three parts: the group name itself, the LISTSERV site, and **.bitnet**. For instance, the address of the group College Activism/Information List is **actnow-l@ brownvm.bitnet**. **Actnow-l** is the name of the group, and **brownvm** is the name of the site.

The term "LISTSERV" actually refers to the software used to administer these groups. Although there are several different versions, they work in very similar ways.

A *site* is a computer that has the LISTSERV program, and handles one or more LISTSERV groups. In fact, a site may have dozens of groups. The **brownvm** site, for instance, also maintains the ACH-EC-L, AFRICA-L, and AGING-L forums, among about 70 others.

So Where's the List?

You can have Bitnet send you a current list of LISTSERV groups. Send an e-mail message to **listserv@bitnic.educom.edu**. In the body of the message (not the subject) type **list global**. That's all you need. You'll automatically get an e-mail message containing the new list.

Let's Do It—Subscribing

Once you've found a LISTSERV group to which you want to subscribe, you must send an e-mail message to the LISTSERV site (not to the group itself), asking to subscribe to the list. Send a message with the following text in the body (not the subject) of the message.

SUBSCRIBE *group firstname lastname*

For instance, if I wanted to subscribe to the **actnow-l** list at the **brownvm** LISTSERV site, I could use UNIX mail to send a message like this:

```
teal% mail listserv@brownvm.bitnet
Subject:
SUBSCRIBE actnow-l Peter Kent
.
Cc:
teal%
```

Notice that you send the message to **listserv@***sitename***.bitnet**, and that the SUBSCRIBE message only contains the name of the group (not the entire group address).

You may (or may not) receive some kind of confirmation message from the group. Such a message would tell you that you have subscribed, and would provide background information about the group and the different commands you can use.

Some groups are listed as **peered**. A peered LISTSERV group is the same as a moderated newsgroup: someone's checking the mail and deciding what stays and what's trashed.

Once you've subscribed, you can either sit back and wait for the messages to arrive, or you can send your own messages. Simply address mail to the full group address (in the preceding case, to **actnow-l@ brownvm.bitnet**).

Enough Already!—Unsubscribing

When you're tired of receiving all these messages, you'll have to unsubscribe. Send another message to the LISTSERV address. This time, it'll lock like this:

```
teal% mail listserv@brownvm.bitnet
Subject:
SIGNOFF actnow-l
.
Cc:
teal%
```

Again, make sure you address it to **listserv@**, not to the group name itself. And make sure the group name—but not the entire group address—appears after SIGNOFF (the instruction to unsubscribe).

Getting Fancy with LISTSERV

There are a few neat things you can do with LISTSERV. By sending e-mail messages to the LISTSERV site, you can tell the LISTSERV software how you want to handle your messages. You

Even if you have only a mail connection to the Internet, you can still subscribe to LISTSERV groups. However, you may not want to. Some mail connections charge for each message you receive. If you join a busy group, you'll go broke.

can ask LISTSERV to send you an acknowledgment each time you send a message (by default most groups won't do this). You can find information about another group member—or tell LISTSERV not to provide information about you to other users. You can tell LISTSERV to stop sending you messages temporarily (perhaps when you go on vacation) or tell it to send only the message subjects, instead of the entire messages. You can request a specific message, and can even search the archives for old messages.

In addition, you can combine these commands, as I've done in this example:

```
teal% mail listserv@brownvm.bitnet
Subject:
list
query groupname
info ?
.
Cc:
teal%
```

This tells LISTSERV to send you a list of the groups handled by this site (**list**), tells you what options you have set (**query *groupname***), and sends you a list of information guides (**info ?**). It's a good idea to use this last command to find out what user documentation they have available, and then use the **info *documentname*** command to get the site to send you specific documents. (At some sites, sending e-mail to the LISTSERV address with the message **INFO REFCARD** will get you a document outlining the commands.)

The Least You Need to Know

➤ In rn, use the **s** *filename* command to save a newsgroup message.

➤ Reply to messages with the **f** command; use the **F** command if you want to include the original message.

➤ You may be able to start a discussion from your newsreader; check the documentation. If not, you may have a **Pnews** command or similar command that lets you send a newsgroup message from the UNIX shell.

➤ Subscribe to a LISTSERV group by including the command **SUBSCRIBE** *groupname firstname lastname* in the body of a message to **listserv@***sitename***.bitnet**.

➤ To unsubscribe, send the command **SIGNOFF** *groupname* in the body of a message.

➤ When you join a group, send a message with the command **info ?** in the body to find out what documentation they have available.

Telnet: Inviting Yourself onto Other Systems

There are millions of computers connected to the Internet, and some of them have some pretty interesting stuff. Wouldn't it be neat if you could "reach out" and get onto those computers, to take a look at the games and databases and programs on computers around the world?

Well, you can. At least you can get onto computers whose administrators want you to get on, and there's a surprisingly high number who do. A special program called telnet lets you turn your computer into a telnet *client* to access data and programs on a telnet *server* somewhere. Because you are logging into a computer other than the one you connect to normally, "telneting" is sometimes known as *remote login*, though this really refers to a command called **rlogin**, which is similar to—yet slightly different from—telnet.

Many Internet users have private telnet accounts. A researcher, for example, may have several computers he works on regularly, and may have been given a special login name and password by the administrators of those computers. But many computers also allow "strangers" into their systems. This is done on a purely voluntary basis, depending on the good will of the people who own or operate a particular computer. If a telnet server is open to the public, anyone can get on the system and see what's available.

Let's Go Telneting!

Telneting, as it's known, is surprisingly easy. All you need to know is the host name of the computer you want to reach and (perhaps) a login name it will accept. Then you'll issue this command:

```
telnet hostname
```

The Internet has a simple menu system, called Gopher, that can help you find and connect to telnet sites. Gopher is a great way to see what's available, to cruise around in Gopherspace looking for telnet sites. (Take a look at Chapter 21 for more information.) We'll look at an example of a service provider's menu system based on Gopher later in this chapter.

When you connect to the computer, you may be prompted for a login name. You can enter the one you know is acceptable, or if you don't have a login name, just type your own name. In some cases, you won't even have to log in; the computer just lets you straight in without any kind of checks.

How do you know what to use as a login name? Often, you'll see a telnet site listed in a directory, file, or e-mail somewhere. If so, this will tell you to use a particular login name. In other cases, the introductory screen you see may tell you what to use. And sometimes, as in this example, when you connect, you go straight into the program without logging in.

Let's take a quick look at how it works. I'm going to telnet to the Conversational Hypertext computer, an experimental system owned by the Government of Canada. It contains databases that you can "talk" to: you type questions in plain English, and the databases answer you.

```
CNS> telnet debra.dgbt.doc.ca 3000
Trying 142.92.36.15 ...
Connected to debra.dgbt.doc.ca.
Escape character is '^]'.
```

```
NOTE: use BACKSPACE (Control-H) to erase characters
CHAT Version 8.1.4  %G%
Copyright 1989-1992 Government of Canada
```

You'll see some more introductory screens, telling you what the system is and does. Then you'll see a list of choices:

```
There are information files available on the following topics:
    - AIDS (Acquired Immune Deficiency
      Syndrome)
    - Epilepsy
    - Alice (A simulated conversation)
    - Maur (A simulated conversation
      with a dragon)
    - Spectrum Management Program of
      Industry and Science Canada
  Please specify which information file you would like:
Select an Information File:
```

Let's have a word with that dragon. We type **Maur** and press **Enter**, wait a few moments, and then we see this:

```
[This is an experimental simulation of a conversation with a dragon,]
[and it is STILL UNDER CONSTRUCTION.                                ]
[                                                                   ]
[If you don't already know, communicate with the dragon with plain ]
[English.  Adventure game commands like "run away" will NOT work.   ]
[Also please note that you CANNOT browse in this conversation, as   ]
[you can in other databases.                                        ]
[                                                                   ]
[A word of warning:                                                 ]
[This dragon is mean and nasty.  Be creative and inventive and try
to come out of it alive - it IS possible.                          ]
Press <Return> to continue.
It seems like you have been wandering through these dark tunnels
for years. They hadn't seemed so bad when you and your companions
had entered the deserted mine, led by a rumour that the Hero's
Crown might have come to rest here.
```

blah, blah, blah... lots more; then,

185

```
The voice says:
Well, well, a visitor.  It has been a long time since anyone has
come down this way.
You say:  who's there?
```

It may take a while, but eventually you'll see this:

```
The voice says:
Long ago my name would have meant something to you.  Whole villages
fled at my coming; at least they tried...  my name is Maur.
You say:  Maur? What kind of stupid name is that?

Maur says:
Yes, Maur.  You are rather irritating, you pitiful human!  I may
very well burn you to a crisp this instant!
You say:  I'd like to see you try, you over-inflated pile of $%#@!
Maur says:
See for yourself. (About ten meters into the gloom, ahead of you
and to the right, two huge red reptilian eyes flick open....)
```

Well, I think the computer got a little confused by my last statement. Still, it's an experimental system.

Can't see what you type when you are in a telnet session? See the information on the **set echo** command later in this chapter.

Once you are connected through telnet, what you see depends on what sort of system is set up on that computer. It might be a series of menus that let you select options, or it might be a prompt at which you type. You're simply logging onto a different computer, and each system varies a little.

You may need to specify a port number in addition to a host name. Simply leave a space and type the number. For instance, **telnet hellspark.wharton. upenn.edu 6969** takes you to a telnet site where you can play Go with other users.

I will warn you about one thing: Telnet can be slow—*very* slow— sometimes. On occasion, you may type something, and not see what you have typed for several seconds or even several minutes. It depends on the amount of network traffic going that way, the number of people working on that machine at that time, and the amount of traffic on your service provider's computer. If you find a particular task to be too slow, you should probably come back later. If it's always slow at that telnet site, maybe you can find another site with the same services.

What Type Is Your Terminal?

Sometimes you'll be prompted to enter a terminal type before you start a telnet session. If you enter a terminal type that the other system doesn't recognize, you may not be able to see what's displayed on your screen. The most common terminal type, one that virtually all systems can use, is VT100. (Some communication programs have VT102 instead of VT100; they're pretty much the same.) Make sure you set your communications software to the same terminal type that you tell the telnet site to use.

Waving Goodbye to the Telnet Site

Once you've logged on to a telnet site, you're in that computer's system, and each system is different. How do you leave the telnet site? Try **quit**, **exit**, **Ctrl-d**, or **done**, in that order. One of those will probably end the session and return you to the **telnet>** prompt, or take you all the way back to the UNIX prompt if you used the **telnet** *host* command to start the session. If none of these work, try **Ctrl-]** followed by **close**.

Commanding Telnet to Do Your Bidding

As you've seen, you can start telnet and go to a computer directly from the UNIX prompt. You can also start telnet and go to the **telnet>** prompt simply by typing **telnet** and pressing **Enter**. If you do this, you'll have to use the **open** command. You can't just type **telnet** *hostname* at the **telnet>** prompt; you'll have to use **open** *hostname* instead. Here are a few other commands you should know:

> **close**   Closes the connection to the telnet server. Use this if you get stuck somehow on the other computer, and it doesn't seem to let you log out. Press **Ctrl-]** and type **close**. If you issued the **telnet** command from the UNIX shell prompt, you'll go back there. If you used the **open** command, you'll go back to the **telnet>** prompt.

Ctrl-]   Use this to send an *escape character* (a way of halting a telnet session temporarily) but still remain in telnet. For instance, if the telnet server just locks up, and you can't even issue the **close** command, try **Ctrl-]** instead. Then use the **close** command to actually close the session with that telnet site, or press **Enter** to return to the session. Ctrl-] won't always do the job. Some computers use a different character, but there will normally be some kind of notice (when you log in) explaining what to use.

set escape *character*   This command changes the escape character to whatever you choose. You might want to use this in the case of a telnet session in which you log into one machine, and then telnet from there to another machine. (You probably won't do so often.) If you used **Ctrl-]**, it would take you all the way back to the first machine, instead of the second. So you can set a different character for just the first session. Press **Ctrl-]**, type **set escape** *character*, and press **Enter** to return to the session and telnet to the next site. (You can type ^ to indicate the Ctrl key: **^a** for Ctrl-a, for example. Or you can simply type the command and press **Ctrl-a**.)

set echo   Telnet usually works with remote echoing. When you type, the characters are sent to the server, which then sends them back; only then are they displayed on your screen. If they are not sent back (you notice that you don't see the command when you type it, but the command is still used by the telnet server), you can turn on local echoing with the **set echo** command. Press **Ctrl-]** to get back to the **telnet>** prompt, type **set echo**, press **Enter**, and press **Enter** again to return to the session. Repeat the process to turn local echoing off. You'll also use the **set echo** command to turn off local echo if everything you type appears twice.

?   This command displays a list of telnet commands. However, you can only issue it at the **telnet>** prompt; again, press **Ctrl-]** before typing **?**.

z   This command lets you suspend the telnet session, do something on your own system, and then return to where you were in the telnet session. To use this system, first press **Ctrl-]** to return to the **telnet>** prompt. Then type **z** and press **Enter**. You'll be back at the UNIX shell prompt. How you return to the telnet session depends on the type of system you are running. You'll probably use the **fg** command at the UNIX shell. In some other shells, you may have been working in a "subshell," and have to close it before you can return automatically to the telnet session. And some systems simply won't work with the **z** command (try it and see).

quit or **q**   Use this to end your telnet session and return to the UNIX shell. You may also be able to use **Ctrl-d**.

IBM Mainframe Telnet Sites

Some telnet sites are on IBM mainframes running "3270" software. If you try to telnet to a site and find the connection is instantly closed (even before you get to the login prompt), it may be a 3270 site (though there's no guarantee of it). If you log in and see this:

```
VM/XA SP ONLINE-PRESS ENTER KEY TO BEGIN SESSION
```

you've definitely reached a 3270 site. Leave the site (press **Ctrl-]**, type **q**, and press **Enter**). Now use this command: **tn3270** *host*. For example, you might have telneted with this command:

```
telnet vmd.cso.uiuc.edu.
```

If so, you saw this:

```
Trying 128.174.5.98 ...
Connected to vmd.cso.uiuc.edu.
Escape character is '^]'.
VM/XA SP ONLINE-PRESS ENTER KEY TO BEGIN SESSION .
```

Leave the session; then do this:

```
teal% tn3270 vmd.cso.uiuc.edu
```

You'll see this:

```
VM/XA SP ONLINE
        University of Illinois  Computing Services Office
            3081-KX Serial 24222        VM/XA SP 2.1
  9205
```

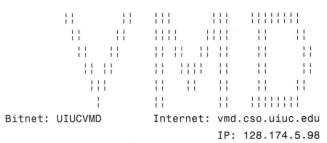

```
                       Bitnet: UIUCVMD          Internet: vmd.cso.uiuc.edu
                                                          IP: 128.174.5.98

          Fill in your USERID and PASSWORD and press ENTER
          (Your password will not appear when you type it)
          USERID   ===>
          PASSWORD ===>
          COMMAND  ===>

                                              RUNNING    VMD
```

Now you are into the site using the 3270 mode. You can type **?** and press **Enter** to see a help screen, or type **logoff** and press **Enter** to end the session.

In 3270 mode you usually type something at a prompt and press **Enter** or a function key (a *PF key* in 3270-speak). If you find a 3270 site you need to work with, see if your service provider can find you some program documentation that explains how to work in this mode.

The HYTELNET Directory— Finding What's Out There

To get a taste for what's available in the world of telnet, telnet to **access.usask.ca** and log in as **hytelnet**. You'll see this:

```
                  Welcome to HYTELNET version 6.6.x
                     Last Update: November 15, 1993


          ->   What is HYTELNET?     <WHATIS>
                    Library catalogs    <SITES1>
                    Other resources     <SITES2>
                    Help files for catalogs   <OP000>
                    Catalog interfaces <SYS000>
                    Internet Glossary  <GLOSSARY>
                    Telnet tips         <TELNET>
                    Telnet/TN3270 escape keys <ESCAPE.KEY>
                    Key-stroke commands        <HELP>
```

```
Up/Down arrows MOVE    Left/Right arrows SELECT   ? for HELP anytime
m   returns here      i  searches the index        q  quits
              HYTELNET 6.6 was written by Peter Scott
              E-mail address: aa375@freenet.carleton.ca
```

You'll notice that **<WHATIS>** is highlighted. You can move the highlight up and down with the arrow keys and press **Enter** to select an option. Return to this menu by pressing **m**. When you get down the "menu tree" you can use the left arrow to move back to the previous menu.

Play around in here. You'll find descriptions of various resources—electronic books, NASA databases, library catalogs, the Biotechnet Electronic Buyers' Guide, the Business Start-Up Information Database, and on and on—and which telnet site you have to go to find them.

Easy Street: Telneting from a Menu

If you're lucky, your service provider has set up some kind of menu system—possibly based on Gopher (explained in Chapter 21)—that leads you to various telnet sites. On the system I'm working with, for example, **<TEL>** appears at the end of various menu options as an indication that the option will use telnet to take me somewhere. For example, if I select **15. Tools for Information Retrieval**, I see several options with the **<TEL>** indicator. There's

```
1. HYTELNET Directory of Telnet Accessible Resources <TEL>
```

(We just learned about HYTELNET.) There is also

```
4.  Services - An Interactive Directory of Internet Resources <TEL>
```

which takes you to **library.wustl.edu**, where you can access library databases all over the world. Then there's this one:

```
6.  World Wide Web (WWW) <TEL>
```

You'll learn more about WWW in Chapter 23.

What happens when I select **1. HYTELNET Directory of Telnet Accessible Resources <TEL>**? I see the following box:

```
+------HYTELNET Directory of Telnet Accessible Resources------+
¦ Warning!!!!!, you are about to leave the Colorado SuperNet ¦
¦ Supermenu and connect to your selection.  If you get stuck ¦
¦ press the control key and the ] key.  If you immediately   ¦
¦ return to SuperMenu the line may be busy.                  ¦
¦                                                            ¦
¦                                                            ¦
¦ Connecting to access.usask.ca using telnet.                ¦
¦ Use the account name "hytelnet" to log in                  ¦
¦                                   [Cancel - ^G] [OK - Enter] ¦
¦                                                            ¦
+------------------------------------------------------------+
```

Notice that this tells me where I'm going (**Connecting to access.usask.ca using telnet**) and how to log in (**Use the account name "hytelnet" to log in**). All I need to do is press **Enter**, and away I go. Within a few seconds, I find myself at the HYTELNET login prompt.

The Least You Need to Know

➤ Start a telnet session by typing **telnet** *hostname* or **telnet** *hostname port* and pressing **Enter**.

➤ To connect to a telnet site while at the **telnet>** prompt, type **open** *hostname* or **open** *hostname port*.

➤ Get back to the **telnet>** prompt without ending the session by pressing **Ctrl-d**.

➤ To close the telnet session and return to the **telnet>** prompt try **quit**, **exit**, **Ctrl-d**, or **done**.

➤ Use the **close** command to close the connection to the telnet site.

➤ Press **Ctrl-]** to return to the **telnet>** prompt, and then use the z command to temporarily suspend the session. In most cases, you'll use the **fg** command to return.

➤ Close telnet using the **quit**, **q**, or **Ctrl-d** commands.

➤ Take a look at HYTELNET to find out what's available by telneting.

Grabbing the Goodies: Downloading Files with FTP

In This Chapter

➤ Using a menu versus using a UNIX prompt

➤ Clues that will help you find files

➤ Knowing your file formats

➤ Searching with grep

➤ Grabbing files from here and there

➤ Dealing with compressed files

Let's say you've discovered a really neat file on a computer in Albania, or Australia, or Alabama, or somewhere. Perhaps someone told you where it was, or you saw a message in a newsgroup about it. It might be a public domain or shareware program, a document containing information you want for some research you're working on, a picture, a book you want to read, or just about anything. Now, how do you get the file from that computer to your computer?

You use a system called *file transfer protocol*, or *FTP* for short. You'll often see the term **ftp** or **FTP**. In a directory or mail message, you might be told to "ftp to such and such a computer to find this file." That simply means use the FTP system to grab the file.

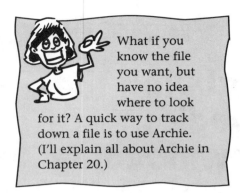

What if you know the file you want, but have no idea where to look for it? A quick way to track down a file is to use Archie. (I'll explain all about Archie in Chapter 20.)

In some cases, you may have specific permission to get onto another computer and grab files. A researcher, for instance, may have been given permission to access files on a computer owned by an organization involved in the same sort of research (another university or government department, for example).

In other cases, however, you'll just be rooting around on other people's systems without specific permission. Some systems are open to the public: anyone can get on and grab files that the system administrator has decided should be publicly accessible. This is known as *anonymous ftp* because you don't need a login name to get onto the computer, you simply log in as anonymous. For a password, you normally enter your mail address.

Before we get started, a word about when you should use FTP. Many systems don't like people digging around during business hours. They would rather you came in during evenings and weekends. So you may see a message asking you to restrict your use to after hours, or the FTP site may not let you in at all during certain hours.

FTP is relatively easy to use, once you know what you are doing. But like everything else on the Internet, it's not designed to look like it's easy to use. There's no fancy graphical user interface (or even a menu system) built into FTP; however, there is something called Gopher which can automate FTP for you to some degree (more on that in a moment).

Menus, If You're Lucky

If you're lucky, your service provider has set up a menu system to make FTP easy to work with, possibly using a Gopher (see Chapter 21) to help you find your way through the Internet to FTP sites. On my service provider's menu system, I can select **8. File Transfer (FTP)/** to see an FTP menu. From there I can choose from such options as **Connect to a specific ftp host** and **Ftp sites in alphabetical order by hostname**. The first option expects me to enter the FTP site name; the second displays hundreds of different FTP sites in alphabetical order. It even has a word or two indicating what I might find there. For instance:

```
                        a FTP sites

—>1.  a.cs.uiuc.edu 128.174.252.1   TeX, dvi2ps, gif, texx2.7,/
   2.  a.psc.edu 128.182.66.105  GPLOT, GTEX/
   3.  aarnet.edu.au 139.130.204.4   Australian AARNET network/
   4.  ab20.larc.nasa.gov 128.155.23.64 amiga, comp.sources.amiga,/
   5.  acacia.maths.uwa.oz.au 130.95.16.2    unknown/
   6.  acfcluster.nyu.edu 128.122.128.11 VMS UUCP, news, DECUS library/
   7.  acns.nwu.edu 129.105.49.1    virus info/programs, maps/
```

Whichever way I choose to get to one of the FTP sites, the system handles all the logging on for me, and displays file directories in the form of a menu like this:

```
a.cs.uiuc.edu 128.174.252.1   TeX, dvi2ps, gif, texx2.7,

      1.  .cshrc.
      2.  .hushlogin.
      3.  .login.
      4.  adm/
      5.  bin/
      6.  dev/
      7.  etc/
      8.  files.lst.
      9.  files.lst.Z <Bin>
     10.  lib.
     11.  ls-lR.
     12.  ls-lR.Z <Bin>
     13.  msgs/
  —> 14.  pub/
```

I can select the **pub** directory just as I would select any menu option. If I want to read a text file, I just select it from the menu. To *get* the file, i.e. copy it to my service provider's computer, I press **qs** while reading the file. To see information about a file, I just put the arrow on it and press =. To transfer a binary file, I select it from the menu.

Remember, these commands are case sensitive. That is, an uppercase D is not the same as a lowercase d.

I can even download a file directly from FTP to my computer. I select the file I want to get, and type **D**. I see something like this:

195

```
+---------medit001.zip----------+
¦                               ¦
¦                               ¦
¦   1. Zmodem                   ¦
¦   2. Ymodem                   ¦
¦   3. Xmodem-1K                ¦
¦   4. Xmodem-CRC               ¦
¦   5. Kermit                   ¦
¦   6. Text                     ¦
¦                               ¦
¦   Choose a download method:   ¦
¦                               ¦
¦   [Cancel ^G]  [Choose 1-6]   ¦
¦                               ¦
¦                               ¦
+-------------------------------+
```

I select my transfer mode, and away I go. (We'll look at file transfers in more detail in Chapter 19.)

This system makes running around an FTP site much easier than using FTP itself (which you'll soon realize as you read on). The menu system makes it much easier to view directories and text files, transfer files back to my service provider's computer, and even transfer them back to my system. However, you may not have such a system available; and even if you do, you may still find you want to use FTP yourself sometimes. You may not be able to get to some systems or some files using the menu system. So we're going to take a detailed look at FTP and how to use it.

Hitting the FTP Trail

Okay, you've discovered that a file you want lies somewhere on a computer in, say, London. You've got the hostname of the FTP site, but you don't know exactly where on the computer the file is. We'll track it down (maybe). To get started, go to the UNIX prompt, type **ftp** *hostname*, and press **Enter**. (You can actually start the FTP program by simply typing **ftp** and pressing **Enter**, but including a hostname starts FTP and tells FTP to connect to the named host.)

However, let's say you mistyped the name. You'll see an **unknown host** message, and the prompt changes to **ftp>**. To connect to a host from the **ftp>** prompt, you'll have to use the **open** command. Type **open** *hostname* and press **Enter**. Let's see an example:

```
ftp> open ftp.demon.co.uk
Connected to newgate.demon.co.uk.
220 newgate.demon.co.uk FTP server (Version 5.60 #1) ready.
Name (ftp.demon.co.uk:peterk): anonymous
331 Guest login ok, send ident as password.
Password: (type your e-mail address as the password)
230 Guest login ok, access restrictions apply.ftp>
```

We used the **open** command to connect to this host because we were already running FTP. Notice that this hostname (**ftp.demon.co.uk**) starts with **ftp**. Because many FTP sites start their hostnames with **ftp**, to get to them from the UNIX prompt, you would have to type **ftp ftp.***etcetera* (**ftp ftp.demon.co.uk**, in this case).

In the example above, we saw a message saying that we had connected, another line saying that the system was ready, and then a line asking for our Name. We logged on using the name **anonymous**. In some cases you may want to ftp to a system that doesn't let just anyone in. In this case, you'll have to get permission from the system administrator, who will provide you with a login name. If you log in using **anonymous**, the system will usually ask you to enter your real "ident" (or something similar). Enter your e-mail address as the password. (You can see in the example where the remote system asked for the Password, but because that system doesn't echo it back, you can't see what I actually typed.)

Made a mistake when you typed the login? You'll get a message saying that the login failed. Don't worry, you're not stuck. Type **user anonymous** (or type the login name you've been assigned) instead of "anonymous" and press **Enter**. Although this won't always work (the remote system may close the connection), it's worth a try.

After entering your login name, you'll see a line telling you that you got through (**Guest login ok**), and you'll probably see a message telling you that **access restrictions apply**. This simply means you will be able to go only where the system administrator allows you to go, and do only what he allows you to do, and no more.

Finally, you'll see the **ftp>** prompt again. You're on. Now what?

Finding That Pot o' Gold

Now that you're on, you want to find the file that you know lies somewhere on this system. Where do you start? Well, FTP has a number of commands available to you, some of which are the same as the standard UNIX commands. You might start with **pwd**. That will show you where you are; you are probably in the root directory (/).

File names in UNIX are not quite the same as file names in DOS. DOS files have not only a name, but an extension (three characters that appear at the end of the name preceded by a period). For instance in THISFILE.TXT, the TXT is the extension. UNIX file names don't have extensions. Sure, a name might have a period in it, but it could have several periods; a period does not signify the beginning of an extension.

Next you might use **dir**. The **dir** command shows you a list of files and directories, although the actual form of the list varies between systems. (FTP's **dir** command simply tells the system to send the information, and the system decides in which format to send it.) You can also use the **ls** command to do a simple name-only listing.

Remember that UNIX uses a forward slash to separate directory names, unlike DOS, which uses a backslash.

However, there is a problem with FTP's listing commands: a long directory will shoot by faster than you can read it. There are a few ways around this problem. (None are ideal, of course, but you're in the UNIX world now; this is normal.)

First of all, you can use the command **ls -l** "**|more**" to show the list one page at a time. Alternatively, you could do a multi-column listing: type **ls -C** and press **Enter**, and the listing is placed in several columns across your screen (though you'll get file names only, no detail).

You could then limit the listing to only those files in which you are interested, using the * wild-card character to limit the search a little. If you type **dir** *thisfile* and press **Enter**, for instance, you'll see information about *thisfile*. If you type **dir *txt** and press **Enter**, you'll see a listing of all the files that end in the characters *txt*. The * simply means "anything might be here."

You could also type **dir p*** to search for all files beginning with *p* (or **dir P*** for all files beginning with *P*). However, the **dir** command

198

also lets you specify which directory you want to list: **dir *directoryname***. So if there are any directories beginning with *p* (or *P*), you'll also see a listing of the files in those directories.

You can also do a *recursive* directory listing. Type **ls -lR** and press **Enter**, and FTP displays a list of all the files and subdirectories in the current directory, plus all the files and subdirectories in those directories, and so on. This will often be much too big and fast to read online, so type **ls -lR *filename*** to copy it to a file. Because this file is placed on your system, you will have to close FTP to read the file, but it may help you track down what you want a bit more quickly.

Perhaps the easiest way to deal with long listings is to use your communications program to save them. For example, most communications programs let you copy all the incoming data to a text file. If you are using a Windows communications program, you could then go to File Manager and double-click on the text file to open and read it (assuming it's got the extension .TXT). Some communications programs even let you scroll back to earlier portions of the session, so if the text runs past, you can scroll back up to view it.

Look for Clues

Some system administrators will place clues to help you figure out what can be found where. You may see a file called README, READ.ME, README.TXT, INDEX, or something similar. Such a file is likely to give you a listing of what you can take and where to find it.

Also, did you see a directory named **pub**? That's the public directory, where the system administrator has probably placed all the files that outsiders are likely to want. Go into that directory to see what's there, or simply type **dir pub** to list the contents of the pub directory.

You'll often find that directories have names that describe their contents (hey, we may be working with UNIX, but not everything has to be difficult). **slip** will probably contain SLIP software, **mac** will have Macintosh software, **xwindows** will have X Windows software, **windows** will have Microsoft Windows software, **gif** will contain GIF-format graphics, and so on. If you know what you are looking for, you can often figure out what the directory names mean.

Some systems let you run multiple sessions in multiple "windows." You won't be able to do this if you have a dial-in terminal connection, but you may be able to do it if you have a SLIP or PPP connection, depending on the software you are using. If so, you can transfer a file to your system, and then read the file in another window—without leaving FTP.

Why Don't You Read the Index?

Let's say you find an index file of some kind, a file named README, INDEX, or whatever. How can you read it? Unfortunately, you can't use the UNIX **cat** and **more** commands (at least not directly). Here are some commands you can use:

get *filename* -   The **get** command is normally used to transfer a file from the remote system back to yours. But if you place a space and a hyphen after the file name and press **Enter**, the remote system displays the text file. If it's short, that's great: you can easily read it. If it's not, you might try pressing **Ctrl-s** to stop the text flow and **Ctrl-q** to restart it when you're ready (although that might not work).

If you tried **Ctrl-s** and **Ctrl-q**, you might be returned to the **ftp>** prompt, but your keyboard might not work. Press **Ctrl-q** again.

get *filename* "|more"   This command sends the file to the **more** command so that (if you are lucky) you can read the file in the usual UNIX way: by pressing **Spacebar** to move from page to page. To stop the file display, press **Ctrl-c** (not **q**).

get *filename*   If the first two systems don't work, and if you can't use your communications program to save incoming text in a text file for you, your only hope is to transfer the file back to your system, and go back and read it there. We'll look at how to transfer files in a moment.

grep to It!

There's another useful command for finding information: **grep** (which we already looked at in Chapter 9). You can use **grep** while working in

FTP, but in a slightly different way: you combine it with the **get** command. For example, consider this command:

```
get wizoz10.txt "¦grep Dorothy"
```

This searches a file called wizoz10.txt to see if the word "Dorothy" appears anywhere. If it does, grep displays each line in which it is found. If grep displays lots of lines, you can press **Ctrl-c** to end the list. You may also be able to use **Ctrl-s** and **Ctrl-q** to stop and restart the list, though there will probably be a significant time lag.

In addition, you can use some (but not all) of grep's permutations. For instance, if you are not sure of the capitalization of the word you are looking for, type

```
get wizoz10.txt "¦grep -i dorothy"
```

to have grep find any lines that contain "dorothy," whether the word is capitalized as Dorothy or dorothy (or DOROTHY, or DoRoThY, or whatever). Remember, however, that when you use the **-i** switch, grep also displays lines containing words of which the specified word is just one part. (For example, if you were searching for "she" with the **-i** switch, you'd get lines containing "she" and lines containing "sheet.")

Unfortunately you won't be able to search for a "string" of words. For instance, if you entered the command,

```
get wizoz10.txt "¦grep "she was in""
```

grep would find all lines with the letters "she."

Moving Around

You can move around the remote computer's directory system in a way very similar to that in which you move around in directories on your own DOS system. You'll use the **cd** command, although it doesn't work quite the same in FTP as it does in plain ol' UNIX. You can't just type **cd** and press **Enter** to move to a "home" directory; if you try this, the FTP site will probably prompt you for a directory name. So it's a good idea to use the **pwd** command now and again to figure out where you are, and you can always use **cd** to get you back there. For example, if you were in the / directory (the root) when you got onto the FTP site's machine, you can type **cd** / and press **Enter** to go back to it from your adventures in its subdirectories.

201

Changing Your Directory

When you are working in FTP, the **cd** command changes the directory on the FTP site's machine. The **lcd** command, a "local change directory" command, changes the directory on your host machine (such as from C: to A:). This is useful when you want to transfer files, because it lets you define the directory into which you want to place the file. The **lcd** command works the same as the usual **cd** command, as I described in Chapter 9.

Grabbing Files—What Format?

When you've found a file you want, you'll use the **get** command to grab it. But first, let's consider the type of data you are going to grab. The data might be *ASCII* or *binary*. (Although ASCII files are also binary files—all computer files are stored as a collection of binary digits—we're concerned here with how the files are going to be transferred. Read on and you'll understand the distinction.)

ASCII or Text Files

By ASCII we mean a file that contains plain text (no pictures, no sounds, no program). Plain text is just that. It's not a word processing or spreadsheet file (with all the fancy formatting that comes with such files); it's just letters, numbers, and a few special characters, which include punctuation, %, $, #, and so on. Most documents you find on the Internet are ASCII files.

FTP automatically assumes that you want to transfer your files in ASCII (text) format. (If you want to use binary format, you'll have to tell FTP first. We'll get to that in a moment.) When FTP sends a file using an ASCII-type transfer, it doesn't really send the file at all; it sends the individual letters, numbers, and characters. The machine receiving the data then saves it in a text file in the appropriate format. A UNIX machine saves it in a UNIX format, a Macintosh saves it in Mac format, and so on.

Because different computers store information in different ways, a Macintosh can't read a UNIX text file. But if you use an ASCII transfer, you're not transferring the file itself, you're transferring the text, which is stored in the receiving computer's format.

Binary Files

Sending a binary file is different. The sending machine looks at every *bit* and sends exactly the bits (the 1s or 0s) it sees. It doesn't care what the data means. In effect, it tells the machine receiving the data that "This is a 1, this is a 0, this is a 0, this is a 1, this is a 1," and so on. With an ASCII transfer, it would be telling the receiving computer that "This is a p, this is an l, this is an e, this is an a," and so on.

Why is this distinction important? Because when FTP transfers an ASCII file, it makes sure that the machine reading the file can put it in a format that can be used on that machine. But when it transfers a binary file, it really doesn't care; it transfers the file exactly as it appears at the FTP site and assumes that the user (you) will know what sort of machine the file can be used on. So if you are transferring a DOS program, you must use the program on a DOS machine, not a UNIX computer or a Macintosh.

> A **bit** is a Binary digIT, the smallest piece of data that a computer can store. Each bit is represented by a 1 or a 0. The binary number system has only two digits, one and zero, thus binary digit. It takes eight bits (known as one byte) to store one letter, number, or character.

Decisions, Decisions: Choosing the Transfer Type

What sort of transfer will an FTP site use as its default? That depends. Some use ASCII, and some use binary, so it's a good idea to check first. To check, enter the **type** command, and FTP will tell you the type of transfer it's going to use. To change to a binary transfer, use the **binary** command. FTP, characteristically obtuse, will then display **Type set to I**. Don't worry, **I** (for *image*) means binary.

To convert back to an ASCII transfer, use the **ascii** command. This time FTP displays **Type set to A**.

> If you try to send a non-text file by an ASCII transfer, FTP will get upset. It might lock up, and it could even lock up your computer. Be sure that you use ASCII transfer for text files, and binary transfer for everything else.

But how do you choose which type of transfer to use? Generally, this is easy. If you are transferring a document, use ASCII. If you are transferring just about anything else—a program, picture, sound, word processing document, spreadsheet, database—use binary. There are some exceptions, of course, such as those listed here:

Database file   These might be text files. If the file was created by a mainstream database program (such as dBASE, Access, or FoxPro), it's a binary file. But it's quite possible to create a database in an ASCII file, using commas, tabs, or other characters to separate the data.

Spreadsheet file   A spreadsheet file is almost certainly a binary file (although, again, it's possible to create a spreadsheet file as an ASCII file).

Word processing file   A word processing file is, almost by definition, a binary file, because it contains all sorts of formatting codes. Virtually all word processing applications (Word, WordPerfect, Q&A Write, WordStar, and so on) create files that should be regarded as binary files. Don't confuse word processing applications with text editors: although a text editor is a program that lets you write (as is a word processing application), it stores the text in an ASCII file. The earliest word processing applications were little more than text editors, and stored their data in an ASCII format.

Program file   Programs are almost always transferred as binary files. However, program *source code* is generally ASCII, and programs themselves may be text files if they are *scripting* files (for example, DOS batch files and UNIX script files are ASCII).

Source code is what a programmer actually writes; it's just words and numbers in a text file. Source code is then compiled into the program file (the file that actually does the work).

E-mail file   Internet e-mail messages are generally stored as ASCII.

Compressed file   A compressed file, one that has been "squeezed" to take up less room, is always a binary file.

Uuencoded file   A file that has been converted to ASCII using UUENCODE or something similar (as we discussed in Chapter 12), is, of course, ASCII.

PostScript file   These files, used to print on laser printers or to store graphics, are ASCII files.

UNIX tar file   A file ending with .tar is a tape archive file created with the UNIX **tar** command. This command is used to store various files in a single .tar file (which may or may not be on tape!). These are binary files.

If You're Not Sure What It Is...

If you're not sure what type of file it is, you might try these rules of thumb:

➤ If you think the file's a text file (and you've no reason to think otherwise), transfer as ASCII. To be sure, you can use the **get** *filename* "**|more**" command first.

➤ If you think the file's a program, database, spreadsheet, or word processing file (and you've no reason to think it might be ASCII), transfer as binary.

➤ If you know it's a graphic, sound, compressed file, or tar file, it's binary.

➤ If you know it's PostScript, e-mail, or a uuencoded file, it's ASCII.

UNIX actually has a command that helps you find out the type of file: not surprisingly, it's the **file** command. (To use it, type **file** *filename*.) Problem is, you can't use this in FTP.

Getting the File

When you're ready to get the file, transfer using the **get** command: **get** *filename*. For instance, **get README** transfers the file called README. It's that simple. You can even rename the file while you're transferring it, with the command **get** *filename newfilename*.

You can also get more than one file at a time by using the **mget** command: **mget** *filename filename etc*. For instance:

```
ftp> mget dm930119.doc dm930119.exe
```

This tells FTP to get both dm930119.doc and dm930119.exe. You could also use a wild-card character, like this:

```
ftp> mget d*
```

205

This tells FTP to get all the files starting with d. Of course, you could do it the other way around: **mget *.txt** would get all the files with .txt at the end. You can use wild cards in other ways, too. For example, the ? replaces a single character, so **get dm93811?.exe** would get dm938111.exe, dm938112.exe, dm938113.exe, and so on. But be warned: the rules for using wild cards vary from system to system.

Here's another pair of handy commands. Before doing a file transfer, use the **hash** command; this tells FTP to display hash marks (#) to show that it's actually doing something during transmission (so you don't think it's locked up). Use the **prompt off** command if you are using **mget**, so FTP doesn't ask you to confirm each file transfer.

When you finally press **Enter** and FTP starts to get your files, you'll be able to confirm that you want each one. FTP names each file before transferring it, and asks whether you really want it (for example, **mget dm930119.doc?**). You can type **y** and press **Enter** to continue, or type **n** and press **Enter** to skip to the next file.

You Might Be Able to Do This...

Most people will use *anonymous* FTP most of the time. That is, they'll be "guests" on someone else's system, able to do little more than look around and "get" files that have been placed there for public use.

In some cases, though, you may be working on a system on which you have more rights. You may be able to place files there (using the **put** and **mput** commands), create new directories, or even delete files. The **put** and **mput** commands work in the same way as the **get** and **mget** commands, and the other commands are the same as in UNIX. (See Chapter 9 for more information.)

Compressed (Squeezed) Files

Many files on FTP sites are *compressed*. That is, special programs have been used to "squeeze" the information into a smaller area. These files can't be used in their compressed state, but it's a great way to store and transmit them, because it saves disk space and transmission time. A compression program can reduce files to as little as 2% of their normal size, depending on the type of file and the program used. (However,

40% to 75% is a more normal range.) If you decide you need one of these compressed files, transfer it as binary. You'll have to uncompress it at some point before you can use it.

If you are a DOS user, you'll find that most of the compressed DOS files are in .ZIP format, a format created by a program called PKZIP. There are other programs, however. You may also see .ARJ (created by a program called ARJ) and .LZH (created by LHA).

> An **archive file** is one that contains one or more other files, generally in a compressed format. Archive files are used for storing infrequently used files or for transferring files from one computer to another.

Here are some other compressed formats:

.Z	UNIX, compress
.z	UNIX, pack
.shar	UNIX, sh (shell archive)
.sit	Macintosh, Stuffit
.pit	Macintosh, Packit
.zoo	zoo210 (available on various systems)
.tar	UNIX tar
.arc	DOS, PKARC (an older method, predating PKZIP)

You may even see programs that have been compressed twice. For example, you might find a file called **sliphack.tar.Z**. First you should use the UNIX **uncompress** program (**uncompress sliphack.tar.Z**). The files inside this file are extracted. You'll then find that one or more of those files are .tar files, so you'll use the **tar** command: **tar xvf sliphack.tar**. This command simply tells tar to extract the files from sliphack.tar and display the file names as it does so. If you just want to see what's inside, use **tar tf** *filename*.

You may occasionally run into *shell archives*, files that end with .shar. These are UNIX files that have been archived with a shell script (a script in UNIX is kind of like a batch file in DOS). You run the script to extract the files: **sh** *filename*.

Finally, there's something called a *self-extracting archive*. Programs such as PKZIP and ARJ can create files that can be executed (run) to extract the archived files automatically. This is useful when you're sending a compressed file to someone but you're not sure if they have the program to uncompress the file (or would know how to use it). For instance, PKZIP can create a file with an .EXE extension; such a file can be run directly from the DOS prompt, just by typing its name and pressing **Enter**. When you do so, out pop all the compressed files.

So Long, Farewell

How do you leave FTP? Well, to leave the FTP site you are logged onto, you can type **close** and press **Enter**. This will take you back to the **ftp>** prompt (if you used the **open** command to start the session) or to the UNIX prompt (if you used the **ftp** command to start the session). To leave the FTP site and close FTP at the same time, you can use the **quit** command or the **bye** command, or press **Ctrl-d**.

The Least You Need to Know

➤ If your service provider has a menu system for FTP, get to know it. It can save lots of time and trouble.

➤ Start an FTP session from the UNIX prompt by typing **ftp** *hostname*. Start from the **ftp>** prompt by typing **open** *hostname*.

➤ Use **cd** and **pwd** to move around in the directories.

➤ The **ls -x** command lists all the files in several columns so you can see them all.

➤ Read a text file using **get** *filename* "**|more**".

➤ Transfer a file to your system using **get** *filename*.

➤ If the file's anything other than a text document, use the **binary** command before **get** *filename* to set FTP to a binary transfer. Use **ascii** to change it back.

➤ Close the FTP session using the **close** command.

➤ Close the FTP session and close FTP itself with **qui** or **by** or by pressing **Ctrl-d**.

## Chapter 19

More Neato FTP Stuff

In This Chapter

➤ Grabbing the CIA *World Factbook*

➤ File transfers with xmodem or zmodem

➤ Speeding logins with .netrc

➤ Meeting your FTP hosts

➤ FTP by mail

➤ Avoiding computer viruses

By this time, you should know that FTP is a *file transfer protocol*, not a rude noise. (For your reference, the rude noise would look something like "pfttph." Go ahead and say it if FTP has been a struggle up to now.) Anyway, in Chapter 18, we spent a lot of time getting an overview of FTP and what it does. In this chapter, we're going to look at a few more details. But first, let's actually do something with FTP.

Grabbing Files from Project Gutenberg

In this example, we're going to take a look at Project Gutenberg's files, and grab a free copy of the CIA's *World Factbook*. It's large (approximately 1 MB in compressed form or 2.5 MB uncompressed), so if you see something you'd rather have, grab that instead.

Here we go. In the following listing, the commands that you type are in **bold**. The rest is what you'll see from the other computer. First, let's start by ftping to the host that has Project Gutenberg's files:

```
teal% ftp mrcnext.cso.uiuc.edu
Connected to mrcnext.cso.uiuc.edu.
220 mrcnext.cso.uiuc.edu FTP server (Version 5.1 (NeXT 1.0) Tue Jul
21, 1992) ready.
Name (mrcnext.cso.uiuc.edu:peterk): anonymous
331 Guest login ok, send ident as password.
Password: (I typed my e mail address here; you won't see it, so type
carefully.)
230 Guest login ok, access restrictions apply.
ftp>
```

I don't really know where everything is, so let's take a look at the directory. (I'm not going to show you the entire directory.)

```
ftp> dir
200 PORT command successful.
150 Opening ASCII mode data connection for /bin/ls.
total 137
-rw-r—r—  1 187     micro     1579  Jun  4    2000 README
-rw-r—r—  1 109     micro     1798  Jan  4    2000 README.bak
drwxrwxr-x 2 root    micro     1024  Oct  4    1999 amiga
dr-xr-xr-x 2 root    micro     1024  Jul 14    2000 bin
```

Did you notice the README file? Let's take a look at what it has to say:

```
ftp> get README "|more"
200 PORT command successful.
150 Opening ASCII mode data connection for README (1579 bytes).
This is an '040 NeXT cube with a 660 Meg hard drive.  In this public
directory is an NFS mount of the ftp directory on ftp.cso.uiuc.edu,
128.174.5.59, labelled "ux1".  It contains a lot more than 660 Meg.
```

```
Files/directories of interest:
amiga
        A few files for Amigans.  Look in ux1/amiga for more.
apple2
          For necromechanomaniacs.
Bible
          A copy of the KJB can be found on uxc.cso.uiuc.edu
drivers.zip
          A bunch of packet drivers for PC versions of Telnet.
cwp.zip
          Chinese Word Processor.  This is NOT a product of the
          University of Illinois, and we're NOT doing support for
          it.
          It is nonetheless useful, and it's here.
etext
          Michael Hart's Project Gutenberg electronic text
          collection.
```

There's more, but we're interested in the etext directory. Let's go there now and take a look at what's in it.

```
ftp> cd etext
250 CWD command successful.
ftp> dir
200 PORT command successful.
150 Opening ASCII mode data connection for /bin/ls.
total 54
-rw-r—r—     1 24      wheel    14300   May  1    07:03    0INDEX.GUT
-rw-r—r—     1 24      wheel      300   Sep 28    2000     ETEXT92
-rw-r—r—     1 24      wheel     9214   Jul 19    1998     LIST.COM
-rw-r—r—     1 24      wheel     4420   Jun  3    2000     NEWUSER.GUT
drwxr-xr-x   3 24      wheel     1024   Apr 29    17:00    articles
```

Again, there's more, but let's take a look at 0INDEX.GUT.

```
ftp> get 0INDEX.GUT "¦more"
200 PORT command successful.
550 0INDEX.GUT: No such file or directory.
```

211

Oops! I typed an O (capital "oh") instead of a 0 (zero). Let's try again.

```
ftp> get 0INDEX.GUT "|more"
200 PORT command successful.
150 Opening ASCII mode data connection for 0INDEX.GUT (14300
bytes).
etext93:
total 36522
-rw-r—r—  1 hart      1166473    Mar  1     1993    2sqrt10.txt
-rw-r—r—  1 hart       552131    Mar  1     1993    2sqrt10.zip
-rw-r—r—  1 hart       247391    Jun 29    17:10    32pri10.txt
-rw-r—r—  1 hart       124130    Jun 29    17:10    32pri10.zip
-rw-r—r—  1 hart       637842    Aug 31    22:56    7gabl10.txt
-rw-r—r—  1 hart       276240    Aug 31    22:57    7gabl10.zip
-rw-r—r—  1 hart        38818    Mar 31     1993    alad10.txt
```

It turns out that this file is a list of the Gutenberg files—not much use to us right now, because we don't know which is which. When we did a **dir** earlier, though, we saw another file called gutmar3.3. Let's see what that says.

```
ftp> get gutmar3.3 "|more"
200 PORT command successful.
150 Opening ASCII mode data connection for gutmar3.3 (14005 bytes).
****This is the Project Gutenberg Newsletter for March, 1993***
Our Goal, To Give Away One Trillion Etexts By December 31, 2001
*[10,000 titles to 100,000,000 people equals 1,000,000,000,000]
```

This file has more background information. Later in the file, we find a listing of some of the books available. The list includes this line:

```
Jan 1993 The World Factbook        (world192.xxx)
```

Unfortunately, this file doesn't show a complete listing; to find that, we'd probably have to spend more time digging around. Still, it shows us that *The World Factbook* is in a file called world192.xxx, and was put there in January of 1993. (The gutmar3.3 file lists other things, too: *Dr. Jekyll and Mr. Hyde, Far from the Madding Crowd*, Sophocles' *Oedipus Trilogy, The Time Machine* by H.G. Wells, The 1990 U.S. Census, *Alice in Wonderland*, and more.)

So, let's go get that *World Factbook*. First, we'll go to the etext93 directory, where the documents added in 1993 are stored.

```
ftp> cd etext93
250 CWD command successful.
```

Now we'll look for the *World Factbook*. This command will list all the files beginning with *world*:

```
ftp> dir world*
200 PORT command successful.
150 Opening ASCII mode data connection for /bin/ls.
total 9432
-rw-r—r—  1 24      wheel    2473400   Jul  6  2001  world192.txt
-rw-r—r—  1 24      wheel    1006254   Jul  6  2001  world192.zip
-rw-r—r—  1 24      wheel    2423749   Jun 19  2001   world92.txt
-rw-r—r—  1 24      wheel     992943   Jun 19  2001   world92.zip
-rw-r—r—  1 24      wheel    2638067   May  1 19:43   world93.txt
-rw-r—r—  1 24      wheel    1080105   May  1 19:46   world93.zip
226 Transfer complete.
remote: world*
414 bytes received in 0.15 seconds (2.7 Kbytes/s)
```

The gutmar3.3 file told us that the *World Factbook* was in world192.xxx. The *xxx* means the last three characters may vary; as you can see, there's a .txt version (ASCII text) and a .zip version (compressed using PKZIP). But you'll notice also that there's a version called world93.txt, probably the next year's version. Let's look:

```
ftp> get world93.text "¦more"
200 PORT command successful.
150 Opening ASCII mode data connection for world93.txt
(2638067 bytes).
**Welcome To The World of Free Plain Vanilla Electronic Texts**
**Etexts Readable By Both Humans and By Computers, Since 1971**
*These Etexts Prepared By Hundreds of Volunteers and Donations*
Information on contacting Project Gutenberg to get Etexts, and
```

213

This file goes on with introductory stuff, but finally, we see:

```
*The Project Gutenberg Edition of the 1993 CIA World Factbook*
Central Intelligence Agency
The World Factbook 1993
```

That's it, exactly what we're looking for. You can browse through the file a little way, and when you're ready to transfer it back to your own system, press **Ctrl-c**.

```
^C
426 Transfer aborted. Data connection closed.
226 Abort successful
local: |more remote: world93.txt
12679 bytes received in 3.9 seconds (3.2 Kbytes/s)
```

Now we're ready to transfer the file. We'll transfer the ZIP version; it's much smaller, and we can "unzip" it when we get back. (That's assuming you've got a DOS-based PC and a copy of PKUNZIP. If not, you'll want to use the text version.) However, we first have to change to a binary format using the **bin** or **binary** command. (If you're transferring text, don't use this command.)

```
ftp> bin
200 Type set to I.
ftp> get world93.zip
200 PORT command successful.
150 Opening BINARY mode data connection for world93.zip (1080105
bytes).
226 Transfer complete.
local: world93.zip remote: world93.zip
1080105 bytes received in 28 seconds (38 Kbytes/s)
```

We're finished in FTP, so let's get out:

```
ftp> bye
221 Goodbye.
```

If you've got a dial-in terminal connection, you still have to get the file from the service provider's computer back to yours. So let's look at file transfers.

File Transfers

If you have a dial-in terminal account, you are working at home or at your office on your computer, which is connected to your service provider's computer. When you get files using FTP, where do they go? Back to your directory on the service provider's computer. The question is, how do you get them back to your computer?

There are a few ways. Since most communications programs will let you do an xmodem transfer, we'll look at that first.

Xmodem

Most communications programs can work with xmodem to transmit files. It's quite easy. First, make sure your communications program is set up to receive files by xmodem. If you are using Windows Terminal, for example, select **Binary Transfers** from the **Settings** menu and click on the **Xmodem** option button.

At the UNIX shell, you'll enter the **xmodem** command by typing **xmodem**, followed by one of these:

sb Send binary: Use this if you are sending a binary file (see Chapter 18 for a discussion of binary vs. ASCII).

st Send text: Use this if you are sending a text (ASCII) file to an MS-DOS computer.

sa Send Apple: Use this if you are sending a text (ASCII) file to an Apple computer.

After you add one of the commands above, type the filename. Your complete command will look something like this:

```
xmodem st zap.txt
```

This sends the file named zap.txt in ASCII format to your computer. After you type the command and press **Enter**, you'll see this:

```
XMODEM Version 3.9 (November 1990) — UNIX-Microcomputer File
Transfer Facility
File zap.txt Ready to SEND in text mode
Estimated File Size 2K, 15 Sectors, 1845 Bytes
Estimated transmission time 2 seconds
Send several Control-X characters to cancel
```

215

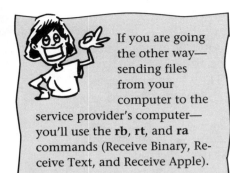

If you are going the other way—sending files from your computer to the service provider's computer—you'll use the **rb**, **rt**, and **ra** commands (Receive Binary, Receive Text, and Receive Apple).

You then tell your communications program to receive the file; in Windows Terminal, you would select **Receive Binary File** from the **Transfers** menu (even if you are sending a text file, you are using a binary transfer method to send it). You'll have to tell your communications program what file name to use. When the transfer is complete, you'll be returned to the UNIX shell prompt.

There are a lot of options available with the **xmodem** command (to read the xmodem manual pages, type **man xmodem** at the UNIX prompt and press **Enter**). For example, you can tell it to use *xmodem/crc* when receiving files (this isn't necessary when sending files because the receiving software will request that type of error-checking; Windows Terminal uses xmodem/crc). You can also use the **xmodem** command to send files using another protocol, ymodem, which many communications programs can use.

Zmodem

The xmodem and ymodem protocols are not necessarily your best options. Zmodem is actually much better. It's quite a bit faster, and while xmodem can send multiple files with a lot of messing around (assuming your communications software can accept multiple files, which it may not be able to do), zmodem makes it much easier to send several files at once.

Be careful when transferring files. These systems will usually overwrite files that have the same names as the ones being transferred. If you use zmodem, you can use the -p switch (as in **sz -p** *filename*) to make sure files aren't overwritten; but test this first, as it may not work with some systems. See the next section.

To run zmodem, begin by setting up your communications program to receive zmodem transfers (Windows Terminal can't use zmodem). Then use the command **sz** *filename*.

You can actually send several files at a time. For instance, **sz *.txt** sends all the .txt files in the directory; **sz file1 file2** sends both file1 and file2.

The nice thing about zmodem is that once you issue the command, that's it. You don't have to tell your system anything about the incoming files. As long as you've got zmodem receive set up, it will detect when the service provider's computer is sending data, and will even figure out the file names automatically. Zmodem is also

To see a summary of all the options, type **sz** and press **Enter** at the prompt.

simple to use for transferring files from your computer to the service provider's computer. You begin the transfer from your communications program; the service provider's computer detects it, and begins receiving automatically. Also, in some cases, zmodem can continue a download after the connection has been broken. For example, the next time you try to transfer the same file, zmodem may be able to recognize it as the file it hadn't finished transferring, and complete the previous operation.

There are a few command switches you need to know about when using zmodem:

-b Sends the file in binary format. This is the default anyway, so you won't normally need to use this.

-a This, in effect, sends an ASCII file to a DOS machine; it converts the UNIX new line character at the end of each line to the DOS carriage return/line feed characters.

-p This tells your computer not to overwrite any existing files with the same name. However, this option may not work with all systems, so experiment with it before you rely on it.

If you need to use more than one switch, you can combine them. For instance, type **sz -ap** *filename* to send a text file and ensure that it doesn't overwrite a file of the same name.

If you want more information about zmodem, use the **man sz** command to see the online manual.

Sending the CIA World Factbook

Because it's fast, I'm going to use zmodem to get the CIA *World Factbook* off my service provider's computer. If you don't have zmodem, use xmodem (type **xmodem -st world93.zip**, press **Enter**, and tell your communications program to get ready to receive the file). Using zmodem, my session looks like this:

```
teal% sz world93.zip
rz
*B0000000000
teal%
```

That's almost it. If you transferred the .zip version, you now have to unzip it. Go to the DOS prompt, change to the directory containing the file (make sure that you have a copy of PKUNZIP in that directory), and type

```
C:\DOWNLOAD>pkunzip world93.zip
```

Now press **Enter**. (Okay, you don't have to put the files in the same directory if you type a full path for each one, but this is the easy way.) That's it. In a few seconds you'll have an (almost) free copy of the CIA's 1993 *World Factbook*. You can open it in any word processor, and use the word processor's search feature to track down anything you need to know about Albania, Australia, or Zimbabwe.

Speedy Logins: Using the .netrc File

If you find yourself going to a particular FTP site frequently, maybe you should automate the login procedure. Use a text editor (such as vi) to create a file called .netrc in your home directory. Then enter this text:

```
machine hostname
login loginname
password password
```

Here's an example:

```
machine ftp.demon.co.uk
login anonymous
password peterk@csn.org
```

The next time you ftp to this site, here's what you'll see:

```
teal% ftp ftp.demon.co.uk
Connected to newgate.demon.co.uk.
220 newgate.demon.co.uk FTP server (Version 5.60 #1) ready.
331 Guest login ok, send ident as password.
230 Guest login ok, access restrictions apply.
ftp>
```

The .netrc logs in for you. It's quicker, and it doesn't make mistakes.

But Mine Doesn't Work That Way...

I've explained standard FTP, but there are variations. As you may remember, I told you that when you use the **dir** command, FTP asks the host to send a directory listing, and the host decides what to send. That means you'll see some differences between systems. The following sections outline some important things to remember.

DEC VMS Systems

File names on VMS systems consist of the name itself, an extension, and a version number (for example, READTHIS.TXT;5). You can ignore the version number. If the extension is .txt, the file is a text file you can read. If the extension is .dir, it's not a file at all, it's a directory. To change directories, use the **cd** command and the name without the extension (for example, **cd files**, not **cd files.dir**). Also, VMS systems separate subdirectories with periods, not slashes; DIR1/DIR2/DIR3 appears as DIR1.DIR2.DIR3. In addition, the **cd** command may not work normally for you on a VMS system. Instead of **cd ..**, you may need to use **cdup**. You may also have to name the subdirectory you want to move to (as in **cd [dir1.dir2.dir3]**), although the normal **cd dir1/dir2/dir3** may work on some systems.

DOS Systems

If you are a DOS user, you'll feel right at home when ftping to a DOS host (there are a few). DOS names consist of a name (up to eight characters) and an extension (up to three characters). In directory listings, directories will be indicated by **<dir>**. Also, you may be able to change disks to get to more directories while working on a DOS system (type cd *n:* where *n* is the disk letter). And while DOS uses backslashes to separate directories (dir1\dir2\dir3), you must use the forward slash when using the **cd** command in FTP (cd dir1/dir2/dir3).

IBM/VM Systems

VM machines store files on disks instead of in a directory system, and each disk requires that you log in. So to change to another disk, you type **cd** *login.disk*, where *login* is your login name for that disk, and *disk* is the disk itself. Then type **account** *password*. (If you are using anonymous FTP, you won't need the password.) File names on VM systems have two parts: the name itself and a file type. These parts are separated by spaces. When you use the **get** command, however, you'll separate the two parts with a period (**get** *name.type*).

Macintosh

On a Macintosh system, directories (or *folders* in Mac-speak) are indicated by a slash at the end of a name. In addition, file names may contain spaces. To work with a file that has spaces in its name, enclose the entire name in quotation marks (as in **get "this file" "|more"**). When you transfer such a file, you should rename it while transferring (use the command **get "this file" thisfile**).

FTP by Mail?

If you don't have access to FTP (many Internet mail-only users don't), there's still hope for you. It's possible to work by mail using *FTPmail*. Digital Equipment Corporation (DEC) kindly maintains a system that will ftp to any site for you. You just send FTPmail an e-mail message telling it what you want it to do, and away it goes. You'll send your message to **ftpmail@decwrl.dec.com**.

If you'd like to try this, send an e-mail message to this host. Don't include a subject, just write **help** at the beginning of the first line of the message. You'll get back a list of commands. For example, it will explain how to find a listing of a particular directory (using the index command).

Note that you might find FTPmail tricky to use. You need to know where (in which directory) the file you want is. That's not always easy, because people aren't always specific when they tell you to get something from an FTP site (either they don't remember exactly where a particular file is, or they figure that you'll be able to find it anyway). Even if they are specific, the file may get moved, or they may get the case wrong (remember that you need to spell the file name exactly as it really is, using uppercase and lowercase correctly). FTPmail is like working blind, but it may be worth a try if it's your only option.

To get a file from FTPmail, you'll put something like this in the body of a message:

```
connect hostname
chdir directorypath
binary
get filename
quit
```

Of course, if you want the file sent as ASCII, you'd omit the **binary** command. See the FTPmail help document for more information.

More Files by Mail: Special Servers and LISTSERV

There are two other ways to get files by mail: using various special servers, including LISTSERV servers (we looked at LISTSERV in Chapter 16). These are mail servers set up especially for distribution of files. You may see these sites mentioned elsewhere, with instructions to get a particular file from a particular mail address.

Some mailservers require that you send a message with the command **send** *filename* as the subject. Leave the body of the message blank. The file name may need to include the directory path. If you're not sure where the file that you need is, send a message with **help** as the subject.

When you are trying to grab mail from LISTSERV servers, put the command **get** *filename filetype* in the body of the message—not the subject. The files distributed by the LISTSERV servers use the IBM VM file name format, in which each file name has two parts: the name itself and the file type. To get a file, you have to know both parts.

It's Alive! Viruses and Other Nasties

If you haven't been alone in a cave for the past six or seven years, you've probably heard about computer viruses. A *virus* is a computer program that can reproduce itself, and even convince unknowing users to help spread it. It spreads far and wide, and can do incredible amounts of damage. As is true of real viruses, the effects of a virus on your system can range from almost unnoticeable to fatal. A virus can do something as harmless as display a Christmas tree on your screen, or it can destroy everything on your hard disk.

Viruses hide out in a variety of places. *Boot sector* viruses hide in a disk's boot sector, the part of the disk read into memory when the computer starts. From there, they can copy themselves onto the boot sectors of other disks. *File* viruses hide out in program files and copy themselves to other program files when someone runs that program.

Viruses and other malevolent computer bugs are real, and they do real damage. In 1988, 6,000 computers connected to the Internet were infected with a worm. (The Internet has grown tremendously since then; the numbers are surely higher today.) Just recently, a service provider in New York had to close down temporarily after its system became infected.

The term virus has become a "catch-all" for a variety of different digital organisms, such as bacteria (which reproduce and do no direct damage except using up disk space and memory); rabbits (which reproduce very quickly); Trojan horses (viruses embedded in otherwise-useful programs); bombs (a program that just sits and waits for a particular date or event before wreaking destruction— these are often left deep inside programs by disgruntled employees); and worms (programs that copy themselves from one computer to another, independent of other executable files, and "clog" the computers by taking over memory and disk space).

Unfortunately, security on the Internet is lax. Some computer BBS services (such as CompuServe) check their own systems for viruses regularly. But on the Internet it's up to each system administrator (and there are thousands of them) to keep his own system clean. If just one administrator does a bad job, a virus can get through and be carried by

FTP all over the world. Some system administrators are reacting by closing off some Internet services (not allowing users to FTP files, for example).

Tips for "Safe Computing"

If you are just working with e-mail and perhaps ftping documents, you're okay. The problem of viruses arises when you transfer programs. (That's not to say your directories on your service provider's system can't get infected, but if you don't transfer programs back to your own computer, it won't get infected; if you don't ftp programs to your service provider's system, you won't introduce viruses. Even so, another user may.)

If you do plan to transmit programs, perhaps the best advice is to get a good anti-virus program. (They're available for all computer types.) Each time you transmit an executable file, use your anti-virus program to check it. Also, make sure you keep good backups of your data. Although backups can also become infected with viruses, if a virus hits, at least you can reload your backup data and use an anti-virus program to clean the files (some backup programs check for viruses while backing up).

For more information about staying safe on the Internet, see Chapter 24.

The Least You Need to Know

➤ Send a binary file with xmodem using this command: **xmodem sb** *filename*.

➤ To send a text file with xmodem, use **st** instead of **sb**. To send text to an Apple computer, use **sa**.

➤ Zmodem is generally quicker and easier to use than xmodem.

➤ Send binary files with zmodem using this command: **sz** *filename filename filename*.

➤ Send text files using this command: **sz -a** *filename filename filename*.

➤ The .netrc file lets you automate your FTP logins; FTP automatically enters the appropriate login name and password for you.

➤ Not all FTP hosts are UNIX machines. VMS, DOS, and Macintosh hosts work in a similar (but slightly different) way.

➤ Viruses are real and dangerous. Use anti-virus software to check files you transfer.

## Chapter 20

Archie the File Searcher

In This Chapter

➤ How Archie indexes files

➤ Using an Archie telnet site

➤ Searching for files

➤ Sending Archie lists home via e-mail

➤ Searching for file descriptions

➤ Using your service provider's Archie client

➤ Mail order Archie

FTP is all very well, but how do you know where to go to find the file you want? Sometimes you'll see the FTP site mentioned in e-mail or a document you found somewhere. But what if you know the file you are looking for, but have no idea where to go to find it?

Archie to the rescue. Designed by a few guys at McGill University in Canada, *Archie* is a system that indexes FTP sites, listing the files that are available at each site. Archie lists several million files at over a thousand FTP sites, and provides a surprisingly quick way to find out where to go to grab a file in which you are interested.

Archie has a *descriptive-index search*. That means you can search for a particular subject and find files related to that subject. (Read more about this later in this chapter.)

More Client/Server Stuff

As with certain other Internet systems, Archie is set up using a "client/server" system. An Archie *server* is a computer that periodically takes a look at all the Internet FTP sites around the world, and builds a list of all their available files. Each server builds a database of those files. An Archie *client* program can then come along and search the server's database, using it as an index.

It's generally believed in Internet-land that it doesn't matter much which Archie server you use because they all do much the same thing; some are simply a few days more recent than others. This isn't always true. Sometimes you may get very different results from two different servers. If, for example, one server finds two "hits," another might find seven.

Getting to Archie

There are several ways to use Archie:

➤ Use an Archie client on your service provider's computer, either from a menu option or a shell command.

➤ Use telnet to get to an Archie server site.

➤ Use e-mail to send questions to an Archie server site.

If your service provider's system has an Archie client setup, you should use it when you can (instead of telneting to an Archie server) because it will cut down on network traffic. However, this arrangement has limitations: it may be much slower than telneting to a server, and you won't be able to do everything you could do if you telneted. We'll take a look at the telnet method first.

Telneting to Archie's Place

Here are a few Archie servers to get you started:

archie.ans.net	147.225.1.2	USA, ANS
archie.internic.net	198.49.45.10	USA, AT&T (NY)
archie.rutgers.edu	128.6.18.15	USA, Rutgers U.
archie.au	139.130.4.6	Australia
archie.th-darmstadt.de	130.83.22.60	Germany
archie.wide.ad.jp	133.4.3.6	Japan
archie.sogang.ac.kr	163.239.1.11	Korea

To find the latest list of Archie servers, send an e-mail message to an Archie server, with this address: **archie@***archieserver* (for example, **archie@archie.rutgers.edu**). In the body of the message, type **servers** on the first line.

All Archie servers are in English, no matter which country they're in. However, the introductory text may be written in the host's native language.

Which should you use? That depends. A general rule is, the closer the better, because it generates less network traffic. (Your message only has to travel over, say, a few hundred miles of the network as opposed to thousands of miles.) But you'll find you won't be able to get onto some of these servers; some may be too busy. Archie is a very popular service, and some servers receive more attempts to get into the system than they can handle. Once they have more than a certain number of people using the system, they simply deny access.

Other systems have a policy of denying everyone access between certain hours (8:00 a.m. and 8:00 p.m., for example). If you are denied, try to use this server again later, or try another one.

How do you get to one of these servers? For example, type

```
teal% telnet archie.rutgers.edu
```

and press **Enter**. When you are asked to log in, simply type **archie** and press **Enter**.

Searching a Server Via Telnet

Before you begin searching for a file name, you should figure out the type of search that you want to use. You have the following choices:

exact You must type the exact name of the file for which you are looking.

regex You will type a UNIX regular expression. That means that Archie will regard some of the characters in the word you type as wild cards. (If you don't understand regular expressions, you're better off avoiding this type of search.)

sub This tells Archie to search within file names for whatever you type. That is, it will look for all names that match what you type, as well as all names that include the characters you typed. If you are searching for *wincode*, for example, Archie will find *wincode* and *wincoded*. Also, when you use a sub search, you don't need to worry about the case of the characters; Archie will find *wincode* and *Wincode*.

subcase This is like the sub search, except you need to enter the case of the word correctly: if you enter *wincode*, Archie will find *wincoded* but not *Wincode*. (By the way, Wincode is a handy little shareware uuencode/uudecode program for Microsoft Windows.)

More often than not, you'll want to use the sub search. It takes a little longer than others, but it's more likely to find what you are looking for.

Each server expects to see a different type of search. If you type **show search** and press **Enter**, Archie will show you which one it assumes you are going to use. In fact, when you first log into Archie, you may see

```
# 'search' (type string) has the value 'regex'
```

or a similar line. To set the search to another form, type **set search** *type* (**set search sub**, for example).

So Where's My File?

Now, to get down to the nitty gritty. Where's the file you want? We are going to use the **prog** command to search. Let's search for *wincode*. First, we're going to set the search type to sub. Then we'll search.

prog is the original Archie command used to find a file. Newer versions can also accept the **find** command. Both do the same thing; it doesn't matter which one you use.

```
archie> set search sub
archie> prog wincode
```

When Archie begins, you may see something like this:

```
# Search type: sub.
# Your queue position: 3
# Estimated time for completion: 00:19
working... ¦
```

Or, you might just see this, which shows you how many files Archie has found, and the percentage of the index it has searched so far:

```
# matches / % database searched:    7 /80%
```

Either way, if you are lucky and Archie finds something, eventually you'll see something like this:

```
Host ftp.utas.edu.au    (131.217.1.20)
Last updated 03:56  7 Oct 1994
    Location: /pc/win31/util/decode
        FILE    -r—r—r—   60519 bytes  19:35 26 Sep 1994  wincode.zip


Host tasman.cc.utas.edu.au    (131.217.10.1)
Last updated 03:55  7 Oct 1994
    Location: /pc/win31/util/decode
        FILE    -r—r—r—   60519 bytes  19:35 26 Sep 1994  wincode.zip
```

That's it. Now you know where to go to find the files you are looking for. Notice the word **FILE** on the left side of the listing. Archie searches for both files and directories that match your criteria. In this case, it has found files, but sometimes you'll also see **DIRECTORY**. Above each listing there's also a **Location**, which shows the directory (or subdirectory) in which you should look for this file or subdirectory. A line or two above there, you'll see the **Host** line; this is the host computer to which you should ftp to get the file. For example, if you wanted to get the first file in our list, you would ftp to **ftp.utas.edu.au** (a computer in Australia), and go into the directory **/pc/win31/util/decode**.

If the list is long, and it shoots by faster than you can read it, use the **set pager** command and run the search again. Now the list will stop after each page. You can press **Spacebar** to see the next page, or press **q** and **Enter** to stop the listing. (Turn off this feature using **unset pager**.) You can also send long lists home using e-mail (see the next section).

You should know, however, that file names are not always set in stone. With thousands of different people posting millions of different files on thousands of different computers, sometimes file names get changed a little. It may be that all these files are actually the same program—or maybe three or four different programs.

Sometimes you'll find clues, though. The Wincode files are in directories that clearly have something to do with Microsoft Windows—notice that one of the directories in the path is win31 (as in Windows 3.1). You'll often find directories with names like Macintosh, DOS, UNIX, and so on.

Sending It Home

If you are doing a lot of Archie searches, or you get a very long list, you can send the information "home" to your e-mail address. To do so, type **mail** *emailaddress* and press **Enter**. The last list Archie found for you will be sent to your e-mail inbox. If you are going to use this feature several times, you can even store your e-mail address (temporarily). First, type **set mailto** *emailaddress* and press **Enter**. Now you can type the **mail** command alone, without bothering to include the e-mail address.

"Whatis" the Descriptive Index?

Archie has a **whatis** search that you might try. This command searches
a *descriptive index*, an index of file descriptions. Not all files indexed by
Archie have a description, but many do. For example, you might type:

```
archie> whatis encryption
```

You would see a list of descriptions like this:

```
codon          Simple encryption algorithm
des            Data encryption system (DES) routines and a login
               front-end
des-no-usa     Data encryption system (DES) code free of US
               restrictions
```

Sometimes you won't be able to figure out how your keyword fits
with some of these files, but that doesn't matter, as long as some of
them look like what you want. Notice the word on the left side of each
line. If you want to find out where the listed file is, type **prog** *name*. If
you type **prog des-no-usa**, Archie would list the DES encryption files
that you can download without worrying about U.S. export restrictions.

When you are finished working in Archie, type **exit** and press
Enter.

But Wait! There's More!

You can, of course, do more with Archie. You can view a list of all the
FTP sites included in this particular Archie server's index: type **list** and
press **Enter**. You can get into what may be a rather confusing "help"
system (**help**), list Archie servers (**servers**—although the list may not
be up to date), limit the number of files Archie will find (**maxhits**
number), and plenty more.

If you want to learn more about Archie, spend a frustrating half
hour in the help system. Type **help** and press **Enter**; you may have to
then press **q** to get to the **help>** prompt. At the prompt, type **?** and
press **Enter** to see a list of help topics. You can now type the name of a
command and press **Enter** to view information about that command.

Press **Spacebar** to go to the next page; press **q** to return to the **help>** prompt. To get back to the **archie>** prompt, type **done** and press **Enter**.

Working with Clients

Many service providers have loaded Archie clients. If your service provider has loaded an Archie client, you don't have to worry about finding a client or a server. You can just select **Archie** from a menu or use a UNIX command to use it. For example, on the system in which I work, I can select **8. File Transfer (FTP)/** from the menu; then **5. Search FTP sites (Archie)/** to get to Archie. I can select from two types of searches (Exact search or Substring search), and I'll see a box in which I type the file name for which I want to search.

You may also be able to type **archie** *searchstring* at the command prompt to start your search.

Using your service provider's client will be a little different from using the Archie server itself. You won't use the **prog** command, and you won't set the type of search before searching. Instead, you'll specify it at the same time, as in this example:

```
teal% archie -s wincode
```

This starts a sub search for *wincode*; that is, it tells Archie to look for any file name that contains *wincode*, and it doesn't care about case. As a result, Archie would find **Wincode** or **wincoded**. (For a description of the four search types—exact, regex, sub, and subcase—see the telneting section earlier in this chapter.)

So here's how you can enter a command. You'll always start with **archie**, and you'll finish with the name for which you are searching. Everything in between is optional. You can select the type of search with these options:

-e   Archie will do an exact search.

-r   Archie will do a regex search.

-s   Archie will do a sub search.

-c   Archie will do a subcase search.

If you don't use one of these options, Archie will do an exact search. What, then, is the point of having an -e option, if omitting it does an exact search anyway? Because you could include -e and one of the other three. By doing so, you tell Archie to do an exact search, and do one of the other searches if it doesn't find anything. Note, however, that you can't combine the other three.

There are a few more options you can use with Archie:

-h*hostname*   If you want, you can tell the Archie client which Archie server to use. Each client is set up with a default server, but if you have a reason to search a particular server, you can enter **-h***hostname* to tell it which one to go to.

-m*number*   This tells Archie to limit the number of files it will find. If you use **-m1**, for example, it will stop when it finds the first match. If you don't use this option, it will stop at the 95th match.

Unfortunately, using Archie from your service provider's system can prove to be very slow. You might even imagine it has locked up (who knows, it might have!). Maybe you can start Archie running and find something else to do for five (or ten) minutes. If you get tired of waiting, pressing **Ctrl-c** should stop it.

-l   You'll see a simplified output, with one line (consisting of a time and date, file size, host name, and file or directory name) for each entry.

Saving It in a File

If you want, you can copy the search results into a file by following the name you are searching for with >*textfilename*, such as:

```
archie -s wincode >wincode.txt
```

This tells Archie to do a sub search for *wincode*, and copy the output into a file called wincode.txt. This is useful when you are likely to get a big list, or if you want to save the information and use it later.

Mail Order Archie

If you don't want to spend time looking for an Archie server you can use, or waiting while it works, you may want to send an e-mail message to an Archie server and wait for the response. You could also use Archie by mail if you don't have access to telnet (some Internet users don't).

Using Archie by mail is actually quite simple. You send a message to **archie@***archieserver*. You can choose whichever Archie server you want.

Leave the **Subject** line blank, but put the commands in the body of the message. Each command must be on a separate line (you can put as many commands as you want in a message), and the first character of each command must be the first character on its line. Here's a sample message created with UNIX mail.

```
teal% mail archie@archie.rutgers.edu
Subject:
servers
prog wincode
whatis encryption
.
Cc:
teal%
```

The first command, **servers**, asks Archie to send you a list of Archie servers (remember, this list may not be complete; you may want to try several different servers to get a complete picture). The **prog** command tells Archie to search for *wincode*, and the **whatis** command tells Archie to search for the description *encryption*, as we saw earlier.

How soon will you get a response? Some responses may take just a few minutes. Others (even responses to commands in the same e-mail message) may take hours. Archie says that if you wait two days without any response, there's probably a problem, and you may want to try the **set mailto** command to make sure Archie has your correct e-mail address.

You can also use the following commands:

set search *type*   As we saw earlier, this command tells Archie which type of search you want to do: exact, regex, sub, or subcase.

compress   Tells Archie to compress the listing before sending it to you. You'll have to uncompress it to read it (see Chapter 18 for more information about uuencoding). You may want to use this option if you expect the list to be very large.

help   Sends a Mail Archie user guide.

site *host*   You can enter a host IP address (the numbers that describe a host's location) or domain name, and Archie will send a list of all the files held at that FTP site.

quit   This tells Archie to ignore everything that follows in the message. If you have a mail system that inserts a signature file automatically at the end of each message, use **quit** to make sure you don't get the help information each time you send an Archie request. (If Archie sees any command it doesn't understand, it automatically sends the help information.)

set mailto *mailaddress*   If you find your Archie requests go unanswered, it may be because your mail program is not inserting enough information in the **From** line. You can use this command to enter the path to which you want Archie's response sent.

If you like the idea of working with Archie through the mail, send the **help** command to get the user's guide. There are plenty of little tricks you can use with this system.

The Least You Need to Know

➤ Archie servers index available files at over a thousand FTP sites periodically. Archie clients can read the indexes.

➤ It's important to know which type of search you are doing; type **show search** and press **Enter**. To change the search type, type **set search** *type* and press **Enter**. The *type* can be exact, regex, sub, or subcase.

➤ Use the **prog** *filename* command to search for a file.

➤ Use the **mail** *emailaddress* command to send a list to your e-mail inbox.

➤ Use the **whatis** *description* command to search for a file description.

➤ Your service provider probably has a client setup you can use from a menu or the UNIX prompt (although it may be slow).

➤ Using Archie by mail can be easy and convenient. Send the message to **archie@***archieserver*. Put the commands in the body of the message.

Digging Through the Internet with Gopher

Having seen how complicated the Internet can be, you may be happy to learn that it doesn't always have to be so difficult. You can use a *Gopher* to help you find your way around. No, a Gopher is not a furry garden pest; it's a menu system that helps you find telnet and FTP sites.

The Gopher system is based on several hundred Gopher servers (computers that contain the indexes) and thousands of Gopher clients (computers that are running the Gopher menu software that accesses the server's indexes). All servers are public, so any client can access the information from any server.

Each time a client starts, it has to get the information it needs from the server. In other words, when you start the Gopher menu (I'll explain how in a moment), the menu software goes out onto the network and grabs all the information it needs from one of the servers. You can even use *bookmarks* to create your own menu of places you frequent.

Where does all the information come from? Well, first a system administrator decides to make areas on his or her host computer available to the public (so users can come in and take files, run databases, play games, and so on). Then the host administrator informs the Gopher server administrators, so they can add the information to their indexes.

Which Gopher Do You Want to Use?

There are hundreds of Gopher servers, and thousands of Gopher clients. Unless you install a client (which I'll explain in a moment), you don't have to worry about the servers. But which client are you going to use? You have a few options:

Why **Gopher**? For three reasons. First, it was originally developed at the University of Minnesota, home of the "Golden Gophers." Second, as most Americans know, "gofer" is slang for someone who "goes fer" things—and Gopher's job is to "go fer" files and stuff. And third, the system digs its way through the Internet, like a gopher in a burrow. By the way, when you use Gopher you are traveling through **Gopherspace**.

Maybe your service provider's system is based on Gopher. Some service providers have based their own user interface on the Gopher system (the menu system we looked at in Chapter 8).

You can run Gopher from the UNIX prompt. While you may not see the Gopher menu when you log in, it may be available when you type **gopher** and press **Enter** at the UNIX shell.

You can telnet to a Gopher site. Some computers will let you log in on a telnet connection and use their Gopher system. However, this practice is falling out of favor because it creates a lot of network traffic, and many administrators feel you should set up your own Gopher client (or get your system administrator to set up a Gopher client). Some systems that (until recently) allowed telnet users to use their Gopher system are now denying access to outsiders.

You can set up your own Gopher client. If you have a permanent connection or a dial-in direct account, you can set up your own Gopher client. There's software available for just about any type of computer. We'll look at where to find it a little later.

Using Your Service Provider's Gopher

Most Internet users will work with their service provider's Gopher, the one already installed on their systems. When you log in, you may find you are already in Gopher. If you see a menu system like the following, there's a good chance you are in a Gopher.

```
                    << SuperMenu Main Menu >>
    —>   1.  About SuperMenu.
         2.  Search SuperMenu Titles <?>
         3.  Commercial Services/
         4.  Communities/
         5.  Databases/
         6.  Education/
         7.  Events & Entertainment/
         8.  File Transfer (FTP)/
         9.  Help/
        10.  Libraries/
        11.  Mail/
        12.  News and Weather/
        13.  Phone Books/
        14.  SuperNet Services/
        15.  Tools for Information Retrieval/
   Help ?   Quit q   Main-Menu m   Menu-Up u   BackPg <   NextPg >  Page:1/1
```

Notice that some of the menu options have a slash (/) at the end; that's a typical Gopher indication that selecting this option leads to another menu, a *submenu*. Notice also the commands at the bottom. These are typical Gopher menu commands. In addition, there's even an About option right at the top. If you select this option (at least on this particular system), you'll find that this is, indeed, a Gopher system.

Starting from the UNIX Shell

If you don't see a Gopher menu when you log in, you may be able to start Gopher from the system prompt (the UNIX shell if you are

You can also use this command method to define where you want to go. For example, **gopher yaleinfo.yale.edu 7000** will take you to a Yale University Gopher site.

working on a UNIX host). Simply type **gopher** and press **Enter**. We can hope your service provider has set up a Gopher client. If so, they will have defined the **gopher** command so that it goes out to a Gopher server somewhere, grabs the relevant information, and builds the Gopher menu for you. Again, you'll see something similar to the menu we just looked at.

Maybe your service provider does it differently. Perhaps you don't run a command from the UNIX prompt; instead you might have to select a command from a different menu system. If you can't find Gopher, ask your service provider how to get to it, or check the documentation you got when you first opened your account.

Using Someone Else's Gopher Through Telnet

It's possible your service provider's system administrator hasn't set up Gopher. If not, ask if he or she could do so. In the meantime, see if you can use someone else's Gopher. It used to be that you could telnet to another computer and use Gopher from there. It's still possible, but with the incredible increase in Internet traffic in the past year, it's becoming more difficult. Some Gopher sites that used to allow public access now limit Gopher use to their own accounts. Still, if you want to telnet, you can try these sites:

consultant.micro.umn.edu　Log in as **gopher**. This system says it will accept outside gophering, but it may not actually do so. The system may simply "timeout" before you are connected. They are trying to discourage telnet users from gophering. (This is the University of Minnesota, the home of the Gopher.)

hafnhaf.micro.umn.edu　Log in as **gopher**. This is the University of Minnesota again.

pubinfo.ais.umn.edu　The University of Minnesota yet again, but this host is a 3270 host, so you get there using the **tn3270** command instead of telnet (**tn3270 pubinfo.ais.umn.edu**).

library.wustl.edu　No login required (Washington University, St. Louis, Missouri).

ux1.cso.uiuc.edu　Log in as **gopher** (University of Illinois).

panda.uiowa.edu   No login required (University of Iowa).

gopher.sunet.se   Log in as **gopher**. (This is in Sweden, but the menus are in English.)

info.anu.edu.au   Log in as **info** (Australia).

gopher.chalmers.se   Log in as **gopher**. (This is in Sweden, and the menus are in Swedish and English. This can be confusing if you don't speak Swedish, because the Swedish comes first.)

tolten.puc.cl   Log in as **gopher** and press **Enter**. (This is in Chile, and it's mainly in Spanish, with a little English.)

pinto.isca.uiowa.edu (USA) and **ecnet.ec** (in Ecuador)   You can, reportedly, gopher to these sites, but I haven't managed to get through. All the others, at the time of writing, did accept telnet gophering.

Here We Go—Let's Gopher It!

Let's do a little gophering. In all my examples, I'm going to assume you are using the most common type of Gopher client, known as the Curses Gopher.

Whichever method you use (telnet or your service provider's Gopher), you're going to arrive at a screen that is something like this:

```
              Internet Gopher Information Client 2.0 pl10
                 Root gopher server: hafnhaf.micro.umn.edu


    —>   1.   Information About Gopher/
         2.   Computer Information/
         3.   Internet file server (ftp) sites/
         4.   Fun & Games/
         5.   Libraries/
         6.   Mailing Lists/
         7.   News/
         8.   Other Gopher and Information Servers/
         9.   Phone Books/
         10.  Search Gopher Titles at the University of Minnesota <?>
         11.  Search lots of places at the U of M <?>
         12.  UofM Campus Information/


Press ? for Help, q to Quit                            Page: 1/1
```

The main menu screen may have some kind of system title—Washington University Libraries, Cornell University, Electronic Library Information System at ANU, or whatever. In the example, it simply shows the root server, the location of the Gopher server that is providing the information.

> While working in the Gopher menus, you don't need to press **Enter** to carry out a command (unless you're told to do so). For example, to go to the previous menu, simply press **u**. There's no need to press Enter after the u.

Below the title lines are the menu options, each one numbered. You can type the number you want to select, or move the arrow (—>) to it, and press **Enter** or the right arrow to select it. Move the arrow using your keyboard's up and down arrow keys. If they won't work, try the j and k keys. Here are some other commands you'll need:

u or left arrow	Return to the previous menu
m	Return to the main menu
Spacebar or > or + or **PgDn**	View the next page in long menus
b or < or - or **PgUp**	View the previous page in long menus
q	Exit Gopher (the system will ask you to confirm)
Q	Exit Gopher immediately (no confirmation)

Play with these commands for a few minutes, and you'll soon get the hang of it.

What Are the Symbols at the Ends of Menu Options?

Notice that each menu option has some kind of symbol or word at the end. These symbols and words are described in the following list. The example on page 241 shows only the first two of these, but you may see the others elsewhere.

/	This indicates that selecting the menu option displays another menu (that it is a *directory*).
<?>	Select one of these menu options, and you'll be able to enter a search word.
. (period)	Select this option, and Gopher will display a document.
<TEL>	Selecting this option telnets you to another computer system.
<bin> or <PC Bin>	This marks a DOS file that has been compressed with an archive program such as PKZIP.
<Movie>	This signifies a video file.
<Picture>	This represents a graphics file.
<HQX>	This leads to a BinHex file, a Macintosh file that has been converted to ASCII so it can be transferred as e-mail.

There are plenty of other such indicators, some of which are numbers or letters. You can check what an item is by using the = command. Just place the arrow next to the item in question and press =, and you'll see something like this:

```
Name=disinfectant33.sea.hqx
Type=4
Port=70
Path=ftp:ftp.acns.nwu.edu@/pub/disinfectant/disinfectant33.sea.hqx
Host=gopher1.cit.cornell.edu
```

At the top, it shows you the menu option name (which we know already, of course). The next line shows the item type. These are the types you may see:

0	A text file. Select it and you'll be able to read the file page by page. This is the same as a period (.) at the end of the menu option.
1	A directory. Selecting this option leads to another menu. This is the same as a slash (/) at the end of the menu option.

243

2   A menu option that leads you to a CSO "phone book" you can use to find Internet users.

4   A BinHex Macintosh file.

5   A DOS compressed file, such as a ZIP or ARC file. This is the same as <PC BIN> at the end of the menu option. (You'll need the appropriate decompression utility to use the file unless it's a self-extracting archive file, in which case it has the extension .EXE.)

6   A UUENCODed file. You'll need UUDECODE to convert the file to its original format.

7   Select this option and you'll be prompted to type a search word. This is the same as <?> at the end of the menu option.

8   This menu option takes you to a telnet session.

9   Select this option, and you'll be sent a binary file. You don't necessarily want to do this unless your system is set up to receive such a file.

T   This menu option takes you to a tn3270 connection (an IBM 3270 equivalent of the telnet session).

s   A *mulaw sound file*. Your system may not be set up to use this.

g   A GIF graphics file.

M   An e-mail file in MIME file-transfer format.

Some of the fancier Gopher clients have various "viewers" that can accept the more unusual types of data. For example, if a client has a *GIF viewer*, and you select a GIF graphics file, you'll actually be able to see the picture on your screen. The basic Curses Gopher client cannot do that. In fact, you'll be better off if you don't try getting data types that your Gopher client can't handle. At best, it's a waste of time. At worst, your computer may crash.

The information that appears after the type line varies, but it will often help you find a file if you can't transfer the file using Gopher. For example, if you can find the host and path, you may be able to use FTP to get to the host, and use the **cd** command to go directly to the directory containing the file.

244

Saving Stuff

Of course, traveling through Gopherspace is all very well, but what about saving what you find? There are ways to save files and documents, depending on where your Gopher client is.

If you are using a client on your own computer (or your service provider's computer), you will be able to save stuff. If you are using a telnet Gopher session, your options are more limited. I'm going to assume you are working with your own or your service provider's Gopher; some of what I describe next won't work if you are telneting.

Saving a Document

There are several ways to save a document. First, you can save it while you are reading it. Press **q** to stop reading it, and you'll see this:

```
— —Press <ENTER> for next page, q to exit— —q
Press 's' to save this file or any other key to continue:
```

Press s and you'll see this:

```
+ — — — — — — — — — — — — — — — — — — — — — — — +
¦ Save in file:    Lawyer-Jokes                 ¦
¦                              [Cancel ^G] [Accept · Enter] ¦
+ — — — — — — — — — — — — — — — — — — — — — — — +
```

Simply press **Enter**, and you've saved the file. If you are working with your service provider's Gopher client, it's in your home directory.

In most cases, you can simply press **s** instead of pressing **q** first. Try it. You can even use this method at the menu itself. Just place the arrow (—>) next to the menu option and press **s** (remember that menu options that end with . are documents).

If you are working on a dial-in terminal connection with your service provider's Gopher client, you may want to send the data back to your system. Type **D** to see the following box:

```
                        Humor
      1.  Alice in UNIX Land.
      2.  Backwoods Fusion.
      3.  Beer_vs_Cucum+ — — — —Lawyer Jokes— — — — —+
      4.  Berkeley.      ¦                             ¦
      5.  C-Programming¦   1. Zmodem                   ¦
      6.  C-Shell.      ¦   2. Ymodem                   ¦
      7.  Car-Acronyms.¦   3. Xmodem-1K                 ¦
      8.  Chai's C Bibl¦   4. Xmodem-CRC                ¦
      9.  Final Exam.   ¦   5. Kermit                   ¦
     10.  Hacker Test.  ¦   6. Text                     ¦
     11.  How To Take N¦  Choose a download method:     ¦
 —>  12.  Lawyer Jokes.¦  [Cancel ^G]   [Choose 1-6]    ¦
     13.  McDonnell Dou+ — — — — — — — — — — — — — — —+
```

If your communications program is set to a particular type of file transfer, type the number associated with it, and away you go. In the case of zmodem, your program will start automatically. In other cases, you'll have to tell it to begin (see Chapter 19 for more information about file transfers). When the transfer is finished, press **Enter** to return to the Gopher menu.

Saving Files

In some cases, you can use Gopher in place of FTP to transfer files across the world. (If you telnet to a Gopher client, you won't be able to do this.) The procedures are similar to those used for grabbing text files. Simply select the option that leads to the file from the menu: type its number and press **Enter**, or place the arrow next to it and press **Enter** or **s**. You'll see the same **Save in File** box we looked at a moment ago. To download using a file transfer method such as zmodem or xmodem, place the arrow next to the option and press **D**.

Make sure you press **D** and not **d**! The **d** command removes menu options (we'll learn more about that when we discuss bookmarks, in a moment). If you did press **d**, your menu option probably disappeared. To get it back, you'll have to go back one menu (**u**) and then return (**Enter**). If you remove it from the main menu, though, you'll have to leave the Gopher client and restart it.

Searching for Entries

In long menus, you can search for a particular menu option by pressing / and then typing the word you are looking for. When you do, you'll see something like this (I'm searching for *bio* in this example):

```
+ — — — — — — — — — — — — — — — — — — — — — — — — — — +
¦ Search directory titles for    bio                 ¦
¦                               [Cancel ^G] [Accept - Enter] ¦
+ — — — — — — — — — — — — — — — — — — — — — — — — — — +
```

When you press **Enter**, the arrow will move to the first entry that matches what you typed. Press **n** to move to the next matching entry. In this way you can search for all entries related to a subject (in this case, biology—EMBnet Bioinformation Resource, Center for Genetic Eng. & Biotech, and so on).

Create Your Own Menu: Placing Bookmarks

While you're working in Gopher, you might want to place *bookmarks*. Bookmarks let you create a list of menu options in which you are interested. You can travel around and mark the things you think you may want to check into further, and then come back and examine each one in more detail.

Use these commands to place bookmarks (remember, they're case-sensitive):

a   Adds the selected menu item to the bookmark list.

A   Adds the current menu to the bookmark list.

v   Displays the list of bookmarks.

d   Deletes a bookmark from the list.

For example, when you find something you want to mark, press **a**. You'll see something like this:

```
+ — — — — — — — — — — — — — — — — — — — — — — — — — +
¦ Name for this bookmark:                           ¦
¦   Lawyer Jokes                                    ¦
¦                    [Cancel ^G] [Erase: ^U] [Accept - Enter] ¦
+ — — — — — — — — — — — — — — — — — — — — — — — — — +
```

Press **Enter** to place the bookmark. (If you want to enter a different name for the bookmark, press **Ctrl-u** and then type the new one.)

Later, when you want to view all the bookmarks, just press **v**. You'll see something like this:

```
          Internet Gopher Information Client 2.0 pl10
                             Bookmarks
     —>   1.   University of Western Sydney/
          2.   Empire of the Petal Throne/
          3.   Virtual Spaces at U Texas/
          4.   Guns n' Roses.
          5.   Killer Dwarfs.
          6.   X.500 Gateway/
          7.   Lawyer Jokes.
```

This is just like any other Gopher menu (you select items in the same way), but it's a menu that you created.

Of course, if you are using a menu on another system, these bookmarks will be lost when you leave the system. If you are using a Gopher client on your own computer—or even on your service provider's system—the bookmarks will be saved, which is very convenient. In effect, you can build your own menu of frequently used menu options, and view the menu at any time by pressing **v**.

Finding your way back to somewhere you've been before in Gopherspace can be very frustrating. If you think you may need to return, create a bookmark and enter your own title if you wish (something you're more likely to remember).

Using Veronica

There are hundreds of servers in Gopherspace, and even a system that's intended to make the Internet easier to use could do with its own system to make itself easier to use. Enter *Veronica*, a frequently updated index system that you can search.

Veronica is an example of that American habit of picking a word to be an acronym, and *then* finding the words to fit. Veronica means Very Easy Rodent-Oriented Net-wide Index to Computerized Archives, and is named after Archie's girlfriend. Recently, a new, similar search tool has appeared; it's called Jughead (named after one of Archie's friends) and is also a strange acronym.

Most Gopher systems will have a menu option for Veronica some-where (something like **3. Search Topics in Gopherspace Using Veronica/**). Select this option, and you'll see something like this:

```
Search Gopherspace using Veronica
—>1.   Search gopherspace at NYSERNet <?>
   2.   Search gopherspace at PSINet <?>
   3.   Search gopherspace at University of Pisa <?>
   4.   Search gopherspace at University of Cologne <?>
   5.   Search Gopher Directory Titles at NYSERNet <?>
   6.   Search Gopher Directory Titles at PSINet <?>
   7.   Search Gopher Directory Titles at University of Pisa <?>
   8.   Search Gopher Directory Titles at University of Cologne <?>
   9.                                                          .
  10. *** 100% Experimental WWW indexer (NorthStar) ***/
  11.                                                          .
  12. FAQ:  Frequently-Asked Questions about veronica (1993/08/23).
  13. How to compose  veronica queries (NEW June 24) READ ME!!.
            Search Topics in GopherSpace Using Veronica
```

There are different Veronica servers—hosts that maintain Veronica databases. The four shown here are not the only ones; you may find different ones on your Gopher client.

You can even place the result of a Veronica search into your custom menu using the **A** command (to create a bookmark). If you are using your own Gopher client or your service provider's, this will be saved when you close the client and will be there the next time you return. However, what is actually being saved is the search statement. Each time you select it from your Bookmarks menu, the search is carried out. Therefore, if you deleted any menu options the last time, they'll be back. Still, you can always add individual menu options to your Bookmarks menu using the **a** command.

Notice that there are two sorts of searches: you can search all titles or directory titles. The former will search for all information stored in Gopher servers: menu names (a menu is, in effect, the same as a direc-tory), telnet connections, FTP connections, file names, and so on. The directory titles search looks only at the menus, not at the files.

Therefore, a title search will result in a larger number of hits than will a directory titles search. Where the directory title list might be one page long, the titles search might be a dozen pages.

To search using Veronica, simply select the menu option, and type into the box the word or words for which you want to search; for example:

```
+— — — — — — — — — — — — — — — — — — — — — — — — — — — —+
¦ Words to search for  Electronic books                 ¦
¦                                [Cancel ^G] [Accept - Enter]  ¦
+— — — — — — — — — — — — — — — — — — — — — — — — — — — —+
```

Press **Enter**, and Veronica's off and running. In a few moments you'll see a new menu:

```
Search DIRECTORY Titles in GopherSpace via NYSERNet database:
electronic books

—> 1.  Phone Books/
    2.  E-mail Addresses and Telephone Books/
    3.  Online Books, Images, Journals, Preprints, Publishers,
        Tech Report../
    4.  Books/
    5.  Books and Literary Events/
    6.  Electronic Books/
```

(This search actually found me 12 pages of entries.)

If one of the hits interests you, select it as you would any menu option, and you'll be taken directly there. Alternatively, you can place the arrow next to it and press = to see some information about it (such as the host name).

Veronica is a fantastic tool for finding information in Gopher-space. In effect, you are very quickly creating a menu of options (options that may be spread across several continents and dozens of countries) in which you are interested.

You will usually find plenty of entries that you don't want. For example, when searching for Electronic Books, I found Phone and Address Books, E-mail Addresses and Telephone Books, and so on. You can remove an entry by placing the arrow next to it and pressing **d**.

Finding Gopher Software

If you have a dial-in direct account, you may want to find your own Gopher client software. You don't have to; you can run the Gopher software made available by your service provider. But you may prefer to get some neat-looking software that fits the way you are used to working (Macintosh software that looks like Macintosh software, Windows software that looks like Windows software, and so on).

As I've mentioned elsewhere in this book, experimenting with Internet software is not for the weak of heart or the inexperienced. As the READ-ME file at **boombox.micro.umn.edu** states, "There is minimal documentation for the software; but have faith, we are working on it." Still, if you use Gopher a lot, you might want to install your own client. If you don't, or if you hate tinkering with your computer and software, use someone else's client.

If you want the most recent releases of shareware Gopher software, use anonymous ftp (or Gopher itself) to go to **boombox.micro.umn.edu**. You'll find various subdirectories in the **/pub/gopher** directory. You'll find directories that contain various Gopher client and server programs for such systems as Macintosh, NeXT, PC, UNIX, Microsoft Windows, OS/2, VM/CMS, and VMS. Also, see *The Complete Idiot's Next Step with the Internet* for more information about graphical Gophers.

The Least You Need to Know

➤ Travel through Gopherspace by selecting menu options. Type the number and press **Enter**, or move the arrow to the option and press **Enter**.

➤ Go back the way you came by pressing **u** or left arrow, or by pressing **m** to return to the main menu.

➤ To find out more about a menu option, place the arrow next to it and press =.

➤ To save a text document or file, place the arrow next to it and press **s**. To transfer it back to your computer (if using a dial-in terminal connection) press **D**.

➤ To search a menu, press /.

➤ Create your own menu by adding bookmarks. Add a menu to your custom menu by pressing **A**. Add a menu option by moving the arrow to it and pressing **a**. View your custom menu, by pressing **v**.

➤ Veronica is a powerful tool you can use to search through thousands of miles of Gopherspace at once. Look for a Veronica menu option somewhere in your Gopher menu.

➤ Leave a Gopher client by pressing **q** or **Q**.

## Chapter 22

Finding Your WAIS Around

In Chapter 21, I showed you how Gopher can help you dig your way around the Internet, burrowing for whatever may interest you. In this chapter, you'll learn about *WAIS*, or *Wide Area Information Server*, a system that helps you search for documents containing the information you want.

WAIS does the work for you (well, part of it). Instead of simply providing a menu that lets you travel around the world, WAIS provides a list of databases, lets you select the ones you want to search, and carries out a search for you. If it finds what you want, it can then save the documents and send them to you via e-mail (or, if you're using a WAIS server on your computer or on your service provider's computer, it can save them to a file). Not bad, eh?

While I was writing this book, the number of databases WAIS can search rose from 497 to 624!

WAIS can search through more than 620 databases (probably more by the time you read this). In the past year, the number more than quadrupled. Those 620 databases contain tens of thousands of documents, from the archives of various newsgroups to weather reports, ZIP codes, computer archaeology, and kids' software reviews. While most of the files contain text documents, you may also find sounds, graphics, and so on. As with other aspects of the Internet, you name a subject, and it's probably out there somewhere.

Getting Started

As with Gopher, there are several ways to run WAIS:

➤ Telnet to **quake.think.com** or **nnsc.nsf.net** and run WAIS from there.

➤ Run WAIS from a menu option on your service provider's system.

➤ Run WAIS from a Gopher menu option.

➤ Set up a WAIS client on your own computer (if you have a permanent or dial-in direct connection).

In case you're interested, WAIS uses the American National Standard Z39.50: Information Retrieval Service Definition and Protocol Specification for Library Applications standard, revised by the National Information Standards Organization. (No, you don't need to remember that.) Z39.50 is a method for connecting different computer systems and databases. It provides a standard for storing and accessing database information.

As usual, there are various types of WAIS interfaces available. The one you can get to by telnetting is *swais*, a UNIX-based WAIS server. There are WAIS systems available for just about any computer system:

DOS, Windows, Macintosh, X Windows, NeXt, and so on. They all work differently, and some have more features than others. We're going to look at the swais version, because it's one of the simplest. Ask your service provider what you have available.

Let's Try It!

Let's take a look at WAIS. We're going to use telnet to get to a WAIS server. You can telnet to **quake.think.com** or **nnsc.nsf.net** and login as **wais**.

```
teal% telnet quake.think.com
Trying 192.31.181.1 ...
Connected to quake.think.com.
Escape character is '^]'.
SunOS UNIX (quake)
login: wais
Last login: Tue Nov 16 10:44:41 from forsythe.Stanfor
SunOS Release 4.1.1 (QUAKE) #3: Tue Jul 7 11:09:01 PDT 1992
Welcome to swais.
Please type user identifier (optional, i.e user@host): pkent@lab-
press.com
TERM = (vt100) (I pressed Enter here)
Starting swais (this may take a little while)...
```

Next you'll see an introductory message. When you've read it (and pressed **q**) you'll be shown the search screen, which looks something like this:

```
SWAIS                      Source Selection      Sources:  1
  #      Server                      Source                Cost
001:  [  quake.think.com]  directory-of-servers        Free




Keywords:

<space> selects, w for keywords, arrows move, <return> searches,
q quits, or ?
```

A Good Server Is Hard to Find

One problem you'll find with WAIS is figuring out which databases contain what data. The names are often quite obscure. (For instance, what is bib-ens-lyon? It's the Ecole Normale Superieure de Lyon, and has databases on the sciences—geology, math, physics, chemistry, and so on.) Fortunately, WAIS has a database called the *directory of servers* that you can use to narrow the search a little.

In fact, the directory of servers is probably the first thing you see when you enter WAIS, though at one time a full database listing was displayed. Just press **Enter** to select the directory of servers and highlight the **Keywords** line. Type a general keyword, such as **biology**, and press **Enter** again, and WAIS will search for databases with biology-related subjects. When it has found matches, it will show you a list, something like this:

```
SWAIS                              Search Results              Ite
  #     Score     Source                 Title              Lines
001:   [1000]  (directory-of-se)  biology-journal-contents    20
002:   [ 500]  (directory-of-se)  Cell_Lines                 117
003:   [ 389]  (directory-of-se)  ANU-Ancient-DNA-Studies     90
004:   [ 389]  (directory-of-se)  IUBio-fly-clones            59
005:   [ 389]  (directory-of-se)  com-books                   99
006:   [ 389]  (directory-of-se)  environment-newsgroups      39
007:   [ 333]  (directory-of-se)  ANU-Ancient-DNA-L           86
008:   [ 333]  (directory-of-se)  ANU-Complex-Systems         67
```

You can move the highlight to an entry and press **Spacebar** to see a description of the database's contents. If it's one that you are interested in, press **q** to remove the description and press **u** to add the database to the main list. Continue in this manner, until you find all the databases you want to search. When you've picked the databases you want, press **s** to return to the first screen—the Source Selection screen.

Back at the Source Selection screen, deselect the directory of servers (press =) and select the databases you picked (highlight each entry and press **Spacebar**). When you're ready to search, press **w**, press **Backspace** several times to clear the original search word, and press **Enter**. If Backspace doesn't work, try **Delete**. (By the way, you may not be able to see the original search word. Just press **Backspace** until the text cursor is immediately after **Keywords:**, and type a new search word.)

Here are the commands you can use in Source Selection list:

j or down arrow or **Ctrl-n**	Moves the cursor down one entry
J or **Ctrl-v** or **Ctrl-d**	Moves the cursor down one screen
k or up arrow or **Ctrl-p**	Moves the cursor up one entry
K or **Ctrl-u**	Moves the cursor up one screen
number and **Enter**	Moves to a particular line
v or **,** (comma)	Displays information about the highlighted database (**q** and **Enter** to return to the listing)
Spacebar or **.** (period)	Selects an entry (or deselects a selected entry)
=	Deselects all selections
Ctrl-j	Selects an entry and moves to keywords field
/*word* and **Enter**	Searches for a listing
w and **Enter**	Enables you to enter keywords on which to search (press **Ctrl-c** to cancel)
Enter	Searches selected entries with keywords
s	Returns to the listing
h or **?**	Displays the Help screen
q	Quits

Use the various commands to move the cursor through the list, and press **Spacebar** or **.** (period) to select the entries you want to search. (You can select as many as you want.) If you see an entry you think might be useful, move the highlight to it and press **v** or **,** (comma) to read a description of the database (press **q** and **Enter** to return to the list).

Picking Your Keywords

What sort of keywords can you use? You can enter several words, separated by spaces. Note that you can only do a simple keyword search this way; WAIS will search for each word you enter, so you can't do the sort of *Boolean* search that many computer databases use. For example, in a Boolean search if you entered *MATH AND SPELL*, the system would search for documents that contained both *MATH* and *SPELL*. However, with WAIS, the AND will be ignored (because it's a *stop* word, a common word that is not indexed). Therefore, WAIS will find any documents that contain either *MATH* or *SPELL* (or both).

Keywords must start with a letter, not a number. And you may use only one type of punctuation character inside words, such as the period in "I.B.M."

Some words (such as *and*, *or*, *though*, and so on) are stop words because they are common. Other words may be stop words because they are common in a particular database. For example, the word *software* may be a stop word in a database that is related to computer programs.

Reading and Saving the Info

You can now move through this list in the same way you moved through the previous list. However, this time the list is of documents, not databases. When you press **Spacebar** or **Enter**, you'll be able to read the highlighted document.

To be more exact, you *may* be able to read the document. Sometimes documents will be displayed jumbled up slightly, so the lines are not consecutive. If that happens, try this. Go to the list and highlight the document you want to read. Then press | (the vertical "pipe" character), type **more**, and press **Enter**.

What if you want to save the information? You can send the document to yourself (or anyone else, for that matter) using e-mail. Press **m**. You'll be prompted for an e-mail address. Type the address, press **Enter**, and it's on its way. If the WAIS client is on your service provider's computer or on your own computer, you can use the **S** command to save the document in a file.

Using Gopher

There's a simpler way to use WAIS—through a Gopher menu. This might be through your service provider's menu system (if they have set up a menu based on Gopher) or through a Gopher client you telneted to (see Chapter 21 for more information about Gopher).

On my service provider's system, I can select **15. Tools for Information Retrieval/**, followed by **5. Wide Area Information Servers (WAIS)/**. I then have the option of telneting to **quake.think.com** or **nnsc.nsf.net**. Alternatively, I can select **1. Search WAIS using Gopher/**. This selection leads me to several more options. I can select **2. List of all WAIS Sources/** (to see a list in numerical order), **3. WAIS Databases sorted by Letter/**, or **4. WAIS Databases sorted by Subject/** (an experimental system in Sweden). This is especially useful, because the menu system helps me find databases that are relevant to the subject in which I'm interested: Archaeology, Religion, Math, and so on. Whatever I choose, eventually I can find my way to a particular database. Selecting the database displays a box into which I can type a search term.

Gopher is a very convenient way to search through WAIS, but it has one significant drawback. You can search only one database at a time. As we've already seen, if you telnet to a WAIS site, you can select any number of databases and search all of them at once.

Be Your Own Client

The following info is for dial-in direct or permanent connection users only. The rest of you can skip right to the end of the chapter (or stick your fingers in your ears and hum, if you prefer).

If you decide you like using WAIS but don't like the user interface you're forced to work with, you can set up your own WAIS client. You can find WAIS software in several places. Try ftping to **wais.com**, go into the **pub/freeware** directory, and search around for client software for your computer. There are directories for various types of systems, including Windows, NeXt, Sun, and Motif.

> If you just want a different user interface to work with, you need **WAIS client software**. If you want to set up your own indexed database and make it available to the Internet, you need **WAIS server software**.

You may also be able to find WAIS software at **sunsite.unc.edu**, **think.com**, **quake.think.com**, and **cnidr.org**.

The Least You Need to Know

➤ Run WAIS from your service provider's menu or from the UNIX shell.

➤ You can also telnet to a WAIS server at **quake.think.com** or **nnsc.nsf.net**.

➤ Press **m** to send a document to yourself via e-mail. If the WAIS client is on your service provider's system, save the document as a file with **S**.

➤ Refer to the directory of servers to narrow your search to those servers with information that interests you.

➤ WAIS accepts only simple keyword searches, not Boolean searches.

➤ To search the highlighted database, press **Enter**, type a keyword, and press **Enter** again.

➤ To search several databases at once, highlight each one and press **Spacebar**. Press **w** and type the keyword. Then press **Enter**.

➤ Probably the easiest way to search WAIS is through a Gopher menu.

## Chapter 23

Think Global: World Wide Web

> **In This Chapter**
>
> ➤ Getting to a WWW browser
>
> ➤ Finding your way around the Web
>
> ➤ Viewing topic lists
>
> ➤ Searching for info on the Web
>
> ➤ From Web to Gopher, WAIS, FTP, and whois

Here's another Internet tool that can help you search for what you need. *World Wide Web* (also called *WWW*, *The Web*, or sometimes even *W3*) is a *hypertext* system that helps you travel around the world electronically, looking for information.

WWW is very easy to use—probably the easiest Internet system you'll find. Instead of searching for a keyword, as you would with WAIS, with WWW you follow a "trail" of linked words. You select a topic that interests you, and view related information; from there you select another topic that interests you, and view information related to that topic. In this way, you move from one topic to another, hopefully

What is **hypertext**? If you've ever used a Windows Help file or a Macintosh HyperCard file, you've used hypertext. A hypertext document lets you jump from place to place in the document using links of some kind. Instead of reading the document from front to back, you can select a word and move to related text elsewhere in the document.

moving closer to where you want to be. (You'll see exactly what I mean in a moment.) If you ever decide you've taken the wrong trail, you can quickly return whence you came.

World Wide Web is made up of documents with built-in links. If you are using the basic line-mode Web browser program, each link has a bracketed number, like this: [3]. For example, when you are reading a menu of options, you'll see something like this:

```
The Virtual Library[1]
A classification by information by subject.
Includes links to other known virtual
libraries.
```

The [1] after the title means you can type **1** and press **Enter** to move to this "Virtual Library."

The topic number doesn't have to be in a header; it could appear after a word anywhere in a document's text. A document may have dozens of these topics, each leading somewhere different.

Getting to the Web

As usual, there are several ways to use the Web:

➤ You can telnet to a WWW browser.

➤ There may be a menu option in your service provider's menu system. The menu option may be a shortcut that uses telnet automatically to get you to a WWW browser, or your service provider may have installed a WWW browser on their system.

➤ From the UNIX shell, you can use a command that your service provider has set up to connect to a WWW browser automatically. You may be able to type **www** or **lynx** to start the browser.

➤ If you are using a dial-in direct or permanent connection, you can install your own WWW browser.

Whichever method you use, you will be using a *browser*, a program that knows how to search through the hypertext files. We're going to look at the simplest browser, a text-based system (the *line-mode browser*) that you may be using. However, there are others around, some of which are quite fancy, appearing more like Windows Help systems with underlined text (instead of bracketed numbers) to denote topics you can select. (SuperHighway Access includes a program called Tapestry, which is a graphical Web browser. See Chapters 26 and 27.)

 Everyone seems to have heard of Mosaic. It's a graphical browser available for X Windows, Microsoft Windows, and the Macintosh. However, you *cannot* run it on a dial-in terminal account. You need a permanent or a dial-in direct connection.

What About Lynx?

We're going to look at the line-mode browser because it's available to any Internet user who can telnet, even if their service provider hasn't loaded a Web browser. However, there's another popular browser, called Lynx, which is easier to use. With Lynx, you press the **Tab** and arrow keys to move through the document, and press **Enter** to select links.

If your service provider has only the line-mode browser—or worse yet, no browser at all—ask them to install Lynx.

Off to the Alps—Using WWW

To show you how to use WWW, we're going to take a quick trip to Switzerland to **nxoc01.cern.ch** (that's a zero before the 1, not an *o*) at the European Particle Physics Laboratory (CERN). We're going to use telnet to get there. (I'm using this method because it allows people to use the Web even if their service provider doesn't have a Web browser. If your service provider does have a Web browser, use that instead.)

```
CNS> telnet nxoc01.cern.ch
Trying 128.141.201.214 ...
Connected to www0.cern.ch.
Escape character is '^]'.
```

```
UNIX(r) System V Release 4.0 (www0)
            Welcome to the World-Wide Web
THE WORLD-WIDE WEB

This is just one of many access points to the web, the universe of
information available over networks. To follow references, just
type the number then hit the return (enter) key. The features
you have by connecting to this telnet server are very primitive
compared to the features you have when you run a W3 "client"
program on your own computer. If you possibly can, please pick
up a client for your platform to reduce the load on this service
and experience the web in its full splendor.

    For more information, select by number:
    A list of available W3 client programs[1]
    Everything about the W3 project[2]
    Places to start exploring[3]
    The First International WWW Conference[4]

    This telnet service is provided by the WWW team at the European
    Particle Physics Laboratory known as CERN[5]
    [End]
1-5, Up, Quit, or Help:
```

Notice that we didn't have to log in. When you telnet, you are
placed into WWW automatically. Also, notice all the numbers in
brackets. If you'd like to take a look at the *Places to start exploring
document,* from which you'll be able to search through different subjects you can use as a starting point, type **3** and press **Enter**. If you
want to see a list of the WWW browser programs, type **1** and press
Enter. For whichever option you want to see, simply type the number
and press **Enter**.

WWW Commands

WWW is one of the easiest Internet tools to use. Here are the commands you'll use when moving through the WWW. Type each command and then press **Enter**.

Use this command	To
Press **Enter**	Go down one page
u or **up**	Go to the previous page
bo or **bottom**	Go to the last page
t or **top**	Go to the first page
Type *number* and press **Enter**	Go to a [*number*] reference
f *keywords* **find** *keywords*	Search a document for a keyword (only when you see **FIND** on the prompt line)
l or **list**	See a list of [ ] references
b or **back**	Go to the previous document
ho or **home**	Go to the first document you saw
r or **recall**	List the documents you've seen
r *number* or **recall** *number*	Go to a document in the Recall list
n or **next**	View the next reference from the last document
REF	Refresh the page you are viewing
go *url*	Go to a particular document (I'll explain in detail later)
h or **help**	Display the Help page
m or **manual**	Display the WWW manual
quit	Quit

Play with these commands while you're working in WWW, and soon you'll get the hang of it. Just type the topic number and press **Enter** to select a particular topic. Then move down the topic, whether it's a listing or document, by pressing **Enter**. Move back up a page by pressing **u** and then **Enter**. To go back to where you just came from, use **b** and **Enter**. You get the idea. Take a look at the command list included here, and try navigating through the Web.

Let's Explore

Let's take a look at what you'll find if you select **[3]** from the page we saw earlier (the document entitled *Places to start exploring*). You'll see a list of options. Select **Virtual Library by Subject [1]**, and you'll see the beginning of a list, like this:

```
The World-Wide Web Virtual Library: Subject Catalogue
VIRTUAL LIBRARY THE WWW VIRTUAL LIBRARY

This is a distributed subject catalogue. See Summary[1], and In-
dex[2]. See also arrangement by service type[3]., and other subject
catalogues of network information[4] .
Mail to maintainers[5] of the specified subject or www-
request@info.cern.ch to add pointers to this list, or if you would
like to contribute to administration of a subject area[6].
See also how to put your data on the web[7]. All items starting
with ! are NEW! (or newly maintained).
    Aboriginal Studies[8]
This document keeps track of leading information facilities in the
field of Australian Aboriginal studies as well as the Indigenous
Peoples studies.
    Aeronautics and Aeronautical Engineering[9]
        Separate list
```

We have nine links or topics in this small area alone. We can see summary [1], an index [2], a list of different services available by selecting 3 (World Wide Web servers, WAIS servers, Network News, Gopher, telnet, and so on) or other subject catalogues by selecting 4. We'll also see several other types of indexes of information we can work our way through.

Below the header stuff, we see the beginning of the catalogue itself, starting with Aboriginal Studies and Aeronautics. You'll notice that there are numbers next to both these entries and, below Aeronautics, the words **Separate list** on the description line. This means that if you type **9** and press **Enter**, you'll see a list of aeronautics-related resources: Embry-Riddle Aeronautical University, Aviation and Aerospace Outlook, Penn State University, Aerospace Engineering, and so on. Okay, so maybe you're not interested in aeronautics. Just play with WWW and go where your fancy takes you.

Looking at a Topic List

You can view a list of all the topics or references in the current document. Type **l** and press **Enter**, and you'll see something like this:

```
*** References from this document ***
[1] http://www.biotech.washington.edu/WebCrawler/WebQuery.html
[2] http://rubens.anu.edu.au/prints.xmosaic/inlines.no/Part4.html
[3] http://rubens.anu.edu.au/prints.xmosaic/inlines.no/Part3.html
[4] http://www.eb.com/release.htm
[5] http://www.inhs.uiuc.edu:70/1/edu
[6] http://www.tulips.tsukuba.ac.jp/ndc/200.html
```

If you are in a very big listing or document, you may have dozens of topics, and they'll shoot right by you before you can read them. In a smaller document, the listing may be useful—or it may not. Unfortunately, this is a list of URLs (Universal Resource Locators) and the addresses of the documents, not the document titles. So it's like someone is giving you a list of business addresses without including the business names. Sometimes you'll be able to figure out what all this is, but often you won't.

After viewing the list, either type one of the numbers and press **Enter**, or type **u** and press **Enter** (**u** will just return you to the previous page).

WWW browsers sometimes get a little confused. For instance, you may enter a command and see a long program listing instead of the information you are supposed to see. Or perhaps the browser won't jump to where it's supposed to go, or maybe the **home** command won't take you back to the first document. If you run into problems, try another command: go to a different document or go in a different direction within the same document. The system will eventually get working again. If it doesn't, you may have to close the program and reopen.

That's the One I Want

Most browsers, if not all, let you go directly to a specific document somewhere in webspace. If you are using the line-mode browser, you'll use the **go *url*** command. (A URL is a Universal Resource Locator, a sort of Web address.) As an example, let's say you want to go to the WebCrawler, a giant index of WWW resources. To do so, you would type

```
go http://fishtail.biotech.washington.edu/WebCrawler/WebQuery.html
```

and press **Enter**. You'll shoot off across webspace to the WebCrawler.

If you are working with the Lynx Web browser, you can start it from the command line by typing **lynx *url***. If you are already working in Lynx, simply use the **g** command. Other browsers use different methods, but virtually all allow you to jump directly to a document on the Web.

Finding What You Want

In some areas, you may be able to enter keywords so you can search a document. The fancier browsers have what's known as *forms support*, which means that the user sees a form into which he types information, and buttons that he can click on. So you'll sometimes find documents that tell you that you need a browser with forms support. If you don't have one, you can go to an alternate document to use the basic line-mode searching.

For example, let's say you want to search the WebCrawler that we just mentioned. On the WebCrawler's introductory page, you'll see this:

```
NOTE: if this page doesn't have a place to type your query, try
using this simple search page[6]
```

So you press **6** and press **Enter** to go to the simple search. You'll see another introductory page with this line at the bottom:

```
FIND <keywords>, 1-7, Back, Up, Quit, or Help:
```

FIND <keywords> means you can type words for which you want to search and press **Enter**. For instance, type **conspiracy** and press **Enter**. We'll quickly see a listing, like this:

```
WebCrawler[1] Search Results

The query "conspiracy" found 83 documents and returned 50:
     1000 Conspiracy News Network[2]
     0093 Some Files That I Think Are Neat[3]
     0089 Studio X Table of Contents[4]
     0064 Gunnar's Personal List of Way-Cool music[5]
     0040 Depth Probe Archives [6]
     0029 UWI Shopping Maul[7]
     0029 Web Links[8]
     0028 Depth Probe Home[9]
     0022 NeXT Liberation Front[10]
     0015 Illuminati MC Home Page[11]
     0013 Noel Hunter[12]
```

The numbers in the left column indicate the relevance of the document. The first one has the number 1000 beside it because the word *conspiracy* is actually in the title. The others get lower ratings because they may not match exactly what you are looking for. As the WebCrawler documentation explains, "[The numbers are] not particularly scientific, but it gives you a feeling for just how helpful a document might be."

Save the Info You Find

Saving information from the Web is sometimes a problem. If you are using your own browser, or one set up by your service provider, you can often save the data. However, if you are telneting to a Web browser, you are out of luck.

On UNIX versions of the line-mode browser, you can use the **print** command to print a document or the > *filename* command to save the document in a file. (Use >> *filename* to append it to the end of an existing file.)

If you are working with Lynx, you can use the **p** command to save it in a file. Although other browsers generally have some way to save, they don't always. For example, the current version of Mosaic (one of the fanciest browsers) lets you save a document with all the hypertext coding built in, but it doesn't let you save just the text. However, some other browsers do.

Using Gopher et al

Sometimes you'll find yourself using other resources from the WWW. You may select a topic and notice something like this:

```
gopher://orion.lib.virginia.edu:70/11/alpha/bmcr
```

This tells you that WWW has just hooked into Gopher and taken you to a computer connected through the Gopher menu system. On the other hand, there might be a time when you'll see something like this:

```
Connection Machine WAIS server.
WWW has connected through the WAIS system.
```

Through WWW, you can connect to WAIS, Gopher, FTP, X.500, whois, and so on, and you can use telnet from your own WWW browser (though not from a public one like **nxoc01.cern.ch**). But the simple Web browsers probably won't always work well for you in these other systems. You may be able to view a document through WAIS and Gopher, but you won't be able to download a file. And if you try to view a binary file (through FTP, for instance), your browser may try to do it, but at best you'll see garbage on your screen—and at worst it will crash your computer.

Still, you can use these simple browsers to find what you are looking for. To search directories on a distant computer, for example, it can be easier to use WWW than FTP. Then you can use FTP to go back to that system to grab the files you need. If you want full-blown World Wide Web, though, you'll need one of the more advanced Web browsers.

Loading Your Own WWW Browser

If you are really brave and have time to spare, you can install your own WWW browser. There are currently several dozen browser programs, for MS-DOS, Windows, X-Windows, NeXt, UNIX, Macintosh, and so on. These programs have a wide variety of options, and give you the ability to customize your WWW system. For instance, you can pick a particular document to set up as the one you see each time you start WWW, which saves you from digging your way through the system each time. You can also print documents that you find in WWW or copy them to a text file. You can even set up your own notes with links to the WWW-at-large, so you can view your notes and travel (through links in your notes) to sources of information on the other side of the world.

If you want to find out more about Web browsers, see *The Complete Idiot's Guide to World Wide Web*, due out late January, 1995.

For most browsers you'll need a permanent or dial-in direct connection. Some service providers (such as The Pipeline and NETCOM—see Chapter 25) even give their subscribers software that has a built-in Web browser in order to eliminate the headaches of setting up their own dial-in direct connection. However, if you have a terminal connection, and your service provider only has the line-mode browser, you might want to install Lynx. It's not too hard to install, and it's easier to use than the line-mode browser.

The Least You Need to Know

➤ World Wide Web is a hypertext system that lets you follow cross-references between documents.

➤ You can telnet to **nxoc01.cern.ch** to use a simple line-mode WWW browser, or you can use one set up by your service provider.

➤ With the line-mode browser, follow references by typing the *number* and pressing **Enter**.

➤ To get back to the first page you saw, use the **ho** command.

➤ Travel around in a document with the **top**, **bottom**, and **up** commands. Press **Enter** to go down one page.

➤ Type **l** and press **Enter** to view a list of the document's topics.

➤ If you see **FIND <keywords>** below the document, you can type **f** *keyword* to search the document.

Be Careful Out There!

With a new form of communications comes new problems. Just how safe are you in cyberspace? Granted, you're just sitting at home or in your office, clicking away at the keyboard, but there really are risks. For example, who's reading your e-mail? Who's getting your credit card number? Is the person you've communicated with for a few weeks really who he says he is? And what about protecting the kids from cyber-perverts? We've all heard stories about what a dangerous place the Internet is for kids. What can we do? Read on.

Blind Those Prying Eyes!

There are good reasons for being concerned about the security of your e-mail. Let's say you are doing business via e-mail, and you are sending confidential information across the Internet (information such as credit card numbers, social security numbers, names, addresses, telephone numbers, or profit and loss figures that you don't want read by other people). On the other hand, it might be personal information that you don't want others to read. To quote one encryption program's user manual "you may be planning a political campaign, discussing your taxes, or having an illicit affair... doing something that you feel shouldn't be illegal, but is."

So it might come as a shock to discover that your private correspondence isn't completely private. In addition to you and the message's recipient, there are at least two other people with access to your messages: your system administrator and the system administrator at the other end. However, there may be more people than that. It's a fair bet that most service providers have at least two people—and usually more—with system-administrator privileges (the ability to go anywhere and do anything on the host computer). So now we are up to at least four people who have access, and probably several more.

What about the computer you are using? Do other people have access to your computer? Do other people have access to the computer at the other end? Perhaps the recipient is working on a small network, with a connection to the service provider's computer. Now, in addition to the service provider's administrators, you have the recipient's system administrator (or administrators) to consider. What are we up to now? Six, eight, ten, fifteen?

What about e-mail interception? The vast majority of e-mail crosses the Internet untouched by human command. That is, it's all automatic. But now and again "crackers" get onto the Internet and start digging around, seeing what they can find and what mischief they can get into. Although it may be rare for e-mail to be intercepted, it can happen.

So what can you do about all this? You can *encrypt* your e-mail, convert it into a jumbled mess that is unintelligible, as the world's secret services and governments do with sensitive correspondence. Is this going a bit far? Don't people with something to hide encrypt things? As the PGP encryption program user manual asks (rhetorically), "If you really are a law-abiding citizen with nothing to hide, why don't you always send your paper mail on postcards?"

Can We Trust Uncle Sam?

Spying made easy! Right now, spying on communications is a real hassle for government. Imagine opening all that mail and all those UPS and Fedex packages. But electronic communication simplifies spying in some ways. As more of the nation's messages pass through e-mail, it becomes easier for authorities to set up automated spying systems that can check the e-mail stream and pick out messages from particular people, about particular subjects, or containing certain words. The National Security Agency already does this on international cable-grams. Is e-mail next? It certainly looks that way.

But we can encrypt our e-mail, right? For now. I've heard comments to the effect that "government may encourage us to use their encryption devices, such as the Clipper Chip, but they're not going to outlaw private encryption, are they!" Aren't they! Some of our representatives have already tried. Had Senate Bill 266 passed, it would have forced all manufacturers of secure communications equipment to build "trap doors" into their products. A trap door enables the person with the "key" to the door to read encrypted messages. Who would hold the key? Uncle Sam, of course!

The **Clipper Chip** is an encryption device that the Clinton administration wanted manufacturers to build into their hardware. The device would enable the government to break the code. As this book is being written, it seems probable that the Clipper Chip idea will slowly fade away—and be replaced by a more sophisticated version called Capstone.

The FBI has proposed that communications hardware should include wiretap ports so the FBI could tap into all forms of electronic communication. As for the Clipper Chip, what good is it if nobody uses it? The next step, if the government is able to foist this or another system on us, is to get rid of encryption systems that they can't break. (As this book was going to print, FBI officials were beginning to talk about banning encryption software!)

Why should we care? If we're not doing anything wrong, does it matter if our government can read our communications? All governments spy on their citizens for unwarranted purposes, and the U.S. government is no different from any other. Federal and state authorities in the U.S. have a long history of running illegal spying and harassment operations against American citizens. For years the FBI acted like a "secret police" organization. It's nice to think that "our government doesn't do that sort of thing," but the fact is, they do.

Want to know more about the threats to your online security from your own government? Use a Web browser (see Chapter 23) to read the **http://www.wired.com/clipper/** document.

PGP: Pretty Good Privacy

Okay, my diatribe's over. Let's get down to the nitty gritty. How do you encrypt your correspondence? The most popular freeware encryption program is PGP, Pretty Good Privacy, a program created by Phil Zimmerman's company, Phil's Pretty Good Software.

You can find versions for UNIX, VMS, OS/2, Amiga, and Atari. Although there's currently no true Windows version, there are several Windows "shells" that use the DOS program to do the actual work. You can conveniently acquire PGP by locating a document on World Wide Web at **http://www.mantis.co.uk/pgp/pgp.html**. This has links to various FTP sites from which you can download PGP and its documentation. Alternatively, you can send e-mail to **pgpinfo@mantis. co.uk**. You will automatically get a response with the same document that can be read at the Web site, which contains a list of FTP sites from which you can grab PGP.

If you want a Windows shell, look for WinPGP (shareware), or PGP WinFront or PGP WinShell for Windows (both freeware). You can find these on CompuServe in the NCSAFORUM, or you can search for pgpw, pgpsh, and pfw (the current version is pfw20.zip) using Archie (Chapter 20). Better still, you can get them from the Macmillan Publishing Internet site at **ftp.mcp.com**.

Using PGP

PGP uses *public key encryption*, a system that provides privacy and authentication. To quote the user manual, "only those intended to receive a message can read it ... [and] messages that appear to be from a particular person can only have originated from that person." Thus, not only does public key encryption provide security of the message itself, but it ensures that the message is really from the person it purports to be from.

Unlike *single-key systems*, public-key encryption uses two keys. A key is a number, a code that is used to scramble a message—to convert the message to a form that other people cannot read.

Public-key encryption systems use one public key and one secret key. You publish the public key in a certificate, which other users can download and load into their encryption program. If anyone wants to send you an encrypted message, they can use your public key.

A **single-key system**, such as DES (Data Encryption Standard) works by using just one key (one code) to scramble the message. If Mr. A sends the message to Mr. B, Mr. B needs the key in order to unscramble the message. So the key must somehow be communicated to Mr. B without letting anyone else find out what it is. It's inconvenient and risky.

The encryption program uses the key and a built-in mathematical formula to scramble the message. When you receive the message, you use your secret key to unencrypt it—to convert it back to normal. The message is safe because it can only be converted to its original form with the secret key; the public key can't do it.

The secret key encrypts messages for authentication—not for security. You encrypt the message with the secret key, and send it off in your e-mail. The recipient uses your public key to convert it to normal. If the public key works, the recipient knows that the message was encrypted with the secret key and, therefore, that it came from you. This provides a sort of electronic signature. It's not a secure communication, because anyone can decrypt it; but it is authentic, because only the person with the matching secret key could have created it. Neat system.

There are encryption systems that are easier to use than PGP. For example, some utility programs (such as PC Tools) come with encryption programs. But these are almost always private-key encryption systems, which require that you give someone else your secret password or code.

Forget the Technical Stuff—How Does It Work?

Exactly how does this all work? Let's take a look at the DOS version of PGP. First, installation is very easy. The program is in a .ZIP file, so you use PKUNZIP to extract the files into a directory. The program comes with a user manual in a couple of text files. Unfortunately, it's not organized well, so it can take some time to really understand how to use the program. Read it all; there's some very important stuff in there.

Next, you will create your two keys: the public and private keys. To do so, type **pgp -kg** at the DOS prompt and press **Enter**. You will be asked which form of encryption you want (reasonably secure and very quick, more secure but a little slower, or very secure but slow), and you'll be asked for an ID for your public key. You don't see the actual number used as the key. Instead, you enter your name and e-mail address, which the program converts to your public key when needed (it's easier to remember than a long number).

Once your public key is established, you'll be asked for the password you want to use for your secret key. This is the text you will type when you are decrypting messages sent to you. Again, you don't see the actual number used as the secret key; you use the password or ID instead.

How do you know that the certificate file you've received is the person's real public key, and that it isn't a fake substituted by someone else? (Public key certificate files are often placed on bulletin boards, where they are subject to tampering.) Make sure you get the file from someone you trust—directly from the person who owns the public key or from a mutual friend you trust. In addition, you should read the PGP manual for more information on key management.

Now you've got your public and secret keys. You'll give the public one to people who may want to send encrypted e-mail to you. To do that, you have to give the person your key certificate. That person then uses the **pgp -ka** *filename* command to load the public key into their copy of PGP. If you want to send e-mail to others, you must do the same: load their certificates into your copy of PGP.

To encrypt a file, you type **pgp -ea** *filename publickeyID*. PGP compresses the file and encrypts it in a text file. You can then place the text into an e-mail message and send it off. When you receive a file, you type **pgp** *filename*. You'll be prompted for your secret key password.

There's lots more to PGP. You can add your "authentication" signature, encrypt a file with single-key encryption (to create files only you can open), encrypt a message to multiple recipients, and more. So read the manual carefully.

But Does It Work?

Does PGP work well? Well enough for a Georgetown University professor who has worked closely with the National Security Agency to state that "PGP could potentially become a widespread problem." Why would it be a problem, you might ask? Because the government won't be able to read private communications, that's why!

In a recent Sacramento, CA, police investigation into child pornography, officials were unable to crack a suspect's diaries that had been encrypted with PGP. The FBI and National Security Agency even declined to help the police crack the files—because they didn't know how! (The suspect, by the way, was later convicted based on other evidence.)

If you are a Windows user, you'll have to use the DOS version of PGP; there is currently no Windows version. However, you will probably want to use a Windows shell, a program that uses the DOS PGP program, but provides a Windows interface between you and the program. A DOS shell is much easier to use than the DOS version alone.

We can get into technical discussions of just how secure PGP and similar systems are, but what it often boils down to is "just exactly how many millions of dollars would it cost to break the code?" Yes, it may be possible, given millions (perhaps billions) of dollars of computer time to break some of the encryption systems in use today. But just how secure do you need to be?

Proof! The Law Really Is an Ass!

"If the law supposes that," said Mr. Bumble in Charles Dickens' *Oliver Twist*, "the law is an ass, an idiot." That was written over 150 years ago, but it still rings true today.

What does the law suppose today? In the U.S.A, it supposes that anyone exporting PGP (or other encryption devices) is harming the security of the nation, and that people overseas should not be able to import the product from the U.S.A. That means:

a) If you are in the United States, you cannot send PGP to friends and colleagues overseas, and

b) if you are not in the United States, you can't download PGP from sites within the United States.

It doesn't matter to the law that there are plenty of sites overseas anyway; that "agents of foreign powers" are hardly likely to obey a law that is ridiculously easy to break; that there's no real way to stop foreign Internet users from downloading the program; and that there are lots of powerful encryption programs available throughout the world. Regardless, you can go to jail for breaking it.

There has also been a patent dispute between the distributors of PGP and a company called PKP (Public Key Partners). The Web document Pretty Good Privacy—Legal Issues (**http://www.mantis.co.uk/pgp/pgp-legal.html**) advises the following:

➤ If you live in the USA or Canada, you should buy ViaCrypt PGP or use the PGP version called MIT PGP 2.6. Otherwise, you will be infringing the patents held by PKP, which you merely paid for.

➤ If you live outside the USA or Canada, you can use PGP without having to worry about patent infringement. If you use version 2.6ui, you should have no problems talking to other versions.

➤ It may be illegal to send encrypted messages in some countries or on some networks.

➤ You should not export PGP from the USA or Canada to any other country.

What does the document mean when it says "the patents held by PKP, which you merely paid for"? The technology used in PGP, for which PKP claims to hold the patent, was paid for with U.S. tax dollars and by grants from the National Science Foundation and the Navy. As for ViaCrypt PGP, it's a commercial version of PGP that is quite legal—beyond the patent dispute. In fact, it's identical to the freeware PGP 2.3a program! This all gets a little complicated, so if you want the details, see the **http://www.mantis.co.uk/pgp/pgp-legal.html** document.

More Encryption Stuff

There's another site you might want to check for various encryption programs. FTP to the **ftp.wimsey.com** site and change to the **/pub/crypto/software** directory. Read the README text file; it warns you about all the legal requirements for downloading encryption software. It also tells you the name of the directory (a hidden directory) that contains the software. That is, you won't see it at the FTP site, but you can use the **cd** command to get into it.

What Would We Do Without Credit?

The Internet is becoming America's—and the World's—CyberMall. Many companies are placing electronic storefronts on the Internet that we can drift through and (they hope) buy from.

But how do you buy online? Right now, that's a bit of a problem, because e-mail isn't a secure way to send credit card numbers (as we've just seen). In essence, when you give your credit card number to the store and its employees, which is a risk in itself, you are also giving it to a dozen or so system administrators.

There are ways to get around the problem. Some commercial sites do not take direct orders. For instance, Downtown Anywhere, a commercial Web site (**http://www.awa.com**), tells you to call in your order to a 1-800 phone number. If you want, you can set up an account, and the Downtown Anywhere people will keep your credit card number on file. Then you can safely order online in the future.

Another store using the Internet is the Computer Literacy Bookstore in San Jose, CA (**info@clbooks.com**). They take orders via e-mail, but they recommend that you fax or mail to them first an information sheet containing your address and credit card number.

Of course, there are some systems that take credit card numbers. Many service providers will take credit card numbers online from their subscribers, and some "malls" accept online purchases. For example, the Internet Information Mall (gopher to **marketplace.com** or use your Web browser to go to **http://marketplace.com**) will take online orders. You can enter your credit card number, or, if you prefer, you can set up an account with the Mall offline by fax, mail, or phone, and then order using the account number.

Is this risky? Whenever you use your credit card—in a store, in a restaurant, over the phone, in a letter—there's a risk that the number can be stolen. As for the Internet, "we've found that most people regard sending credit cards over the net as an acceptable risk," Andrew Currie of the Internet Information Mall told me. "There's a vocal minority who raise valid points and believe the risk is unacceptable, so we also offer a way for these people to set up an account offline."

What the Future Holds

Commercial transactions are going to get a little easier online—maybe not right away, but eventually. Systems are being developed to secure credit card transmissions, probably using some sort of public-key encryption system. An online store will have a public key. Anyone wanting to order from the company will encrypt the order using the public key. So the only people who can decrypt the order are the store's employees, the people who have the matching secret key. Other systems in developmental stages, such as DigiCash and Netcash, are new forms of electronic credit—cash, money, or "coupons" that can be used online safely.

Because these systems are still in the development stages, it may be some time before we see them in wide use. For now, you'll have to decide how dangerous you think credit-card transmission really is.

You Don't Know These People!

It's easy to strike up online friendships very quickly. I've done business with a number of people I've met online. In most cases, these are people I've never actually met, but people with whom I've corresponded via e-mail, U.S. Mail, and the phone line. For example, I've been working on a user manual for a large drug company in California for over a year, and I've never met any of the people on the project face to face.

It's quite possible to meet people on the Internet who will turn into clients, friends, lovers, even spouses. But before you jump blindly into online relationships, remember this: Until you've met them, you don't really know them.

I've been lucky with my business relationships. I've been able to verify that the people I'm working with are "on the up and up." But that's not always so in cyberspace. In fact there are probably more frauds in cyberspace than in the real world. Why? Because it provides great cover: if all you can see are the words on your screen, how can you know anything about the person on the other end?

Is the person who is claiming to be a Michelle Pfeifer look-alike really a Roseanne Barr look-alike? Is the kindly gentleman offering friendship to a young boy something more ominous? Is the person you just had "online sex" with really of the gender he/she claimed to be!?

All these "frauds" do occur, and some are more serious than others. There have been cases of pedophiles finding children online, and luring the kids to their homes, for instance. So remember, cyberspace may be real, but it's only one part of reality. Although after a few weeks of e-mail or newsgroup exchanges it's easy to feel that you really know the person, you don't!

Keeping Little Johnny Out of Trouble

Here's an area of "security" that concerns many parents: how do you make sure your kids are not getting into trouble on the Internet?

Of course "trouble" means different things to different people. All parents would regard their child being lured out of the home to visit a pedophile as trouble. Other things may worry some parents and not others. How do you prevent your child from downloading explicit pictures from the **alt.binaries.erotica** newsgroups? How do you make sure he doesn't fall in with the wrong online crowd and end up discussing subjects you feel are "inappropriate" for his age? What can you do?

The easiest way to avoid problems is to make sure that your children don't have access to the Internet. Granted, this seems rather drastic, like banning books from your home just in case a few of them have naughty words in the text or naughty bits in the pictures. As an alternative, perhaps you could also subscribe to an online system that limits access to the Internet—a system such as America Online, which provides newsgroups and some gophering capabilities, but doesn't let them go just anywhere.

Does that stop kids from getting into trouble? Not really. AOL has 12,000 newsgroups, some of which many parents would regard as inappropriate. I don't know of any Internet service provider that has a "parental control" option by which parents can block certain areas and tools to children (although maybe that's coming soon).

Perhaps the only way to make sure your kids are safe in cyberspace is to monitor their use. First, make sure you understand how to use the tools and programs your kids are using. Then look in on them now and again. I'm not suggesting anything more obtrusive than the way you would check in on your kids playing in the backyard or get to know their teachers and friends at school. Make sure you know how your children are using the Internet.

And while it's okay to be cautious, don't get paranoid! Loosen up, relax! The world is a dangerous place, but we don't have to worry about it all day. For every kid getting into trouble in cyberspace, there are thousands getting into real trouble out in the real world. Does it matter if your 15-year old finds a photograph of a couple involved in a gymnastic maneuver involving a bed, a rope, and a couple of pulleys? (Even if you keep your kids from finding this stuff online, do you think you can keep them from seeing it at school?) Does it really matter if your kid runs into a chat group in which participants are using language as foul as that found on the... er... playground?

The Least You Need to Know

➤ By encrypting your e-mail, you can be sure that the only people who can read it are the people you want to read it.

➤ You can place orders by credit card over the Internet.

➤ You can get ripped off placing orders over the Internet (just as you can when using a credit card at a restaurant).

➤ More secure methods for placing orders will arrive someday, but perhaps not for a year or two.

➤ It's easy to feel you know people you've met in cyberspace—but you don't!

➤ If you want to know what your kids are up to online, there's only one way to find out: keep an eye on them.

➤ Relax! Although cyberspace can be dangerous, so can "realspace." Don't get paranoid.

Part IV
Now for the Neat Stuff

In Part IV I teach you how to bring your Internet connection out of the 1960s and into the 1990s. Most users are still digging their way through a user interface based in UNIX, an operating system designed about 30 years ago. Why can't you use a graphical user interface (GUI) on the Internet? You can.

In Chapter 25, I explain a few ways that you might go about upgrading your Internet connection, and I tell you what's going to happen in the near future on the Internet. But that's not all. With this book, we've bundled a disk (you hadn't noticed?!) that contains the SuperHighway Access Sampler, a dial-in direct program from Frontier Technologies Corp. In Chapters 26 and 27, I show you how to install the software, and how to use it.

JERRY REALLY GETS INTO THE ONLINE CHAT ROOMS.

## Chapter 25

Join Us in the 1990s

In This Chapter

➤ Adding offline navigators to your terminal connection

➤ Installing Internet shareware

➤ Running TCP/IP software on a plain terminal account

➤ Installing commercial Internet tools

➤ Using The Pipeline and NetCruiser

➤ Working with a commercial online information service

➤ Seeing the future

The type of user interface most people are working with on the Internet was designed in the 1960s. It's a command-line system: you type the commands you want carried out. On most systems, this command line has been augmented by menus from which you can select options, but still, Internet access is pretty clunky when compared to the slick, graphical software most of us use for our other daily tasks (such as word processing and number crunching).

The proper term for graphics-based software is **Graphical User Interface**, or GUI for short. Examples of GUIs include Microsoft Windows, the Macintosh, and OS/2.

Although most people do the majority of their work in a graphical user interface, they are still stuck at the command line when it comes to the Internet. That's why most of this book is based on the UNIX command line method of working with the Internet.

However, this is changing. In the past 12 months, dozens of GUI-based software products have been released that help make the Internet a more graphical place to be. In this chapter, we'll take a look at the new available software that can help you move your Internet connection into the 1990s.

What Was the Problem?

You are reading the second edition of *The Complete Idiot's Guide to the Internet*. When I wrote the first version late in 1993, there weren't many options for Internet users. Most were condemned to the command line, with little chance of moving to a GUI.

Dial-in terminal account users were at the mercy of their service providers' systems. Since every service provider's system is slightly different, software developers found it difficult to write GUI software to work with more than one of them. A few service providers were ambitious enough to provide GUI software to their users, but that software was limited to that particular provider.

Dial-in direct and permanent connections were generic enough that programmers could write GUI software for use with any service provider—but the software that was available really wasn't very good. Most of it was in a developmental phase. For example, Mosaic (the graphical World Wide Web browser we hear so much about these days) was available in a test (beta) version, but it wasn't very stable.

Users working across telephone lines with a dial-in direct account had an additional problem. They had to install TCP/IP software so they could run a SLIP, CSLIP, or PPP connection. The problem was that these connections were very difficult to set up. As late as March of 1994, *Boardwatch* Magazine described all such software as "barely installable by humanoids."

In addition to all that fuss, SLIP, CSLIP, and PPP connections were expensive: at least $175 for a setup charge (maybe as much as $250) plus, in many cases, higher hourly connect charges than for dial-in terminal connections.

...But It's Different Now

A lot has changed in a year. There are now plenty of really good commercial and shareware GUI programs for the Internet, and they are easier to install than they used to be (though not always a breeze). In addition, dial-in direct accounts have dropped in price tremendously. You shouldn't pay more than $35 to $45 for a setup fee (sometimes a lot less), and the connect charges will probably be the same as dial-in terminal accounts.

Another important change is that the distinction between dial-in terminal and dial-in direct accounts is starting to blur. It used to be that if you wanted the fancy interfaces, you had to have a dial-in direct account (a TCP/IP connection). But now there are neat GUIs available for non-TCP/IP connections. There are also a number of "offline navigators," programs that handle e-mail and newsgroups on a simple terminal connection. One of the more advanced is The Pipeline, which enables you to use a Windows interface for most Internet tools, without the hassle of installing a TCP/IP connection. However, even TCP/IP connections are getting easy to install (well, sometimes). I'd bet that most NetCruiser users don't even realize they are using a TCP/IP connection when they dial into their NETCOM Internet connection. There's no need for them to understand the technology; the NetCruiser installation program takes care of it all.

I'm trying to cover a book's worth of information in one chapter here. If you want to upgrade your Internet connection, read *The Complete Idiot's Next Step with the Internet*. In that book, I provide detailed instructions on installing shareware GUI software for DOS computers, and I tell you where to find good commercial GUIs. Also available soon is *The Complete Idiot's Guide to World Wide Web*, in which I explain how to install Mosaic and other Web browsers on both Macs and PCs.

So, let's look at some of the ways you can bring a GUI to your Internet connection.

Work Online—Offline

If you've used CompuServe, you may have heard the term *offline navigator*. An offline navigator is a program that lets you do most of your work offline—that is, when you are not connected to the system. CompuServe has a few of these offline navigators. Although NavCIS is probably the best, there are also TapCIS, OzCIS, OzWin, WigWam, and more. And now they are appearing in the Internet world.

This is how an offline navigator works. You click on a button or select a command and the program dials into your service provider. When it connects, it grabs your e-mail and newsgroup messages, and then logs off. You read your messages, write responses, and click on the button again. The program logs on again, drops off your messages, and grabs any new messages that have arrived for you since it last logged on.

There are two advantages to this sort of system. First, you spend less time online (and, therefore, less money). Second, the program isn't restricted to the funky interface your service provider provides; it can have any kind of interface its designers want, which means, these days, a GUI.

In the Internet world, there are several such systems, as the next few sections describe.

WinNET News & Mail

Computer Witchcraft, Inc.
330F Distillery Commons
Louisville, KY 40206-1919
800-589-5999
Voice: 502-589-6800
help@win.net

This product is designed for use with the WinNET service, which provides e-mail and newsgroups. The charge is $8/hour with a $9.95 monthly minimum. If you use WinNET's 800 number, you will pay an extra 18 cents a minute for calls made between 8 a.m. and 5 p.m. EST during the week, and 12 cents a minute for calls at other times.

WinNET News & Mail is also available as shareware, for use with UUCP mail accounts (other versions, perhaps a dial-in terminal version, may be available soon). The registration price is $99.

You can get the commercial version of WinNET News & Mail by sending e-mail to **request@win.net**. In the **Subject** line, include **WinNET**. You'll get a reply containing UUENCODED program files, which you'll have to UUDECODE.

To get a copy of the software, send e-mail to **request@win.net**. In the **Subject** line, type **help**, and you'll receive a list of software that you can download. Check to see if there is a dial-in terminal system available. If you want the UUCP version, send e-mail to **request@win.net**, and type **UUCP** in the **Subject** line. You'll get a reply containing UUENCODED program files, which you'll have to UUDECODE.

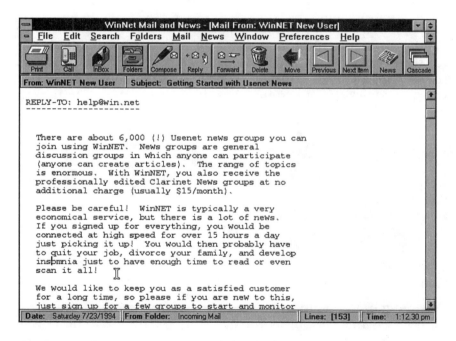

WinNet provides a point-and-click interface to e-mail and newsgroups.

Pronto

CommTouch Software, Inc.
1206 W. Hillsdale Blvd.
Suite C
San Mateo, CA 94403
800-638-6824
Voice: 415-578-6580
Fax: 415-578-8580

Pronto is sold by the CommTouch Software company. Single copies sell for $149. I've worked with an e-mail version, but a version that also downloads newsgroup messages is in the works and may be available by the time you read this.

RFD Mail

RFD Mail is a shareware program ($29.95) that lets you connect to a dial-in terminal account and grab your e-mail. You can find it at the **ftp.std.com** FTP site in the **/customers/software/rfdmail** directory. It comes with a few scripts to make it run on some service provider's systems. Check the **/customers/software/rfdmail/scripts/beta** directory for more scripts, or you can write your own.

Cyberdesk

CyberCorp, Inc.
P.O. Drawer 1988
Kennesaw, GA 30144   USA
Voice: 404-424-6240
Fax: 404-424-8995
cyber@netcom.com
CompuServe: 72662,1267

This program can grab e-mail and newsgroup messages, and also carries out FTP sessions (as long as you give it all the information it needs). It even handles e-mail from other systems, such as CompuServe, MCImail, cc:Mail, and so on. It costs from $179 to $229.

There are limits to how much these programs can do. Because each service provider has a different setup, a dial-in terminal program can't do everything. E-mail and newsgroups are fairly simple to automate, but to add other tools is very difficult. If you need more, you will have to read on.

Dial-In Direct to Your Terminal Account!

Let's say you want to use all the fancy TCP/IP software, but you can't get a dial-in direct line. Perhaps you have an account through work or school, and they simply don't provide TCP/IP connections. Do you just give up? No, there's one more option—The Internet Adapter.

The Internet Adapter is a $25 program (you can try it for free) that lets you run TCP/IP software on a dial-in terminal connection. You have to install a program on your service provider's system, and then install all the TCP/IP software on your own computer. For instance, if you are using Windows you could install Trumpet Winsock.

You use the system by starting the program you loaded at the service provider's end and then starting the TCP/IP software on your computer. The Internet Adapter fools your TCP/IP software into thinking it's running on a TCP/IP connection. If everything's set up correctly, you'll get a fancy interface on a plain vanilla terminal connection.

However, there is one catch (isn't there always?). Installing this stuff is no five-minute job. If your idea of "getting under the hood" of your computer is running a Windows Setup program, you'll find The Internet Adapter a little out of your league. You'll need some patience because everything has to be set up just right. But the program's publisher, Cyberspace Development, Inc., is putting all sorts of documentation online to lead you through the installation procedure. If you want to learn more, send e-mail to **tia-info@marketplace.com** for an automatic response telling you what it's all about, or point your Web browser to **http://marketplace.com/**, or gopher to **marketplace.com**.

Free and Almost Free Software

There are mountains of great shareware and freeware programs on the Internet. You can install GUI programs that will work with your e-mail and newsgroups even on your dial-in terminal account. But if you want a complete suite of shareware GUI Internet tools, you'll need a TCP/IP dial-in direct connection.

If you are working with a PC, install Trumpet Winsock, a $20 shareware program. (See *The Complete Idiot's Next Step with the Internet* for detailed instructions for installing this program.) If you are working with a Macintosh, you need MacTCP from Apple, plus some sort of PPP

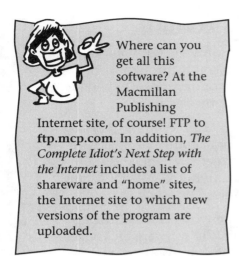

Where can you get all this software? At the Macmillan Publishing Internet site, of course! FTP to **ftp.mcp.com**. In addition, *The Complete Idiot's Next Step with the Internet* includes a list of shareware and "home" sites, the Internet site to which new versions of the program are uploaded.

or SLIP software, such as the freeware programs MacPPP and InterSLIP. (I describe how to install a Macintosh dial-in direct connection in *The Complete Idiot's Guide to World Wide Web*.) Apple includes MacTCP with its most recent operating system, System 7.5.

Once you've got your TCP/IP connection up and running, you can install all sorts of free and low-cost programs, such as WS_FTP (a Windows program that turns FTP into something that's actually enjoyable) or WinWeb, MacWeb, and Mosaic (World Wide Web browsers), and plenty more. There are GUI programs for Gopher, telnet, Ping, Internet Relay Chat (a chat program that lets people all over the world join in discussions over the Internet), Finger, WAIS, e-mail, newsgroups—almost all Internet tools.

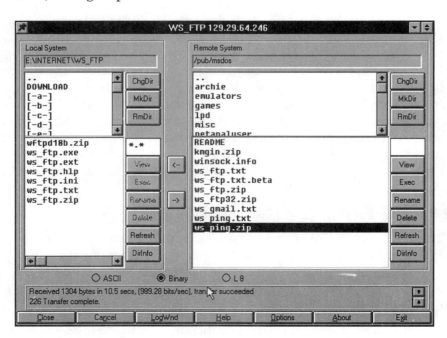

WS_FTP makes FTP sessions simple.

Laying Down the Dough for Software

First, I have to say that some of the available shareware and freeware is excellent—in many cases better than the commercial software. If you can manage to get a TCP/IP connection running, installing the tools is simple, so at least consider using it. (I'm going to make setting up your TCP/IP connection easy with the software on this book's disk. See Chapter 26.)

If you want to take the commercial route, though, there are a number of products available.

Internet Chameleon

NetManage, Inc.
10725 North De Anza Blvd.
Cupertino, CA 95014
Voice: 408-973-7171
Fax: 408-257-6405
info@netmanage.com

Sold by NetManage, this system lists for $199. It includes FTP, telnet, Finger, Ping, Gopher, e-mail, newsgroups, whois, and WWW. Although it has received a lot of criticism for poor interface design, this program is usable.

Internet in a Box/AIR Series

SPRY
316 Occidental Avenue South
Seattle, WA 98104
800-777-9638
Voice: 206-447-0300
Fax: 206-447-9008
info@spry.com

This product is distributed in two ways. In one incarnation, it's known as *Internet in a Box* and can be bought in bookstores and software houses ($149 list price). This version is sold by O'Reilly & Associates. In its other incarnation, it's known as the AIR Series and is sold directly by SPRY, the company that actually writes the software. The AIR Series has various combinations: AIR Connect, AIR NFS, AIR Navigator, and so on. SPRY regards Internet in a Box as a consumer product and the AIR Series as a corporate product.

This system makes setting up a dial-in direct connection very easy. The program has a Web browser, e-mail, newsgroups, FTP, telnet, UUCODE (a UUENCODE/UUDECODE program), and Gopher. Its weakness is that it is not a full suite of tools, and you can't run other Internet programs (shareware or freeware, for instance) using the program's TCP/IP software. However, SPRY says they'll fix that problem soon.

WinGopher

NOTIS Systems, Inc.
1007 Church Street
Evanston, IL 60201-3665
800-556-6847
Voice: 708-866-0150
Fax: 708-866-0178

WinGopher is an excellent Windows gophering tool. WinGopher Complete is $129. If you already have a dial-in direct or permanent connection and don't need the TCP/IP Winsock software, you can get WinGopher for $69.

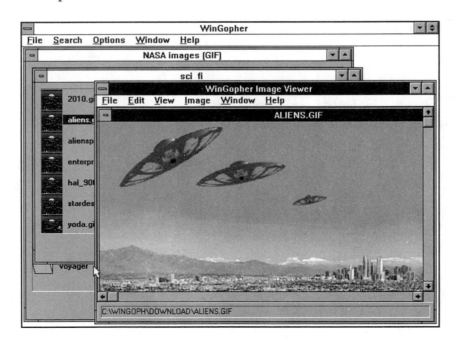

WinGopher has built-in viewers, so you can quickly see your Gopher finds.

SuperHighway Access

This is one of the newest of the bunch, which is due to be released about the time that this book goes to print. It simplifies installation by providing configuration files for most of the service providers in the United States. As an added bonus, you've got a sampler of this program on the disk at the back of this book! For more information, see Chapter 26.

Software/Service Bundles

Another way to get an Internet GUI is to work with a service provider that gives you GUI software designed to work with its system. At the time of this writing, two such notable systems are NetCruiser and The Pipeline.

NetCruiser

NETCOM
3031 Tisch Way, 2nd Floor
San Jose, CA 95128
800-353-6600
Voice: 408-345-2600
Fax: 408-241-9145
info@netcom.com

This Windows system is available from NETCOM (a Mac version should be released in 1995). Its simple installation program installs a PPP connection for you. NetCruiser has a Web browser, FTP, telnet, e-mail, newsgroups, Gopher, and Finger. As with Internet in a Box, you can't add components to NetCruiser; only NetCruiser applications will run over NetCruiser's PPP connection, so you can't add shareware.

There's a $25 registration fee (which gets you the software). Then you'll pay $19.95 a month. For that you'll get 40 "peak" hours and as many hours as you want on weekends and from midnight to 9 a.m. during the week. If you use more than 40 peak hours, you'll pay $2/ hour for those extra hours. At the time of this writing, NETCOM was offering a free first month of service.

The Pipeline

The Pipeline
150 Broadway
Suite 1710
New York, NY 10028
Voice: 212-267-3636
Fax: 212-267-4380
E-mail: info@pipeline.com
Modem: 212-267-6432 (log in as *guest*)
Telnet, Gopher, FTP: pipeline.com

The Pipeline has very easy-to-use Windows and Macintosh interfaces. It's a packet-switching system, but it doesn't use TCP/IP. Instead, it uses a proprietary system called Pink SLIP. Originally intended for use with a service provider called The Pipeline in New York, the software is being licensed and installed by service providers throughout the United States.

If you want to use The Pipeline service itself, these are the charges:

➤ $15/month with 5 free hours, $2/hour for extra hours

➤ $20/month with 20 free hours, $2/hour for extra hours

➤ $35/month, no limit on hours

 You can get The Pipeline software and check it out for free. My "sequel" to this book, the first edition of *The Complete Idiot's Next Step with the Internet* is bundled with The Pipeline software. You can also get the software in *The Complete Idiot's Guide to The Pipeline*, which will be available in April 1995.

These charges are only for connect time, not for phone charges. If you are not within local-call distance, you've got four choices; you can dial long distance, use SprintNet (an extra charge), dial in through a local service provider and use **rlogin** (remote login) to connect to The Pipeline, or dial in to your service provider on a TCP/IP account and connect to The Pipeline.

If you want to use The Pipeline software with a local service provider, contact The Pipeline for the names of licensees.

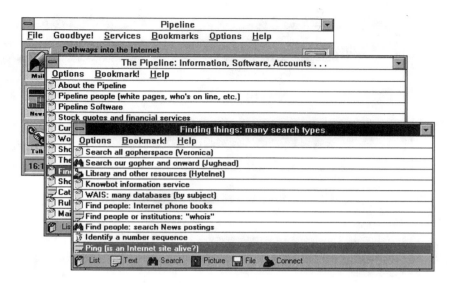

The Pipeline is an all-in-one Internet package.

Delphi

This online service provides full terminal access to the Internet. It has a simple Windows program that helps you work on the Internet, but it's by no means as sophisticated as the interfaces provided by The Pipeline and NetCruiser. See the coupon at the back of this book for contact information and information about getting a free trial.

Online Services: The Big Boys Get In on the Act

The commercial online services are not going to sit on the sidelines and watch the Internet grow. They want part of the action.

At the time of this writing, America Online (AOL) is the largest of the online services to get Internet services running, although it's by no means a full Internet connection. It has about 12,000 newsgroups and a hybrid Gopher/WAIS system. It also has e-mail and mailing lists, of course, but virtually all commercial online systems do these days. However, AOL provides detailed explanations for subscribing to mailing lists. (See the coupons at the back of this book for information about a free AOL trial.)

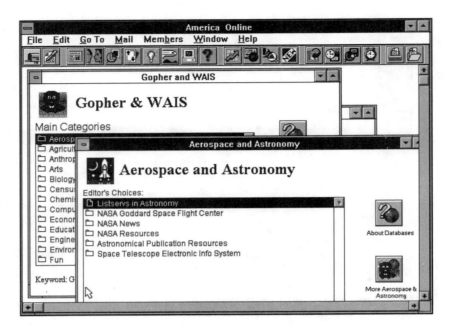

America Online, the first large commercial system connected to the Internet.

CompuServe recently started providing newsgroups, but it doesn't have any other Internet services (at the time of this writing). However, CompuServe is going to expand into the Internet market quickly. By November of 1994, they will be selling PPP Internet access to the Internet. They also claim that CompuServe subscribers will be able to use telnet and FTP by the end of 1994, that more tools will be added in 1995, and that a Web browser and Gopher tool should be working by the middle of 1995. What all this will look like is hard to say.

These two services are not the only ones getting in on the act. You can expect others, such as GEnie and PRODIGY, to add Internet services soon.

What's Next?

How will Internet software develop? Here are my predictions (nothing really psychic here, just stating the obvious).

➤ There are going to be lots more GUI software programs for the Internet. It may take a year or two, but eventually the tide will turn and more Internet users will be working with GUIs than with the command line.

➤ The software is going to become much easier to install. Setting up a dial-in direct account will be pretty simple. (Several products already make it simple, and the others will catch up.)

➤ Packet-switching connections, whether true TCP/IP connections or hybrids like Pink SLIP, will become the most popular connection.

➤ Computers will come bundled with Internet software. In the same way that you get Windows when you buy a PC these days, in 1995 it will become common for computer manufacturers to include a suite of Internet tools. DEC, for example, is planning to bundle Enhanced NCSA Mosaic on its computers. Windows and OS/2 will also soon contain Internet tools.

So Where's Windows 95 and When?

One very important development on the horizon (well, over the horizon, perhaps), is Windows 95. This is the next version of Microsoft Windows, which has been known as Chicago for some time. This was supposed to be released late in 1994, but at the time of this writing, it seems unlikely that we'll see it until the summer of 1995, maybe even fall. In fact, by the time it's released it may have to be renamed Windows $95^1/_2$, or Windows Almost 96.

Anyway, whatever you want to call it, this new operating system will have a very important feature for Internet users: built-in TCP/IP support, including a dialer. In other words, Windows 95 users will be able to connect their computers to a TCP/IP network or a dial-in direct connection, without buying extra TCP/IP software and with (we hope) a minimum of fuss.

Microsoft says they will be including configuration files for many service providers, eliminating the headaches most people get when trying to install TCP/IP software. They are also starting their own online service called *Marvel*. Presumably, connecting Windows 95 to Marvel will be very easy.

Don't Forget OS/2 & Macintosh!

IBM is actually one step ahead of Microsoft, adding Internet tools to OS/2. OS/2 Warp has FTP, telnet, Gopher, e-mail, newsgroups, and a

Web browser. It will also be very easy to connect to IBM's own Internet service, Advantis. OS/2 Warp plus the Internet tools costs approximately $100 and is available now.

And let's not forget Macintosh. As I mentioned earlier, Apple is including MacTCP with System 7.5, their latest operating system.

The TCP/IP connection is still the sticking point for many users. Once you've got your TCP/IP connection up and running, installing your Internet tools is very easy. For example, although installing Mosaic takes no more than 10 minutes, installing the TCP/IP connection might take a few hours (or days?), and many users give up in frustration. Windows 95, OS/2 3.0, and System 7.5 should eliminate this problem for many users.

The Least You Need to Know

➤ You can add offline navigators to a simple terminal Internet connection.

➤ There's plenty of GUI shareware for the Internet, although it's mostly for dial-in direct connections.

➤ You can buy suites of Internet tools for dial-in direct connections.

➤ The Pipeline and NETCOM provide their subscribers with neat user interfaces.

➤ AOL and CompuServe are becoming Internet service providers, and other online services will follow.

➤ Internet access is being built into the next generation of operating systems, such as Apple's System 7.5, Windows 95, and OS/2 Warp.

Loading SuperHighway Access

Now you're to the good part: where you finally learn how to load the neat software on the disk. This software is SuperHighway Access Sampler, a new program from Frontier Technologies Corporation. It's a scaled-down version of the full SuperHighway Access suite of programs, and it contains a TCP/IP "stack" (the program that connects to your service provider and lets you run TCP/IP software), FTP, and a newsreader. There's also a special FTP icon that runs the FTP program and automatically downloads another program from SuperHighway Access called Tapestry. This program is a unique interface combining Gopher, World Wide Web, and a "phone book" application.

Get Ready: What Do You Need?

To run the sampler, you'll need at least Windows 3.1 or Windows for Workgroups 3.1, DOS 5.0, a modem, 3 MB RAM, a 386 microprocessor, and 2 MB free on your hard drive. As is the case with all hardware, more is better.

As for connections, you need a dial-in direct account (SLIP, CSLIP, or PPP) for this software. If you already have a dial-in terminal account, call and ask about setting up a dial-in direct account. (Unfortunately you'll find that Free-Nets and colleges generally won't be able to set up such an account.)

If you want to find a service provider in your area, the SuperHighway Access software can help you. During the installation process, you'll be able to see a list of service providers in your area. You can also get this information by running the file on the installation disk called SHASRVRS.HLP. This is a Windows Help file. Double-click on it in File Manager to open it, and you'll see a map of the United States. Click on a state (or click on the Europe, Alaska, or Hawaii boxes), and you'll see a screen listing service providers in that area. These are not comprehensive lists, and in some cases, the lists may be empty, but these are all the service providers for which SuperHighway Access currently has setup files. If you can't find a service provider in your area, see Chapter 4 for more information about finding one.

Get Set: Gathering the Information

If you are working with one of the service providers included in the SuperHighway Access installation procedure, you probably won't have much work to do. Frontier Technologies has created setup files and login scripts for those service providers, so all you'll need to do is enter a little bit of information—nothing complicated. If you are working with a different service provider, however, you have a little bit more work. (To find out which these are, simply run the installation program. If you find that your service provider is not listed, you can cancel the procedure, go gather the information, and then come back.)

Here's what you need:

Your IP number   Each host on the Internet is identified by an IP (Internet Protocol) number. Your service provider may give you a number that is yours and yours alone. On the other hand, they may use a system called BOOTP, or a system of dynamically providing the number when you log in (in which case, you may get a different number each time you log in). You need to know (a) your IP number, or (b) whether they are using the BOOTP method of IP number assignment, or (c) whether they are dynamically assigning numbers.

The phone number   This is the phone number you must dial to get to your service provider.

SLIP, CSLIP, or PPP   You need to know which type of account you are using: SLIP, CSLIP, or PPP.

User name   You'll need the user name you were given or that you chose when you got your account.

Password   Finally, you need the password you were given or that you chose.

If you are working with another service provider, one that SuperHighway Access does not include in the installation procedure, you also need this information:

The Domain Name   The service provider's domain name by which it is identified on the Internet: **usa.net**, **cscns.com**, **csn.org**, or whatever.

Go: Installing SuperHighway Access Sampler

Okay, let's assume you have a service provider, you have a SLIP or PPP account set up, you have all the information you need, and you are ready to roll.

Follow this procedure to install the Sampler:

1. Place the disk in your disk drive.

2. In Program Manager, open the **File** menu and select **Run**.

3. In the Run dialog box, type **a:install** and press **Enter**. (If your disk drive is not drive a:, substitute the correct drive letter.)

4. You will see a dialog box asking if you already have a service provider. Click on the **Yes** button. (Click on the **No** button to see the list of service providers that we discussed earlier in this chapter.)

5. You'll see a list of service providers and the different types of accounts: SLIP, CSLIP, and PPP (see figure below). Click on your account type and click **OK**. (If you can't find your service provider in this list, select the appropriate **Other** option at the top of the list, and then go to the section entitled "The Tricky Stuff: Setting Up Another Service Provider," later in this chapter.)

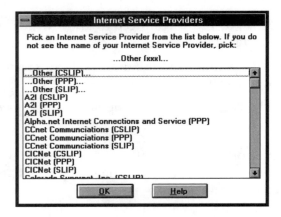

Pick your service provider from a list of dozens.

6. A dialog box appears asking for your user name and password (see figure below). Enter both of these items (be very careful how you type your password, as the text box will only show asterisks, not the actual characters you type), and click on **OK**.

Enter your user name and password.

306

7. Now you'll see a dialog box asking for your modem type (see figure below). Select the one you are using; if you are not sure, select **Other**; then click on **OK**.

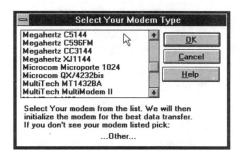

Select your modem.

8. A list of phone numbers appears. These are the numbers that should work for your service provider. Select the one you want to use, and click on **OK**. (You'll be able to change the number later if necessary.)

9. Now a dialog box appears asking for your IP address (see figure below). This is the number that will identify your computer as a host on the Internet. Type the number here or, if your service provider told you to use RARP or BOOTP, type that into the box. (If your service provider says that numbers are dynamically assigned, type RARP; the program will know what to do.) Click **OK**.

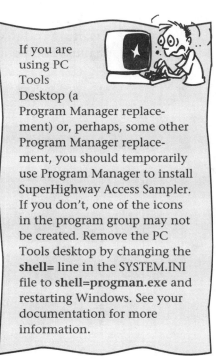

If you are using PC Tools Desktop (a Program Manager replacement) or, perhaps, some other Program Manager replacement, you should temporarily use Program Manager to install SuperHighway Access Sampler. If you don't, one of the icons in the program group may not be created. Remove the PC Tools desktop by changing the **shell=** line in the SYSTEM.INI file to **shell=progman.exe** and restarting Windows. See your documentation for more information.

307

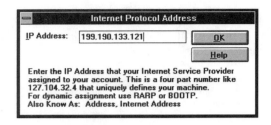

Enter your IP address, or type RARP or BOOTP (if you were told to do so by your service provider).

10. A message box appears. Read the message, and then click on **OK** and check the information in the Install Setup dialog box (shown below). In particular, make sure the phone number is correct. For example, you may have to remove the 1-*area code*, precede the number with **9**, (to get an outside line), or precede it with ***70**, or **1170**, (to turn off call waiting). (Different areas use different call waiting codes. Check with your phone company or in the front of your phone book.)

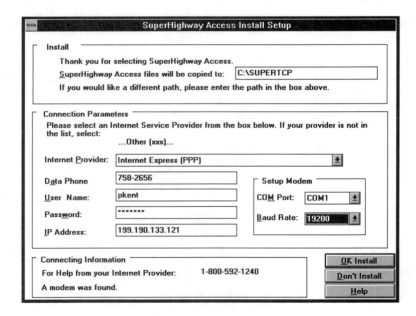

Check the Install Setup dialog box to make sure all the information is correct.

308

11. When you are sure the data is correct, click on the **OK Install** button. The program will install the files on your hard disk and create a program group and icons.

12. A message box pops up, informing you that your AUTOEXEC.BAT file has been modified and a backup has been made. Click on the **OK** button to remove the message.

13. Windows Write opens, displaying the README file. Read the file, and then close Write by pressing **Alt-F4**.

The Tricky Stuff: Setting Up Another Service Provider

If you are working with a service provider that's not on the SuperHighway Access list, you have to do a bit more work. You'll have to enter some configuration information and create a login script. Follow the previous procedure, up to step 5, where you see the list of service providers.

This time, select one of the first three options, **Other (CSLIP)**, **Other (PPP)**, or **Other (SLIP)**. Pick the appropriate one, according to the type of account you have set up with your service provider. Then click the **OK** button and follow these steps.

1. When the Define New Internet Service Provider dialog box appears, type the name of the provider (*Podunk Information Highway Express*, or whatever) and the phone number that you need to dial. You may have to precede the number with **9,** (to get an outside line) or with ***70,** or **1170,** (to turn off call waiting.) (Different areas use different call waiting codes. Check with your phone company or in the front of your phone book.) Click on **OK**.

2. You'll see a dialog box asking for your user name and password. Type both these items (be very careful how you type your password, as the text box will only show asterisks, not the actual characters you type) and click **OK**.

3. Now you'll see a dialog box asking for your modem type. Select the one you are using; if you are not sure, select **Other**; then click on **OK**.

4. Now a dialog box appears asking for your IP address. This is the number that will identify your computer as a host on the Internet. Type the number here or, if your service provider told you to use RARP or BOOTP, type that into the box. (If your service provider says that numbers are dynamically assigned, type RARP; the program will know what to do.) Click **OK**.

5. The Domain Name dialog box appears (see figure below). In the Machine Name text box, simply enter your user name again. (For example, I use pkent.) In the Domain Name box, type the service provider's domain name: **usa.net**, **cscns.com**, **csn.com**, or whatever; then click **OK**.

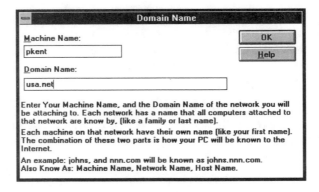

Enter Your Machine Name, and the Domain Name of the network you will
be attaching to. Each network has a name that all computers attached to
that network are know by, (like a family or last name).

Each machine on that network have their own name (like your first name).
The combination of these two parts is how your PC will be known to the
Internet.

An example: johns, and nnn.com will be known as johns.nnn.com.
Also Know As: Machine Name, Network Name, Host Name.

Enter your service provider's machine name and domain name.

6. A message box appears. Read the message, and then click on **OK** and check the information in the Install Setup dialog box.

7. When you are sure the data is correct, click on the **OK Install** button. The program will install the files on your hard disk and create a program group and icons.

For information about contacting Frontier, or about the rest of their products, double-click on the **Read Me** icon.

8. A message box pops up, informing you that your AUTOEXEC.BAT file has been modified, and a backup has been made. Click on the **OK** button to remove the message.

9. Windows Write opens, displaying the README file. Read the file, and then close Write by pressing **Alt-F4**.

Test Start: Will It Work the First Time?

We're ready to try to connect to your service provider. The first time you connect is a test, because we need to check the login script. If you selected one of the service providers in the list box, you'll probably connect on the first try (not necessarily, though, because the service provider may have changed the login procedure). If you had to enter your own service provider, you may be lucky, and the default procedure will work. On the other hand, it may need tweaking.

First, double-click on the **SuperTCP** icon in the SuperHighway Access program group. This will start the SuperTCP Kernel program (the dialer) and open a SuperTCP Kernel message box so you can view the login procedure. You can now watch as the program tries to log on to your system. (If the message box doesn't appear, select **File|Messages**.) You want to see something like this:

```
COMM5001: 0: Waiting for: "ppp".
COMM5005: 0: Received: " ppp"-
COMM5031: 0: Initialized.
PPP5006: Line 1:  COM1 up
PPP5023: Line 1: LCP packet received from the peer
PPP5015: Line 1: LCP phase successfully completed
PPP5016: Line 1: Set new control map for outgoing packets: 0x00000000
PPP5017: Line 1: Begin protocol compression on outgoing packets
PPP5018: Line 1: Begin protocol compression on incoming packets
PPP5019: Line 1: Begin addr/ctl compression on outgoing packets
PPP5021: Line 1: Begin addr/ctl compression on incoming packets
PPP5027: Line 1: Begin Van Jacobson TCP/IP header compression on out-
going packets
PPP5028: Line 1: Local IP address is 199.190.133.121
PPP5029: Line 1: Remote IP address is 165.212.9.10
PPP5030: Line 1: IPCP phase successfully completed
PPP5031: Line 1: Link Open
```

Every line, starting with **COMM5031: 0: Initialized** to the end, is the PPP connection being set up; the **Link Open** at the end lets you know it all went well. (If you are using SLIP, you'll see a much simpler output; look for the **SLIP or COM1 Up** message.) Take a look at the SuperTCP Kernel icon on your desktop. When the connection has been made, the three colored balls are connected by pipes; if the connection didn't work, they just float unconnected. (If you're connected, I give you permission to jump to the next chapter. If not, read on.)

If you see a message that says something like **Peer not listening. Closing LCP** or **Modem Control Failed! Never received text "PPP"** or **Modem Control Failed! Never received an IP address**, the login failed. Click on the **Done** button, click on the SuperTCP Kernel window, and press **Alt-F4** to close both the window and the connection to your service provider.

Write Your Own Script!

If you are unable to connect to your service provider, you probably need to fix your login script. But first, call your service provider. They should be willing to tell you what to enter into the script; after all, if they figure it out once, they can quickly give the information to any other users who request it.

Still, they may not be so helpful. In that case, you're going to have to create your own script (or maybe you should find a friendlier service provider).

Test the Connection

Before writing the script, test the connection using an ordinary telecommunications program such as Windows Terminal, CrossTalk, or HyperACCESS. You can dial into the number given you by your service provider and try to use the dial-in direct logon procedure. You won't be able to get all the way, because these communications programs are not TCP/IP programs, but you will be able to check that you have the correct user name, password, and startup command.

Record the session. Virtually all such programs these days let you record every word that passes over the lines during the session. In Windows Terminal, for instance, use the **Transfers|Receive Text File** command to select a file in which Terminal can store the session.

Here's a sample session I recorded when testing my connection to Colorado Spring's Internet Express, from the point at which it asks for my user name.

```
Username: pkent
Password: (I entered my password here)
Permission granted


                    Community News Service (CNS,Inc.)
                           in affiliation with
                          ==TELEPHONE EXPRESS==
                         If you need assistance,
                        please call CNS at 719-592-1240


Type "c" followed by <RETURN> to continue slip

Switching to SLIP.
Annex address is 165.212.9.10.  Your address is 199.190.133.121.
~E41>@-[b¥#Ç^*y@x$#Ü¦Ä_  (this is where I hung up)
NO CARRIER
```

If I connect using PPP, the last few lines are a little different:

```
If you need assistance, please call CNS at 719-592-1240

Type "c" followed by <RETURN> to continue ppp

Switching to PPP.
~ÿ}#@!}!}!} }4}"}&} } } } }%}&!*}'}"}(}"_«~~ÿ}#*!}!}"} }4}"}&} } }
} }%}&Z__}9}'}"}(}"@©~~ÿ}#*!}!}!}#} }4}"}&} } }}}%}&Ü}?v»}'}"}(}"}+%~
```

In this case, I go straight to PPP, without seeing the **Annex address is** line first.

From these sessions, we can see that the service provider's system is asking for a **Username:** and **Password:**. There's also the line **Type "c" followed by <RETURN> to continue**. I'd type **c** if I wanted to access my dial-in terminal account, but I have to type **slip** and press **Enter** to get into SLIP mode, or **ppp** and press **Enter** to get into PPP. The service provider's system then tells me my IP address (in SLIP mode, but not in PPP mode).

Once in SLIP or PPP mode, I just see garbage. That's okay. I got as far as I needed to, so now I can disconnect using the telecommunications program's hang-up command. In addition to helping me verify that the account was set up correctly, this test gave me something else: the information I need to write a login script.

Now, Where's That Script?

Now we are ready to create the login script. Don't worry, it's relatively easy. Double-click on the **SetupTCP** icon in the SuperHighway Access program group. The SuperHighway Access Sampler for Windows window appears. Make sure the Internet Provider's icon is selected on the left side of this window. Click on the **Advanced** button near the bottom of the window, and click on the **Edit Script** button that appears (it's to the right of the column of icons, near the bottom).

In the Script Editing dialog box, click on the **Initialize** option button, and then click on the **Edit** button. You'll see the Initialization Script dialog box shown below.

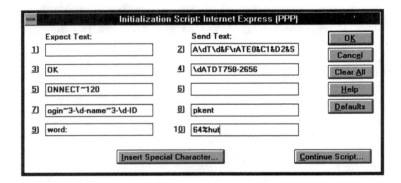

The Initialization Script box provides a relatively easy way to create scripts.

This dialog box shows the text that the program expects to see (the prompts and responses from your modem and service provider's system) on the left, followed by the text that you want to send in response on the right. (Depending on what service provider you selected earlier, the script may look a little different.) Assuming that the program can connect to your system, the information in text boxes 1 through 6 should be correct. These are simply the first few steps in which you dial into the system.

In box 7, you can see that the program is waiting for the login or user name ID: **ogin~3-\d-name~3-\d-ID** means "look for the text *ogin* or *name* or *ID*." So whether your service provider prompts for login name, or user name, or user ID, the program will be able to recognize it. What if your system prompts for something else? Type what it prompts for. For instance, it might have a prompt like this: **Log in>**.

The program won't find that. So replace the text in box 7 with **in>** (you can't enter spaces, so just **in>** will do).

The system prompts in the **Expect Text** column (the left column) are *case sensitive*. In other words, if your system prompts you for Password, you can't enter PASSWORD or password. You must enter it as it appears.

Box 8 should be correct. This is the user name you entered during the installation procedure. In other words, when the program sees the text in box 7 (login, name, ID, in>, or whatever), it sends your user name.

Box 9 is looking for **word**. So when your system prompts for password, SuperHighway Access will see it. If your system prompts for something different (**Login code:**, perhaps), type that instead. Box 10 contains the password you entered into the installation procedure earlier; the program sends that when it sees the text in box 9. When you've finished all the way to box 10, click on the **Continue Script** button to move on to boxes 11 through 22.

Here's where you are most likely to see problems. Box 11 tells the program what to look for next. It may not tell it anything, assuming that the program should simply start the PPP or SLIP connection. However, perhaps in your system, you have to tell the program more. In mine, I have to type **slip** or **ppp** at the **continue** prompt. So here's what my script looks like, starting at box 7:

```
Box 7: ogin~3-\d-name~3-\d-ID      Box 8: pkent

Box 9: word:                       Box 10: 64%hut

Box 11: continue                   Box 12: ppp

Box 13: PPP
```

Scripts can be tricky sometimes. Make sure you enter all the prompts and responses exactly as required. Still need help? Ask your service provider what information should be in the script. Likewise, Frontier Technologies is providing e-mail and fax technical support for the sampler. Contact them at **SuperHighway@FrontierTech. COM**.

In box 11, the program waits for the word *continue* (look back at my sample script, and you'll see **Type "c" followed by <RETURN> to continue**). In box 12, the program types **ppp**. In box 13, it waits until it sees *PPP* (in the script you'll see **Switching to PPP**). And that's the end of the script. (You must end the script with something in the Expect Text column.)

Now, click on the **OK** button several times to close the various dialog boxes, and then click on the **Close** button in the SuperHighway Access Sampler for Windows window. Repeat the test you did earlier, to try to connect to your service provider.

The Least You Need to Know

➤ SuperHighway Access Sampler has dozens of service providers already configured; you may be able to get rolling in ten minutes.

➤ If you connect to another service provider, you may still be able to get rolling quickly.

➤ Although you may have to modify the login script, the program provides tools to make this relatively easy.

YEEEEEEHAAAA!!!

Using SuperHighway Access

SuperHighway Access is a really cool graphical interface that will make working on the Internet much easier than using the UNIX shell. You'll find SuperHighway Access so much easier to use than the UNIX programs or your service provider's system that you may never go back! Here's a quick lesson in using these programs.

Your TCP/IP Foundation: SuperTCP

SuperTCP is the TCP/IP stack that you must have before you can run your programs. If you double-click on the **FTP** or **News Reader** icons,

SuperTCP will start automatically. Alternatively, you can double-click on the SuperTCP icon itself to start it. Note these important menu commands:

➤ **File|Messages**   Displays the box in which you can watch the login process. Remove this box by clicking on the **Done** button.

➤ **File|Make the Icon show Activity**   When this is selected, the program's icon animation is turned on. The icon "flashes" when data is being received.

➤ **File|Dial/Hang up Phone**   When the program is dialing or connected, this menu option has a check mark next to it. Select it to hang up the phone. Select again to reconnect.

➤ **File|Exit SuperTCP**   Closes the program. If you are connected, SuperTCP disconnects first.

Note that, unlike some of the TCP/IP stacks that come in a suite of programs (such as Internet in a Box and NetCruiser), SuperTCP is fully Winsock compatible. That means you can run other Windows TCP/IP programs, such as the many shareware and freeware programs (Mosaic, Cello, Trumpet News, WAIS for Windows, and more) available on the Internet. (See *The Complete Idiot's Next Step with the Internet* for information about these programs; see the forthcoming *Complete Idiot's Guide to World Wide Web* for more detailed information about TCP/IP Mosaic browsers.)

Check the Connection: Ping

Ping provides a quick way to make sure that a connection is up and running. Double-click on the icon to open the application (shown below). Type a host name or IP number into the Hostname text box and click on the **Start** button. The program sends a signal to that host, which responds. You may see a message like this:

```
64 byte response from [192.156.196.1]
usa.net
```

This also provides a quick way to find an IP number if you have the host name, or to find a host name if you have an IP number.

```
┌──────────────────────────────────────────────────────┐
│ ▬                          Ping                     ▼  │
│ File  Number  Specifications  Help                     │
│                                                        │
│  Hostname:  [192.156.196.1]        [Send 1 ping]       │
│  ┌─Status──────────────────────────────────────────┐  │
│  │ 64 byte response from [192.156.196.1]            │  │
│  │ usa.net                                          │  │
│  │                                                  │  │
│  └──────────────────────────────────────────────────┘ │
│  ┌─Packets─────────────────────────────────────────┐  │
│  │  Sent     Rec'd    % Lost    Short    Corrupted  │  │
│  │   1         1         0         0          0     │  │
│  └──────────────────────────────────────────────────┘ │
│  ┌─Time────────────────────────────────────────────┐  │
│  │ Curr: 0.331  Min: 0.331  Max: 0.331  Ave: 0.331  │  │
│  └──────────────────────────────────────────────────┘ │
│            [ Start ]    [ Stop ]    [ Exit ]           │
└──────────────────────────────────────────────────────┘
```

With Ping, you can find out if you can connect to a host.

Grabbing Those Files—FTP Can Be Fun!

You saw in Chapters 18 and 19 just how clunky UNIX FTP can be. Now you are going to find out the advantages of a graphical FTP program. Double-click on the **FTP** icon to open the program. (If SuperTCP is not running, it opens and dials; wait for it to connect before continuing.)

You'll see the Connect dialog box (shown below). In the top text box, type the name of the FTP site to which you want to connect. Click the **OK** button.

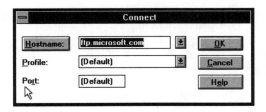

Enter the FTP site to which you want to go. Next time, you'll be able to select from the Profile drop-down list box.

You'll see the Connection Information dialog box (shown on the following page). Enter the user name (usually ***anonymous***) and password (usually your e-mail address) and, if you know it, a startup directory (the FTP site directory that you want to reach). Also, note the

Always Prompt check box. If you leave this checked, each time you connect, you'll see this dialog box and have the option of changing the information in it.

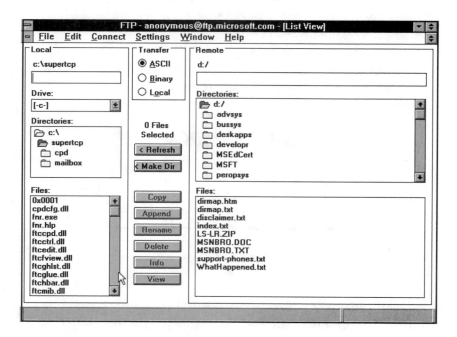

The Connection Information dialog box lets you configure the session

When you click on the **OK** button, FTP starts to make the connection. You'll see messages in the main window, and (if the site is available) when FTP connects, you'll see the List View window (shown below).

The List View brings the GUI to FTP!

Click on the maximize button in the top right corner of the window to expand the window. (At this point it's a good idea to select **File|Save As**, type a profile name in the Save As Profile dialog box for the site you've just selected, and click on **OK**. The next time you use FTP, you'll be able to select that profile to connect to this site.)

Now this is what FTP should look like! In the left column (the Local column), you can see the information about your hard disk. Use this column to select the drive and directory to which you want to copy files. On the right side (the Remote side), you'll see information about the FTP site. Again, use these boxes to select a directory and file.

In the middle, you'll find the transfer methods: ASCII, Binary, and Local. (Local is a rarely employed system used mainly on VMS hosts; you can usually ignore it.) See Chapter 18 for more information about transferring files.

Also in the middle are the buttons that do all the work:

Refresh   Select a directory and click on this to redisplay the contents.

Make Dir   Select a directory and click on this to create a subdirectory.

Copy   Select a file and click on this to copy the file to the other hard disk—from the FTP site to your hard disk (or vice versa if you have permission).

Append   Select a file on your hard disk and then click on this button to copy the file to the FTP site, adding the file to the end of a file of the same name. (Of course you can use this only if you have permission to write files to the site.)

Rename   Select a file and click on this to rename the file.

Delete   Select a file and click on this to delete the file.

Info   Select a file and click on this to view information about the file, including the file size, in the Messages window. (Press **Ctrl-F4** to close the Info window).

View   Select a text file and click on this to read it in Notepad.

When you finish your session, you can either select **Connect|-Disconnect** (and then **Connect|Connect** to go to another FTP site) or press **Alt-F4** to disconnect and close the window.

All the News That's Fit to Print

Let's get the SuperHighway Access News Reader program running. Double-click on the icon and you'll see the Connect dialog box (the same as the one you saw when working in FTP). Again, if SuperTCP isn't already running, it will start. Wait until you are fully connected, and then type the name of the host containing the newsgroups you want to read. Generally, this will be your service provider's hostname: **usa.net**, **cscns.com**, **csn.org**, or whatever. (If you are not sure, ask your service provider what you should type here.)

Click on **OK** and the initialization will begin. This may take some time, as the program is finding a list of all the newsgroups—which could be thousands. It could take as much as five minutes or so; as long as the **Updating Available Newsgroups** message in the bottom left of the status bar is flickering, you'll know something's happening. (Maximize the window, and you'll see the newsgroup count as the program grabs the names.) Just leave your system alone for a while, and eventually you'll see a dialog box with a list of the newsgroups at the host you selected (see figure below).

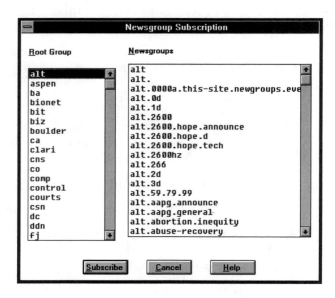

Use the Newsgroup Subscription dialog box to pick your newsgroups.

In the left column, you'll see the Root Group list. Click on one of these to see the groups in that hierarchy in the Newsgroups box. (See

Chapter 15 for information about the hierarchical system of news-groups.) To select multiple groups with a mouse, hold down the mouse button and drag the mouse pointer across the names (to select contiguous groups), or hold down Ctrl while you click on individual groups (to select non-contiguous groups). To select multiple groups with the keyboard, hold down the Shift key and press the down arrow key. Once you have the desired newsgroups selected, click on the **Subscribe** button. The dialog box disappears, and you go to the NNTP Server document window. (You can return to the Newsgroup Subscription dialog box by selecting **Groups|Subscribe**.) Click on the group you want to read, and then click on the **Read** button. The program runs off and gets the messages for you.

You'll see the messages listed in another document window. Double-click on the message you want to read, or click once on the message and click on the **Read** button. The message will pop up in another document window (see figure below).

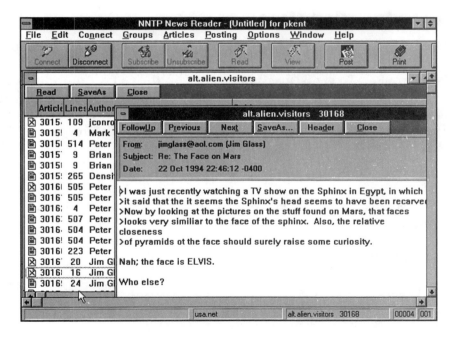

This sure beats rn or nn!

Now you can use the buttons at the top of the document window. Click **FollowUp** to send a reply to the message. Click **Previous** to display the previous message in the list. Click **Next** to display the next one. Click **Save As** to save the message in a text file. Click **Close** to close the document window.

Play around in the News Reader, and you'll find all sorts of neat features. You can save a text file directly from the list of messages—no need to open the message first. (Select multiple messages to save several at a time.) You can set up various configuration options from the Options menu; send new messages using the Posting menu; use the Articles menu to mark all the messages as read or unread; and more. Have fun!

Press **Alt-F4** to close the News Reader. You'll see a message asking if you want to save the profile. Click on **Yes** and type a profile name (**Daily**, for example); then click on **OK** again. The next time you open the News Reader, you'll see your list of newsgroups, ready for you to select and read.

WinTapestry—And More

There's more software just waiting for you at the Frontier Technologies FTP site, including a fully functional demo of Tapestry, a World Wide Web browser. To get it, just double-click on the **Get More Demos** icon in the SuperHighway Access program group. FTP will open and display the Connection Information dialog box. Just click on the **OK** button, and the program will connect to Frontier's DEMO directory at its FTP site.

In that directory, you'll see a file called README.TXT. Click on that file and then on the **View** button, and the file will open in Windows Notepad. This file tells you what demo files you can download. Right now there's a file called SHADEMO2.EXE, which is the WinTapestry demo file. By the time you look in this directory, there may be other files.

Close Notepad (press **Alt+F4**) and use the FTP tools to select a directory into which you want to place the SHADEMO file. You may want to use the Make Dir button to create a new subdirectory. Then click on the SHADEMO2.EXE file and click on the **Copy** button. FTP will start transferring the file to your hard disk (it may take a while; it's a big file).When you've finished, press **Alt-F4** to close FTP, and use File Manager to go to the directory where you placed SHADEMO2. Double-click on the file to extract the archived files inside; then, in File Manager, press **F5** to re-read the directory. In the directory you will now find the program files and a text file. Read the text file for instructions on installing the WinTapestry demo.

As you'll see when you start the program, the heart of Tapestry is the Internet Organizer window, a series of tabbed "sheets" (categories) that point to interesting spots on the Internet. To move to a sheet, just click its tab. To explore an item (bookmark) on a sheet, just double-click on it. You can even add your own bookmarks to a category, or create your own categories, with the Internet Organizer menu. I won't attempt to repeat the full instructions for using Tapestry here and now—you'll find plenty of help in the README.TXT file that comes with it, and in the online help. Just start clicking, and have fun!

When you start Tapestry, you'll see a notice that the demo is for evaluation purposes only, and that it expires on a certain date. That's to encourage people to buy the retail product. But don't fret—if your copy expires before you're done deciding whether you want the retail product, you can always download another copy of the demo. If you are interested in the retail product (it's great deal!), check out the Frontier Technologies special offer in the back of this book.

If You Can't Get the Demo...

As of this writing, Frontier Technologies was in the process of getting a fast, permanent Internet connection set up, to make sure that the Get More Demos program worked as it should. If, for some reason, you can't get the Get More Demos program to work, all is not lost. You can find the Tapestry demo program at a variety of other FTP sites around the world. Use Archie to find files that begin with SHADEMO, or try one of these sites, which at the time this book went to print offered the demo for download. Some of them have directories listed—try these directories first, but keep looking around on the site if you don't see it immediately—it may have simply been moved to another directory.

```
ftp.uu.net     /tmp
ftp.osc.edu /incoming
ftp.execpc.com       /pub
ftp.crl.com /PC-Software/sha
ftp.cic.net /pub/Software/pc/frontiertech
ftp.shell.portl.com /pub/frontier
ftp.onramp.net             pub
ftp.elron.net (Israel)
ftp.msu.edu
```

```
ftp.cica.indiana.edu
ftp.wuarchive.wustl.edu
```

As time goes on, the file name might change a bit—it might be
SHADEMO3.EXE or such. Just look for the SHADEMO part, and you
should find it.

The Least You Need to Know

➤ SuperTCP is the program that sets up your SLIP, CSLIP,
  or PPP connection.

➤ Once connected, you can run other TCP programs,
  such as Ping, FTP, News Reader, and even shareware
  and freeware programs you find on the Net.

➤ Ping provides a quick way to check out a network
  connection.

➤ FTP brings the graphical user interface to file transfers.
  It's a thousand times easier!

➤ The News Reader makes working with newsgroups even
  easier—and more addictive.

## Chapter 28

Things to Do, Places to Visit

This chapter contains a few ideas for playing around on the Internet—places to visit, things to do. This is not intended to be a comprehensive listing of what's available on the Internet; we could fill a book with that (and by the time you read it, it would be out of date). It's simply meant to give you a taste of what's out there. Spend some time with Gopher, HYTELNET, WAIS, and World Wide Web, and you'll find all sorts of amazing things.

Under each entry, I've explained how to get to the resource. **Gopher:** means the resource can be reached from Gopher. Start the Gopher client, go to the menu that lists "all the Gopher servers in the world," and then search for the first name (press /, type the name or part of the name, and press **Enter**). The names after the backslash are the menu options, although they may be changed by the time you get to them, of course. For example, **Internet Wiretap/ Electronic Books at Wiretap** means to go to the **Internet Wiretap** Gopher server and select the **Electronic Books at Wiretap** menu option. There are a lot of Gopher resources in this list, because Gopher's a

Remember that you will often find associated information. For instance, I've mentioned the Children, Youth, and Family Consortium Clearinghouse Gopher server, where you can find articles on raising children. Dig around a little at this site, and you'll also find statistics, as well as information, about services and programs for families.

great tool for finding your way around the Internet. **Telnet:** means the resource can be reached via telnet, and **FTP:** means it can be reached via FTP. In some cases I've included login information.

Aging

A collection of newsgroup messages about aging, from the **bionet.molbio.ageing** newsgroup. Each message is a menu option. Recent messages are grouped by month.

      Gopher: **BIOSCI/AGING**

American Chemical Society

Descriptions of books sold by the American Chemical Society.

      Gopher: **Inforonics' TitleBank Internet Catalog/American Chemical Society - Publications**

American Demographics

The table of contents and article summaries of the latest issue of *American Demographics*. Online articles are also available.

      Gopher: **American Demographics**

Anesthesiology

Book reviews, lectures, and research abstracts related to anesthesiology.

      Gopher: **Anesthesiology Gopher**

Artificial Intelligence Lectures

Mostly in German (this is in Vienna).

      Gopher: **Dept.Med.Cybernetics and Artif.Intelligence**

Astrophysics

Astrophysics databases maintained by the NASA/Goddard HEASARC (High Energy Astrophysics Science Archival Research Center).

Gopher: **High Energy Astrophysics Science Archive Research Center/HEASARC On-Line Data and Software**

CD-ROM

Walnut Creek, a distributor of CD-ROMs, provides an area from which you can download information about authoring and working with CD-ROMs, a list of CD-ROM titles, utility programs for working with CD-ROM drives, and more.

FTP: **ftp.cdrom.com**

Directory: **pub/cdrom**

Child Rearing

Various articles and newsletters on parenting, from caring for babies to dealing with teens.

Gopher: **Children, Youth, and Family Consortium Clearinghouse/Brochures, Newsletters & Short Articles**

Cola Machines

If you are interested in trivial interneting, check out the stock in a distant soda machine:

finger graph@drink.csh.rit.edu

Colorado Alliance of Research Libraries (CARL)

CARL is a great way to do library research at home. Search for books or magazine articles. About 40 city, community college, university, and hospital libraries are connected.

Telnet: **pac.carl.org or 192.54.81.128**

Login: **PAC**

Computer Science Technical Reports from Australia

Read papers such as "An Overview of Secure Electronic Mail" and "Techniques for Implementing the RSA Public Key Cryptosystem."

Gopher: **Australian Defense Force Academy/Research Activities/Computer Science Technical Reports**

Computer World Magazine

A few articles, and the current table of contents, from *Computer World*.

Gopher: **Computer World Magazine**

Consumer Information

Buying cheap air travel, computers, cars, and so on. How to protect yourself when buying and selling.

Gopher: **AMI - A Friendly Public Interface/Consumer**

Diary of the August '91 Soviet Coup

One person's experiences during the coup in Russia.

Gopher: **Internet Wiretap/Various ETEXT Resources/ Historical Texts Archive @ MS State FTP/ diaries/diary.soviet**

Disabilities

A community resource for people looking for information about disabilities: government documents, computing for the disabled, legal issues, and so on.

Gopher: **Cornucopia of Disability Information**

Disaster Information

Reports about disaster management and current disasters all over the world: earthquakes, floods, tropical storms, and more.

Gopher: **Volunteers in Technical Assistance (VITA)/Disaster Situation and Status Reports**

Discovery Channel Magazine

Television program listings for the Discovery Channel. Articles and the table of contents from the latest *Discovery Channel* magazine.

Gopher: **Destination Discovery - Discovery Channel Magazine**

DragonMud

An online, text-based adventure game.

Telnet: **eve.assumption.edu 5000**

Earthquake Information

Recent earthquakes, a "calendar of events" (conferences about earthquakes, not predictions!), the Emergency Preparedness Information eXchange, and more.

Gopher: **Earthquake Information Gopher**

Economic Democracy Information Network

Information on labor issues, human rights, the environment, the economy, and more.

Gopher: **Economic Democracy Information Network**

Economics and Business

Loads of info for economists and businesspeople.

Gopher: **AMI - A Friendly Public Interface/Business Resources and Services**

(The) Economist Magazine

Read articles, check the table of contents, and subscribe to the magazine.

Gopher: **Economist, The (Magazine)**

Einstein Online Service, Smithsonian Astrophysical Observatory

Everything you ever wanted to know about astrophysics.

Telnet: **cfa204.harvard.edu or 128.103.40.204**

login: **einline**

Electronic Books

Over 150 books, such as the CIA's *Psychological Operations in Guerrilla Warfare*, Sir Thomas More's *Utopia*, and Darwin's *The Voyage of the Beagle*.

Gopher: **Internet Wiretap/Electronic Books at Wiretap**

Electronic Frontier Foundation

An organization fighting to "ensure that the principles embodied in the Constitution and the Bill of Rights are protected as new communications technologies emerge."

Gopher: **Electronic Frontier Foundation**

Electronic Periodic Table of the Elements

A periodic table of the elements through which you can navigate and view information about each element.

Telnet: **131.174.82.239 2034**

No login required.

Erotica

Articles and subscription information from *Yellow Silk*, a journal of erotica.

Gopher: **Yellow Silk, Journal of Erotica (Magazine)**

The Flora of Costa Rica

Search for information about plants found in Costa Rica.

Gopher: **Missouri Botanical Garden/Manual of the Plants of Costa Rica**

Flying

Information about recreational flight, including articles, stories, and pictures.

Gopher: **rec.aviation gopher**

Food

Dozens of recipes for Oriental and Italian food, appetizers, breads, casseroles, and so on.

Gopher: **University of Minnesota/Fun & Games/Recipes**

The Future of Computer Networking

Information about how computer communications may be able to enhance communications with the objective of reducing conflict to secure a more promising future.

Gopher: **Communications for a Sustainable Future**

Germplasm

Search for information about "working" collections of bacteria, viruses, fungi, nematodes, and so on. Find the phone numbers and addresses of the researchers working with the germplasm.

Gopher: **Microbial Germplasm Database**

Global Land Information System

GLIS is a source of information for use in earth science research and global-change studies.

Telnet: **glis.cr.usgs.gov or 152.61.192.54**

History of Science

"Classes" in the form of ASCII documents that teach about the history of science.

Gopher: **Scientists on Disk - JHU History of Science and Medicine**

Human Genome Project

Databases of genes, genetic markers, and map locations.

Gopher: **Human Genome Mapping Project Gopher Service (UK)**

The Internet Hunt

A game that builds your research skills. The Hunt provides ten questions. You then use the Internet resources to find the answers.

Gopher: **CICNET gopher server/The Internet Hunt**

Islam

Information about Muslim projects: a Muslim computer network, Muslim TV, an Islamic bank, and Cybermuslim (resources on the Internet for Muslims). You can also find an ASCII copy of the Koran (in English).

Gopher: **ISLAMIC Resources**

Job Openings in Academe

Find a job in the academic world.

Gopher: **ACADEME THIS WEEK/JOB OPENINGS in Academe**

Journals

Electronic journals, including *Gov-Line, Disabilities Newsletter, Advanced Squad Leader Digest, Bangkok Post,* and dozens more.

Gopher: **CICNET gopher server/Electronic Serials**

Lawyer Jokes

A few dozen pages of lawyer jokes.

> Gopher: **University of Minnesota/Fun & Games/Humor/ Lawyer Jokes**

Learning About Chance

A database containing information for teaching about chance and statistics, based on current "chance" events reported in newspapers.

> Gopher: **CHANCE database**

Long-Term Ecological Research

Articles about long-term ecological research.

> Gopher: **Long-Term Ecological Research Network/ LTER Core Dataset Catalog/Files in ASCII text**

Macintosh Freeware and Shareware

Download software for the Macintosh.

> Gopher: **Apple Computer Higher Education/Macintosh Freeware and Shareware**

Magazine Articles

Articles from magazines such as *Worth*, *The New Republic*, *ComputerWorld*, *Financial World, Inc.*, *Yellow Silk (the Journal of Erotic Arts)*, and about 40 others, along with current tables of contents, book reviews, and entertainment reviews.

> Gopher: **Electronic Newstand**

Movies

Select from hundreds of movie reviews ranging from "Buffy the Vampire Slayer" to "Throw Momma from the Train."

> Gopher: **University of Minnesota/Fun & Games/Movies**

National Center for Atmospheric Research

Search NCAR's libraries for papers and books related to the atmosphere.

Telnet: library.ucar.edu

National Institutes of Health Library

Search for health-related publications.

Telnet: nih-library.nih.gov or 137.187.166.250

New Age Magazine

Read articles and the table of contents from, and subscribe to, *New Age Magazine.*

Gopher: New Age Magazine

OS/2 Software

Thousands of files for IBM's OS/2 operating system.

FTP: ftp-os2.cdrom.com or ftp-os2.nmsu.edu

Directory: pub/os2

OSHA Regulations

Read the Occupational Safety and Health regulations.

Gopher: Occupational Safety & Health Gopher (OSHA regulations)/OSHA Occupational Safety & Health Regulations

Papyrus

Research information about papyri held in university papyrus collections.

Gopher: Classics and Mediterranean Archaeology/ Papyrology

Poultry

Information about raising poultry, and pictures of domestic fowl.

    Gopher: **Poultry Science Gopher**

Presidential News

Contains documents from the *Federal Register*, public statements by White House aides, speeches by Bill Clinton, and so on.

    Gopher: **Internet Wiretap/Clinton Press Releases**

Primates

Information about primate research.

    Gopher: **Primate Info Net**

Progressive Club Music

Play music directly from the Internet. Unfortunately, you'll need special software to play these "tribal, trance, and house beats."

    Gopher: **N-Fusion**

Project Gutenberg

Hundreds of books, articles, and speeches in ASCII format, ranging from President Clinton's speeches to *The War of the Worlds*.

    FTP: **mrcnext.cso.uiuc.edu**

    Directory: **/pub/gutenberg/**

Raves

Information about who's holding "raves" and where, about the media perception of the rave "scene," and about techno music.

    Gopher: **Techno/Rave gopher**

"Real Programmer" Jokes

Such as: "Real programmers don't eat quiche. Real programmers don't even know how to spell quiche. They eat Twinkies, Coke, and palate-scorching Szechwan food."

Gopher: **University of Minnesota/Fun & Games/Humor/ Real Programmers**

School Networking

Information about getting a school onto the Internet.

Gopher: **Coalition of School Networking**

SchoolNet

A Canadian network of schools. Information about scholarships and grants, Globe and Mail articles, and so on.

Gopher: **SchoolNet Gopher**

Software

Thousands of shareware and public domain programs for a variety of computers, including MS-DOS, the Macintosh, and NeXT. One of the most popular FTP sites on the Internet.

FTP: **garbo.uwasa.fi**

See also the Microcomputer Software archive at the University of Lancaster in England. It features software for the Amiga, Apple, PC, Atari, BBC, and others.

Gopher: **HENSA micros/The HENSA/micros archive at Lancaster University/Microcomputer Software**

Space Program Graphics

Pictures in a variety of formats from NASA.

FTP: **toybox.gsfc.nasa.gov**

Login: **anonymous**

Directory: **/pub/images**

Space Shuttle

Information about the Space Shuttle's Small Payloads project, including GIF graphics, newsletters, and information on conferences.

Gopher: **NASA Shuttle Small Payloads Info**

Supreme Court Rulings

The "Project Hermes" electronic copies of the U.S. Supreme Court's opinions in various formats (ASCII, WordPerfect, and so on).

FTP: **ftp.cwru.edu**

Directory: **U.S.Supreme.Court**

Teach Yourself Law

The Center for Computer-Assisted Legal Instruction produces software for learning about the law.

Gopher: **CALI - The Center for Computer-Assisted Legal Instruction/Gopher**

The Tropics

A database and electronic publications: a "biodiversity/biotechnology information resource."

Gopher: **Base de Dados Tropical (Tropical Data Base), Campinas, Brasil**

Turkey

Find out about Internet services in Turkey.

Gopher: **Bilkent University, Ankara, (TR)**

UFOs

I couldn't get through to this Gopher site, but it looks fun, so I'm listing it anyway. (Maybe it will be back online by the time you read this.)

Gopher: **UFONet - UFO and Alien information**

United Nations

Keep up to date with what the United Nations does.

Gopher: **United Nations**

Weather Forecasts

Find satellite maps, information about storms and earthquakes, and weather forecasts for anywhere in the United States.

Gopher: **National Center for Atmospheric Research (NCAR)/ National Weather Service Forecasts**

World Health Organization

Information about the programs of the World Health Organization.

Gopher: **World Health Organisation (WHO)**

World Peace

A foundation dedicated to "facilitating positive global change by establishing communications and information systems that inventory and integrate the resources and needs of people, projects, and organizations in service to humanity and the Earth."

Gopher: **Together Foundation for Global Unity**

SPEAK LIKE A GEEK DICTIONARY

Speak Like a Geek: The Complete Archive

AFS   A system (not yet widely used) that allows you to work with files on a remote host as if you were working on your own host. For instance, FTP would not be required to get a file, you could simply copy it to your home directory.

alias   A name that is substituted for a more complicated name. For example, a simple alias may be used instead of a more complicated mailing address or for a mailing list.

America Online   An online information system.

anonymous ftp   A system by which members of the Internet "public" can access files at certain *FTP* sites without needing a login name; they simply log in as *anonymous*.

Archie   An index system that helps you find files in over 1,000 FTP sites.

archive file   A file that contains other files, generally *compressed files*. Used to store files that are not used often, or files that may be *downloaded* by Internet users.

ARPAnet   Where the Internet began; the Advanced Research Projects Agency (of the U.S. Department of Defense) computer network that was the forerunner of Internet.

article   A message in an Internet *newsgroup*.

ASCII The American Standard Code for Information Interchange, a standard way for computers to use bits and bytes to represent characters. An ASCII file contains simple text without any special formatting codes.

backbone A network through which other networks are connected.

baud rate A measurement of how quickly a *modem* transfers data. Although, strictly speaking, this is not the same as *bps* (bits per second), the two terms are often used interchangeably.

BBS See *bulletin board system*.

BIND Berkeley Internet Name Domain, a UNIX implementation of the *DNS* standard.

BITNET The "Because It's Time" network (really!). A large network connected to the Internet. Before the Internet became affordable to learning institutions, BITNET was the network of choice for communicating.

bits per second A measure of the speed of data transmission; the number of bits of data that can be transmitted each second.

bps See *bits per second*.

bulletin board system A computer system to which other computers can connect so their users can read and leave messages, or retrieve and leave files.

chat A system by which two users can "talk" with each other by typing; what you see, the other person sees almost instantly and vice versa. (This is unlike e-mail, in which you send your words, and wait for the recipient to read and respond.)

CIX The Commercial Internet Exchange, an organization of commercial Internet service providers.

client A program or computer that is "serviced" by another program or computer (the *server*). For instance, a *Gopher* client program requests information from the indexes of a Gopher server program.

compressed files Computer files that have been reduced in size by a compression program. Such programs are available for all computer systems (for example, PKZIP in DOS, tar and compress in UNIX, and StuffIt for the Macintosh).

CompuServe A computer information service owned by H&R Block. CompuServe is part of the Internet network (though few CompuServe users realize this).

CSLIP Compressed SLIP. See *SLIP*.

cyberspace The "area" in which computer users travel when "navigating" on a network.

daemon A UNIX *server*, a program running all the time in the "background" (that is, unseen by users), providing special services when required.

DARPANET The Defense Advanced Research Projects Agency network, created by combining ARPANET and MILNET. The forerunner of the Internet.

DDN The Defense Data Network, a U.S. military network that is part of the Internet. *MILNET* is part of the DDN.

dedicated line A telephone line that is *leased* from the telephone company and used for one purpose only. In Internet-land, dedicated lines connect organizations to service providers' computers, providing dedicated service.

dedicated service See *permanent connection*.

DFS A variation of *AFS*.

dial-in direct connection An Internet connection that is accessed by dialing into a computer through a telephone line. Once connected, your computer acts as if it were an Internet host. You can run client software (such as *Gopher* and *WWW* clients), and you can copy files directly to your computer. This type of service is often called *SLIP*, *CSLIP*, or *PPP*. See also *dial-in terminal*.

dial-in service A networking service that is used by dialing into a computer through a telephone line.

dial-in terminal connection An Internet connection that is accessed by dialing into a computer through a telephone line. Once connected, your computer acts as if it were a terminal connected to the service provider's computer. This type of service is often called *Interactive* or *dial-up*. See also *dial-in direct*.

dial-up service A common Internet term for a *dial-in terminal connection*.

direct connection   See *permanent connection.*

DNS   See *Domain Name System.*

domain name   A name given to a host computer on the Internet.

Domain Name System   A system by which one Internet host can find another so it can send *e-mail*, connect *FTP* sessions, and so on. The hierarchical system of Internet host names (***hostname.hostname. hostname***) uses the Domain Name System. The DNS, in effect, translates words into numbers that can be understood by the Internet's computers. For instance, the domain name *firefly.prairienet.org* is translated into 192.17.3.3.

download   The process of transferring information from one computer to another. You *download* a file from another computer to yours. See also *upload.*

EARN   The European network associated with *Bitnet.*

Elm   An *e-mail* program.

e-mail or **email**   Short for *electronic mail*, this is a system that lets people send and receive messages with their computers. The system might be on a large network (such as the Internet), on a bulletin board (such as CompuServe), or over a company's own office network.

emoticon   The techie name for a *smiley.*

etext   Electronic text; a book or other document in electronic form, usually simple ASCII text.

Ethernet   A system by which computers may be connected to one another to exchange information and messages.

FAQ   Frequently-Asked Questions. A menu option named FAQ or Frequently Asked Questions will lead you to a document that answers common questions. You may also find text files named FAQ.

Fidonet   A network connected to the Internet.

File Transfer Protocol   See *FTP.*

finger   A UNIX program used to find information about a user on a host computer.

flame   An abusive newsgroup message.

flamer   Someone who writes a *flame*.

forum   The term used by CompuServe for its individual bulletin boards. In Internet-speak, the term is *newsgroup*.

Free-Net   A community computer network, often based on the local library, which provides Internet access to citizens from the library or sometimes from their home computers. Free-Nets also have many local services, such as information about local events, local message areas, connections to local government departments, and so on.

freeware   Software provided free by its originator. Not the same as *public domain software*, as the author retains copyright. See also *shareware*.

FTP   File Transfer Protocol. A *protocol* defining how files are transferred from one computer to another. FTP is also the name of a program used to move files. FTP can also be used as a verb (often in lowercase) to describe the procedure of using FTP. As in, "ftp to **ftp.demon.co.uk**," or "I ftp'ed to their system and grabbed the file."

FTPmail   A system maintained by Digital Equipment Corporation (DEC) that lets people use e-mail to carry out FTP sessions.

gateway   A system by which two incompatible networks or applications can communicate with each other.

GEnie   A computer information service owned by General Electric.

Gopher   A system using Gopher *clients* and *servers* to provide a menu system used for navigating around the Internet.

gopherspace   Anywhere and everywhere you can go using Gopher is known as *gopherspace*.

Gore, Al   A vice president who believes the "information highway" is critical to the U.S.'s future. Reportedly wants all the United States' high schools connected to the Internet in the next few years.

host   A computer connected directly to the Internet. A service provider's computer is a host, as are computers with *permanent connections*. Computers with *dial-in terminal* connections are not; they are terminals connected to the service provider's host. Computers with *dial-in direct* connections can be thought of as "sort of" hosts. They act like a host while connected.

hypertext   A system in which documents contain links that allow readers to move between areas of the document, following subjects of interest in a variety of different paths. The *World Wide Web* is a hypertext system.

HYTELNET   A directory of *telnet* sites. A great way to find out what you can do on hundreds of computers around the world.

IAB   See *Internet Architecture Board.*

IETF   See *Internet Engineering Task Force.*

interactive service   See *dial-in terminal connection.*

internet   The term *internet* spelled with a small *i* refers to networks connected to one another. "The Internet" is an internet, but it is not the only internet.

Internet Architecture Board   The "council of elders," elected by *ISOC*, who get together and figure out how the different components of the Internet will all connect together.

Internet Engineering Task Force   A group of engineers who make technical recommendations concerning the Internet to the *IAB.*

Internet Protocol   The standard protocol used by systems communicating across the Internet. Other protocols are used, but the Internet Protocol is the most important one.

Internet Society   The society that runs the Internet. It elects the Internet Architecture Board, which decides on technical issues related to how the Internet works.

InterNIC   The Internet Network Information Center. This *NIC*, run by the National Science Foundation, provides various administrative services for the Internet.

IP   See *Internet Protocol.*

ISO/OSI Protocols   The International Organization for Standardization Open Systems Interconnect Protocols, a system of protocols that may someday replace the *Internet Protocol.*

ISOC   See *Internet Society.*

KIS   See the *Knowbot Information Service.*

Knowbot   A program that can search the Internet for requested information. Knowbots are in an experimental stage.

Knowbot Information Service   An experimental system that helps you search various directories for a person's information (such as an e-mail address).

leased line   See *dedicated line*.

LISTSERV lists   Mailing lists (using *mail reflectors*) that act as *newsgroups*. Messages sent to a LISTSERV address are sent to everyone who has subscribed to the list. Responses are sent back to the LISTSERV address.

logging off   The opposite of logging on; tells the computer that you've finished work and no longer need to use its services. The procedure usually involves typing a simple command, such as **exit** or **bye**.

logging on   Computer jargon for getting permission from a computer to use its services. A "logon" procedure usually involves typing in a user name (also known as an account name or user ID) and a password. This procedure makes sure that only authorized people can use the computer. Also known as *logging in*.

login   The procedure of *logging on*.

lurker   Someone involved in *lurking*.

lurking   Reading *newsgroup* or *LISTSERV* messages without responding to them. Nobody knows you are there.

mail reflector   A mail address that accepts *e-mail* messages and then sends them on to a predefined list of other e-mail addresses. Such systems are a convenient way to distribute messages to a group of people.

MB   Abbreviation for *megabyte*.

MCImail   An *e-mail* system owned by MCI.

megabyte   A measure of the quantity of data. A megabyte is a lot when you are talking about files containing simple text messages, but it's not much when you are talking about files containing color photographs.

MILNET   A U.S. Department of Defense network connected to the Internet.

MIME   Multipurpose Internet Mail Extensions, a system that lets you send computer files as e-mail.

modem   A device that converts digital signals from your computer into analog signals for transmission through a phone line (**modulation**), and converts the phone line's analog signals into digital signals your computer can use (**dem**odulation).

navigator   A program that helps you "navigate" your way around a complicated BBS. Several navigator programs are available for CompuServe, for instance. Navigators can save you money by letting you prepare for many operations (such as writing mail) offline, and then go online quickly to perform the operations automatically. Internet navigators are currently in a developmental stage, and not in wide use.

netiquette   Internet etiquette, the correct form of behavior to be used while working on the Internet and Usenet. Can be summed up as "Don't waste computer resources, and don't be rude."

Network Information Center   A system providing support and information for a network.

news server   A computer that collects *newsgroup* data and makes it available to *newsreaders*.

newsgroup   The Internet equivalent of a BBS or discussion group (or "forum" in CompuServe-speak) in which people leave messages for others to read. See also *LISTSERV*.

newsreader   A program that helps you find your way through a *newsgroup's* messages.

NFS   The Network File System, a system that allows you to work with files on a remote host as if you were working on your own host.

NIC   See *Network Information Center*.

NOC   Network Operations Center, a group that administers a network.

NREN   The National Research and Education Network.

NSF   National Science Foundation, a U.S. government agency. The NSF runs the *NSFNET*.

NSFNET   The National Science Foundation network, a large network connected to the Internet.

online   Connected. You are online if you are working on your computer while it is connected to another computer. Your printer is online if it is connected to your computer and ready to accept data. (Online is often written *on-line*, though the non-hyphenated version seems to be gaining acceptance these days.)

packet   A collection of data. See *packet switching*.

Packet InterNet Groper   A program that tests whether a particular host computer is accessible to you.

packet switching   A system that breaks transmitted data into small *packets* and transmits each packet (or package) independently. Each packet is individually addressed, and may even travel over a route different from that of other packets. The packets are combined by the receiving computer.

permanent connection   A connection to the Internet using a leased line. The computer with a permanent connection acts as a *host* on the Internet. This type of service is often called *direct*, *permanent direct*, or *dedicated service*, and is very expensive to set up and run.

permanent direct   See *permanent connection*.

Pine   An e-mail program.

PING   See *Packet InterNet Groper*.

point of presence   Jargon meaning a method of connecting to a service locally (without dialing long distance). If a service provider has a POP in, say, Podunk, Ohio, people in that city can connect to the service provider by making a local call.

Point-to-Point Protocol   A method for connecting computers to the Internet via telephone lines, similar to SLIP (though, at present, less common).

POP   See *point of presence*.

port   Generally, "port" refers to the hardware through which computer data is transmitted; the plugs on the back of your computer are ports. On the Internet, "port" often refers to a particular application. For instance, you might telnet to a particular port on a particular host. The port is actually an application.

posting   A message (*article*) sent to a *newsgroup* or the act of sending such a message.

postmaster   The person at a *host* who is responsible for managing the mail system. If you need information about a user at a particular host, you can send e-mail to **postmaster@*hostname***.

PPP   See *Point-to-Point Protocol*.

PRODIGY   A computer information service.

protocol   A set of rules that defines how computers transmit information to each other, allowing different types of computers and software to communicate with each other.

public domain software   Software that is not owned by anyone. You can freely use and distribute such software. See also *freeware* and *shareware*.

reflector, mail   A kind of public mailing list. Messages sent to a mail reflector's address are sent on automatically to a list of other addresses.

remote login   A BSD (Berkeley) UNIX command (**rlogin**) that is similar to *telnet*.

rot13   Rotation 13, a method used to "encrypt" messages in newsgroups, so you can't stumble across an offensive message. If you want to read an offensive message, you'll have to decide to do so.

router   A system used to transmit data between two computer systems or networks using the same protocol. For instance, a company that has a permanent connection to the Internet will use a router to connect its computer to a *leased line*. At the other end of the leased line, a router is used to connect it to the service provider's network.

Serial Line Internet Protocol (SLIP)   A method for connecting a computer to the Internet using a telephone line and modem. (See *dial-in direct*.) Once connected, the user has the same services provided to the user of a *permanent connection*.

server   A program or computer that services another program or computer (the *client*). For instance, a *Gopher* server program sends information from its indexes to a Gopher client program.

service provider   A company that provides a connection to the Internet. Service providers sell access to the network, for greatly varying prices. Shop around for the best deal.

shareware   Software that is freely distributed, but for which the author expects payment from people who decide to keep and use it. See also *freeware* and *public domain software*.

shell   In UNIX, a shell is a program that accepts commands that you type, and translates them for the operating system. In DOS, a shell is a program that "insulates" you from the command line, providing a simpler way to carry out DOS commands.

signature   A short piece of text transmitted with an *e-mail* or *newsgroup* message. Some systems can attach text from a file to the end of a message automatically. Signature files typically contain detailed information on how to contact someone: name and address, telephone numbers, Internet address, CompuServe ID, and so on.

SLIP   See *Serial Line Internet Protocol.*

smiley   A symbol in *e-mail* and *newsgroup* messages used to convey emotion, or simply for amusement. Create smileys by typing various keyboard characters. For example, :-(means sadness. Smileys are usually sideways; turn your head to view the smiley.

Sprintmail   An *e-mail* system used on Sprintnet. Back when Sprintnet was called Telenet, the mail portion used was called Telemail.

Sprintnet   A network owned by SPRINT. It used to be called Telenet (not to be confused with telnet.)

tar files   Files compressed using the UNIX **t**ape **ar**chiver program. Such files usually have file names ending in **.tar**.

TCP/IP   Transmission Control Protocol/Internet Protocol. A set of *protocols* (communications rules) that control how data is transferred between computers on the Internet.

telnet   A program that lets Internet users log into computers other than their own host computers, often on the other side of the world. Telnet is also used as a verb, as in "telnet to **debra.doc.ca.**"

telneting   Internet-speak for using *telnet* to access a computer on the network.

tn3270   A *telnet*-like program used for remote logins to IBM mainframes.

Token Ring   A system used for creating small local area networks. Such networks may be connected to the Internet.

UDP   The User Datagram Protocol, a *protocol* used in Internet communications.

UNIX   A computer operating system. Most *hosts* connected to the Internet run UNIX.

upload   The process of transferring information from one computer to another. You *upload* a file from your computer to another. See also *download*.

USENET   The "User's Network," a large network connected to the Internet.

UUCP   UNIX to UNIX copy Program, a system by which files can be transferred between UNIX computers. The Internet uses UUCP to provide a form of e-mail, in which the mail is placed in files and transferred to other computers.

UUCP network   A network of UNIX computers connected to the Internet.

uudecode   If you use *uuencode*, you'll use uudecode to convert the *ASCII file* back to its original format.

uuencode   A program used to convert a computer file of any kind (sound, spreadsheet, word processing, or whatever) into an *ASCII file* so that it can be transmitted as a text message.

UUNET   A service provider connected to the Internet.

Veronica   The Very Easy Rodent-Oriented Net-wide Index to Computerized Archives, a very useful program for finding things in *gopherspace*.

virus   A program that uses various techniques for duplicating itself and traveling between computers. Viruses vary from harmless nuisances to serious problems that can cause millions of dollars' worth of damage.

VT100   The product name of a Digital Electronics Corporation computer terminal. This terminal is a standard that is "emulated" (duplicated) by many other manufacturers' terminals.

W3   See *World Wide Web*.

WAIS   See *Wide Area Information Server*.

The Web   See *World Wide Web*.

White Pages   Lists of Internet users.

whois   A program used for searching for information about Internet users.

Wide Area Information Server   A system that can search databases on the Internet for information in which you are interested.

World Wide Web   A *hypertext* system that allows users to "travel through" linked documents, following any chosen route. World Wide Web documents contain topics that, when selected, lead to other documents.

WWW   See *World Wide Web*.

XRemote   A rarely used type of *dial-in direct* connection.

Macmillan Publishing: Stop By and Visit

The Macmillan Internet site is scheduled to be up and running by the middle of December, 1994. (Alpha books, the publisher of this book, is a division of Macmillan Publishing.) You'll be able to ftp to **ftp.mcp.com**, point your Web browser to **http://www.mcp.com**, or gopher to **gopher.mcp.com**.

The Macmillan site will contain various useful items, including programs that are mentioned in this and other Internet books, and the information listed at the top of this chapter. It'll also contain the text files and utilities that appeared on the diskette that came with the first edition of the book.

Right now, structure of the site is still being set up, so I can't tell you which directory to look in for particular files. However, we're going to make sure the site is well documented, so you'll be able to find what you are looking for.

Index

357

359

J-K

L

M

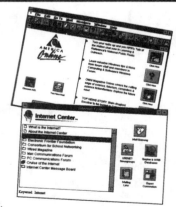

PLUG YOURSELF INTO...

The MCP Internet Site

Free information and vast computer resources from the world's leading computer book publisher—online!

Find the books that are right for you!

A complete online catalog, plus sample chapters and tables of contents give you an in-depth look at *all* our books. The best way to shop or browse!

✦ **Stay informed** with the latest computer industry news through discussion groups, an online newsletter, and customized subscription news.

✦ **Get fast answers** to your questions about MCP books and software.

✦ **Visit** our online bookstore for the latest information and editions!

✦ **Communicate** with our expert authors through e-mail and conferences.

✦ **Play** in the BradyGame Room with info, demos, shareware, and more!

✦ **Download software** from the immense MCP library:
 - Source code and files from MCP books
 - The best shareware, freeware, and demos

✦ **Discover hot spots** on other parts of the Internet.

✦ **Win books** in ongoing contests and giveaways!

Drop by the new Internet site of Macmillan Computer Publishing!

To plug into MCP:

World Wide Web: http://www.mcp.com/
Gopher: gopher.mcp.com **FTP:** ftp.mcp.com

GOING ONLINE DECEMBER 1994!

More Fun Learning from Que!

If you enjoyed this *Complete Idiot's Guide to the Internet,* check out these other books!

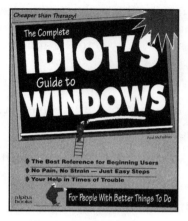

The Complete Idiot's Guide to Excel
ISBN: 1-56761-318-7
Softbound, $14.95 USA

The Complete Idiot's Guide to Windows
ISBN: 1-56761-175-3
Softbound, $14.95 USA

The Complete Idiot's Guide to the MAC
ISBN: 1-56761-395-0
Softbound, $14.95 USA

The Complete Idiot's Guide to Buying and Upgrading PCs
ISBN: 1-56761-274-1
Softbound, $14.95 USA

The Complete Idiot's Guide to Word for Windows
ISBN: 1-56761-174-5
Softbound, $14.95 USA

The Complete Idiot's Guide to WordPerfect for Windows
ISBN: 1-56761-282-2
Softbound, $14.95 USA

The Complete Idiot's Guide to 1-2-3 for Windows
ISBN: 1-56761-400-0
Softbound, $14.95 USA

The Complete Idiot's Next Step with the Internet (with disk)
ISBN: 1-56761-524-4
Softbound, $19.95 USA

Look for these books at your favorite computer book retailer, or call 1-800-428-5331 for more information.

Who cares what you think? WE DO!

We take our customers' opinions very personally. After all, you're the reason we publish these books. If you're not happy, we're doing something wrong.

We'd appreciate it if you would take the time to drop us a note or fax us a fax. A real person—not a computer—reads every letter we get, and makes sure that your comments get relayed to the appropriate people.

Not sure what to say? Here are some details we'd like to know:

- ☞ Who you are (age, occupation, hobbies, etc.)
- ☞ Where you bought the book
- ☞ Why you picked this book instead of a different one
- ☞ What you liked best about the book
- ☞ What could have been done better
- ☞ Your overall opinion of the book
- ☞ What other topics you would purchase a book on

Mail, e-mail, or fax it to:

Faithe Wempen
Product Development Manager
Que
201 West 103rd Street
Indianapolis, IN 46290

FAX: (317) 581-4669
CIS: 75430,174

Special Offer!

Que needs people like you to give opinions about new and existing books. Product testers receive free books in exchange for providing their opinions about those books. If you would like to be a product tester, please mention it in your letter, and make sure you include your full name, address, and daytime phone.